Searching For
Booger County

Ozark Folk Histories

Sandy Ray Chapin

Boogeyman Books

Searching For Booger County
Ozark Folk Histories

Copyright © 2002 Sandy Ray Chapin

Boogeyman Books
Published by Elder Mountain Press

All rights reserved. No part of this book may be reproduced or transmitted in any form or by any means, electronic or mechanical, including photocopying, recording or by any information storage and retrieval system, without written permission from the author, except for the inclusion of brief quotations in a review.

Cover design by Amber Chapin
Edited by Amber and Janet Chapin
Book production by Susie Coobs
First printing 2002
Printed in the United States of America

ISBN 0-9668075-3-7

Publisher's Cataloging-in-Publication Data
Provided by Quality Books, Inc.

Chapin, Sandy Ray.
Searching for Booger County : Ozark folk histories/
Sandy Ray Chapin - 1st ed.
p. cm. Includes bibliographical references and index.
ISBN 0-9668075-3-7

1. Douglas County (Mo.)--History--Anecdotes. 2. Douglas County (Mo.)--Social life and customs--Anecdotes. 3. Folklore--Missouri--Douglas County. 4. Cycling--Missouri--Douglas County. 5. Douglas County (Mo.)--Description and travel. I. Title.

F472.D6C432002   977.8832
                  QBI02-701289

Boogeyman Books   PO Box 184   Mountain Grove, Missouri 65711

Table of Contents

Beginnings	1
Racetrack Hollow	3
Devil's Hill	23
Rippee	39
El Dorado on the North Fork	47
Finding Vera Cruz	57
Uncivil War	65
Baldknobbers	107
Old Richville	121
The Ruins of Omba	129
Champion	139
Topaz	161
Little Yeoman	179
References	196
Index	203

Maps

Booger County	frontispiece
Racetrack Hollow	5
The Forks	10
Braddock Ranch	22
The Sinks	34
Rippee	38
El Dorado	46
Millpond	58
Civil War Roads	62
Redbud	64
The Battle of Clark's Mill	84
Gladetop	108
Richville	120
Omba	128
Champion	138
Ray's Store	160
Seven Springs	167
Satsang	178

Searching For Booger County

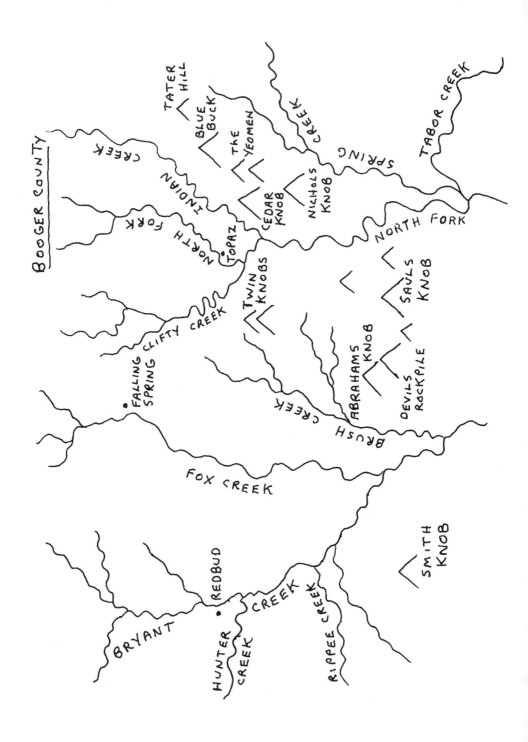

Booger County

Beginnings

Booger County isn't in the atlas. The word booger comes from "booger man," known elsewhere as "bogeyman," the creature of your darkest fears. My friend, the late Otto Loomis, told me that the pioneers inherited the term from the Native Americans, who believed that terrible things happen to people here. The word is old. Some etymologists say it comes from the Irish *bogach* or *bog*, a swamp inhabited by evil apparitions. From it comes *bogey*, *bogy*, or *bogie*, a hobgoblin or malevolent spirit. Others theorize the Celtic *bwg* or *bwgan*, which became the Middle English *bugge* and eventually *bugaboo*, an imaginary terror, or *bugbear*, a frightening phantom, are the origins. I believe booger comes from the Scotch *bogle*, a specter. Scotch-Irish settlers brought the word from the old country. I spell booger with two O's, because that's how it is pronounced.

For generation after generation the people of Booger County have suffered nightmarish hardships. Floods, epidemics, Indian wars, blood feuds, savage barbarity during the Civil War, Baldknobbers who invoked the Lord's will with the bullet, the bullwhip, and the hangman's noose, and the Dust Bowl Drought that uprooted so many families, are just some of the tribulations people here have endured.

Look for Douglas County (Booger County) in south-central Missouri, deep in the Ozarks. Ava, the small county seat, is the only town. Earlier, Redbud, also known as Vera Cruz, was the only town. Partially destroyed during a Civil War battle, Vera Cruz was geographically centered in the county; following the war the "east-enders" and "west-enders" struggled for power amid lawlessness and corruption. Three "commissioners" staked out a new town at a place known as California Barrens or Militia Springs. They broke into the Vera Cruz Courthouse one night, stole the records, and locked them up in the cabin they'd built at the new town site. James Hailey named the new site Ava (pronounced "Avie" by old timers) as a Biblical joke [II *Kings* 17:24] at the expense of the Vera Cruzans: "…and the king of Assyria brought men from Ava…and placed them in the cities of the children of Israel." A wit observed that Ava had a daytime population of three and a nighttime population of zero. The humor was short lived. Someone burned the new "courthouse" and destroyed the documents. Nevertheless, Ava prospered while Vera Cruz faded away.

Though this book is a trail guide for mountain bikers, that's not its purpose. It is for non-bikers who want to "ride" in their imagination. In the chapters ahead we'll cycle through some of the most beautiful countryside in North America. Expect rock-strewn, potholed gravel roads and narrow, winding, brush-choked forest trails. We'll ford streams and pedal laboriously up steep slopes. Caves, sinkholes, "boiling" springs, Civil War battlefields, shoot-out sites, infamous Racetrack Hollow, abandoned homesteads, and Hippie communities are some of the places we'll visit as we travel through Booger County. Along the way I'll tell you about the people who lived and died here: how they raised children, prospered, or struggled simply to feed their families and livestock.

I'm not a writer. I'm a carpenter and gardener. These pages were written painstakingly in longhand over many months. Nor am I a strong, swift cyclist. My wife, Janet, and I became bikers literally by accident when I was on the way to work one morning. A high school boy named Wake drove into our family car. Instead of fixing the crumpled fender, we used the insurance money to buy bikes. Over the years, as we rode through Booger County, I realized how many compelling stories were left by previous generations. My curiosity led to research and eventually to this book.

Before we begin our first mile, realize that although the pages ahead are "true" to the best of my knowledge, much of my information was taken from memoirs, family histories, and interviews. People, even husbands and wives, remember the past differently. The killing of Shelt Alsup, for example, may have as many versions as people who were there that day. Near Buckhart there is an old grave (1816-1884) with two headstones; one is inscribed GEORGE TEDRICK, the other, GEORGE TETRICK. Civil War events in Missouri are interpreted divergently by former Unionists and former Rebels. Inscriptions on gravestones have eroded away; home sites and roads have disappeared; fields have reverted to forest. I do not intend to purposefully malign any person or group, Republicans in particular.

Be cautious out on the county roads. Watch for traffic. Don't forget your helmet, water, pump, and spare tube. You'll need them.

Racetrack Hollow

Fox and Clever Creek bottoms are the focus of our first ride. Are you ready for three hours of cycling up hills, through sand, and over roughly-maintained dirt roads? Start at the Denlow Cemetery at the junction of Hwy 76 and CR 146 five miles west of Hwy 95. The Fox Creek valley is unusually wide, flat, and open. A California based agri-corporation, Sheeks Land and Cattle Company, bought acreage in the 1980's and bulldozed extensive forests to create pastureland. Look east at the concrete pit silo in the hillside. Chop crops grown in these fields are dumped into the pit and used for winter cattle feed.

Ride down to 76, turn right and then immediately left (south) down the valley on CR 243. Denlow is one of the oldest settlements in the county; the springs coming down from the "town" attracted people seeking dependable water and arable land. The next branch on the right is where the Upshaw family camped when they first arrived as hunter/trappers. Further on is the old Upshaw place, now owned by Sheeks. They had a store and blacksmith shop. Family members believe their ancestors used slaves to work these fields in the 1840's and 50's. When the Civil War started, local men created a militia, or Home Guard, and elected John Sevier Upshaw as Captain.

Today, like most days in Booger County, we'll see many beautiful horses. The first settlers who came from Virginia and Carolina by way of Tennessee and Kentucky brought fine "blooded" horses bred over generations for speed and strength. But horses were difficult to keep when the Ozarks was wilderness. Skittish, accident prone, and subject to diseases and parasites, horses needed grain, oats preferably, and high quality hay.

Those first families depended on cattle. They arrived with oxcarts and cleared and plowed these bottoms with oxen. Cattle gave them milk, butter, meat, and leather. Pairs of strong young oxen broken to the yoke brought a premium price from travelers bound for the West Coast over the Oregon Trail. A small herd could be driven to Springfield, Rolla, or St. Louis and exchanged for trade goods: tools, salt, gunpowder, lead, and seed. Cattle are ruminants, cud-chewers with multiple stomachs like deer, goats, and sheep. They can digest low-nutrient food, such as withered grass, efficiently and can tolerate moldy hay, which kills horses.

The Dobbs, Wheats, and Collinses arrived in extended families. Because the Ozarks was a raw frontier with few roads and little government, there was danger from bandits and Indians. The first cabins were built like forts with concealed loopholes in the walls to shoot through and sod roofs immune to fire. Doors were heavy, reinforced, and difficult to batter open.

Yet these people were warm to their neighbors. When a family moved in and claimed squatter's rights, folks gathered for a "house raising." Dinner cloths were spread in the shade for a midday picnic. As the sun went down, a fiddler struck a tune, and the dancing began.

Fun loving, the settlers celebrated whenever they could. There were horse races, wrestling matches, and shooting contests. Men named their rifles Deer Slayer, Indian Killer, and Meat in the Pot. Marksmen attempted to drive a nail into a log by shooting it squarely. Men talked horses: breeding, training, which ones were fastest over which distance and surface. These celebrations were also for business; horses were sold, traded, and commissioned for stud. The night dance was barn style. With a banjo, fiddle, and guitar they played "Sourwood Mountain" or "Sally Ann," and the caller shouted "Circle eight and don't be late, leave that gal, don't hang on the gate." The revelers clapped and stomped in time with the music and sipped from jugs of corn liquor. The dances were one of the few places where young people from distant farmsteads could meet. Casual acquaintances often betrothed in a few days.

Later, after the courthouse was established at Vera Cruz, trials were big entertainment. Families from all over the county would camp along the Bryant. There were horse races, drinking, fighting, game playing, feasting, and dancing. During the trial of an infamous hog thief, someone yelled, "Why he's a damn liar and hog thief." When the visiting judge fined him a dollar for contempt, the man handed the judge two dollars and said, "Judge it will take two dollars to show my contempt for that hog thief."

Early houses were often two separate rooms with a breezeway between them. Sometimes a second story cantilevered over the rooms on every side. Four-poster beds had a rope or hickory bark grid that supported a layer of straw over which lay a mattress filled with feathers or down. Warm handmade quilts or "comforts" covered the bed. Lamps were primitive, just a wick of twisted cloth in a container of

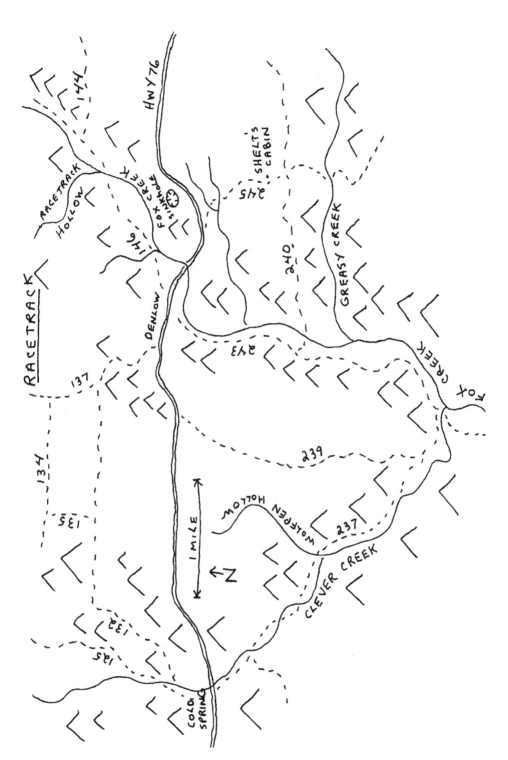

Racetrack Hollow

grease. Some used homemade candles of molded fat. Light was dim; the winter nights, long.

The center of every pioneer home was the fireplace. Iron "cranes" on a swivel were used to hang pots that were swung over the flames. Frying pans were set on iron grills; meat roasted on spits. In her larder the cook kept flour, cornmeal, jerked and smoked beef and venison, smoked and salted ham and bacon, sweet potatoes, turnips, sauerkraut, dried peas and beans, squash, pumpkins, apples, molasses, dried fruit, apple cider and apple vinegar, eggs, milk, butter, and cream.

The most ambitious families looked for sites to build water-powered mills. Water, diverted from a spring or stream into a "race," poured into buckets on the backside of a mill wheel. The weight of the water caused the wheel to turn. A central shaft extended from the wheel into the mill and connected with belts and pulleys that turned stone rollers or drove a circular saw blade. Mill owners took a percentage of the flour, meal, and lumber in exchange for the milling.

Continue downstream on CR 243. CR 240 comes in on the left from Vanzant. The road hugs the west side of the valley and twists through pine-oak woods. Four miles south of Denlow turn right on CR 237 up Clever Creek. If you feel like a soda or snack, it's just a half-mile further down 243 to Henson's Store at Champion. Ride up Clever Creek past 239 on the right and 231 on the left. During the depths of winter these bottoms are filled with the fragrance of blooming Ozark witch hazel. We consider this stretch of gravel road, shaded by oaks and crossing the creek several times, one of the prettiest rides in the county.

The Alsup brothers, Bill, Ben, and Moses (known as Locke) came to Booger County from central Tennessee with their extended family. Contemporaries referred to them as Irish. Beside the wagons trotted racehorses they called "popcorn stock"—short and deep chested with kind eyes, sensitive nostrils, and alert, fox-like ears. Their necks were slightly arched; their hindquarters, powerfully broad. These horses were explosively fast and could pivot and stop with unequalled grace. They tended to be bay (reddish brown with black manes and tails). Legend says that they descended from the English thoroughbred, Jolly Roger. However, the Alsup's stock was a distinctly "American" horse. When the Spanish began the conquest of the New World, Native Americans quickly adopted horses as part of their culture. Breeding stock was traded to tribes further and further north. The

Comanche, Cheyenne, and Crow selectively bred horses adapted to the wilderness of North America. The Appaloosa, developed by the Nez Pierce, is still a popular breed. Eventually, horses were used by the powerful "civilized" tribes of the southeastern United States—Cherokees, Choctaw, and Creeks.

Meanwhile, the English attempted to establish themselves along the warm, humid, bug and disease-ridden tidewater lands of Virginia and the Carolinas. Their horses, native to the cooler climate of Europe, often died. To strengthen their stock, colonial breeders traded with the Native Americans for stallions and created the popcorn horses of Booger County.

Originally the Alsups located near Buckhart, southwest of Twin Knobs. They were contentious men who made enemies quickly. They settled disagreements with "handkerchief" duels; the antagonists each grasped the corner of a large handkerchief with one hand and, without letting go, went at each other with hog-butchering knives until the loser let go of the kerchief.

The Alsups never raced their horses frivolously. Because their steeds were susceptible to hoof and leg injuries, they raced on soft surfaces only, for money and in deadly earnest. During a race with their neighbors the Sheltons, the Shelton boy quirted the Alsup horse across the nose as it tried to pass. In retaliation the Alsup lad struck the Shelton boy across the face with his quirt. At the finish line the Shelton boy pulled a pistol and put a bullet through the heart of the Alsup lad, whose uncle then shot the Shelton boy only to be riddled with bullets in return. It was the beginning of a feud that wouldn't end until the surviving Sheltons were driven out of the county.

Earlier, when news of the California gold discovery reached Missouri, many men contracted gold fever. In the spring of 1849 they assembled along Prairie Creek and formed a company for the long journey to California. Afterwards, the meeting place was called California Springs or California Barrens, and much later, Ava. The men left wives and children behind. Some never returned; others struggled back a few years later hungry, broke, and discouraged. The gold fields were awful. Disease rampaged through the fetid camps; every kind of con man, swindler, gambler, bandit, and desperado preyed on the miners. Prices were astronomical. Only a lucky few made their fortune and lived to bring it home. The richest diggings were bought up, one way or another, by influential mining companies.

Like everyone else the Alsups listened in wonder to the 49ers' tales of the incredible wealth in San Francisco and the scarcity of goods. Supplies had to be shipped around the southern tip of South America or carried across the steamy, unhealthy Isthmus of Panama. Because both the prevailing winds and ocean currents flow north to south off the West Coast, sailing ships were forced to sail far to the west and then double back to San Francisco. Otherwise, there was the California Trail, two thousand miles long.

Talk centered on California as the Alsups plowed, made hay, and cut timber. After lengthy discussions they decided to risk the trip. Locke, his wife, Patsy, and their children would go, as would Bill and his family. The Washington Rileys and the Henry Collins clan joined them. Locke brought a herd of forty-four cattle, three saddle mounts, and two promising young racehorses and filled the wagons with tools and supplies. The Vera Cruz Road out of Booger County was just a trail with deep potholes and many creek crossings; everyone walked at the slow, steady pace of the yoked oxen. While the men hunted and cared for the livestock, the women made and broke camp, built fires, and cooked. At Independence they formed a company with eleven other Missouri families. Locke was elected Captain.

Independence, the jump-off point for Oregon, California, Santa Fe, and the newly discovered gold and silver strikes in the Colorado Rockies, was a boomtown. Steamboats from New Orleans, Pittsburgh, Cincinnati, and St. Louis loaded and unloaded along the riverfront. Emigrants bought supplies and had repairs made to their wagons and gear. "Wild" Indians, gunslingers, slaves, and gamblers walked the muddy streets; just out of town wilderness began.

Getting across the continent alive meant keeping the cattle healthy. If the wagon train started too early in the spring before the ground firmed, the wheels would sink; hard pulling would exhaust the oxen. If it started too late, the livestock ahead would have grazed off the grass. Everyone had heard about the Donner Party; crossing the Sierra Nevada range before the first winter storm was imperative.

At first the route followed the Platte River, "a mile wide and an inch deep, too thick to drink, too thin to plow." Graves lined the trail. The many travelers contaminated the ground water with human waste. Severe diarrhea, dysentery, and cholera were commonplace; the indigenous Pawnee had been decimated by disease. Further on, Native Americans were known to watch for undisciplined wagon trains. At night young warriors slipped in to steal livestock, especially horses, which had become their measure of wealth and social standing. The Alsup men who scouted ahead for water and grass must have felt vulnerable in the immense landscape. The trail was littered with furniture and other belongings that had been thrown out to lighten the loads for the struggling oxen.

The Alsup wagon train crossed the Continental Divide at South Pass and plodded through desolate Wyoming. At the Green River the thirst-crazed stock stampeded, overturned wagons, and caused a delay for repairs. The company crossed the waterless Salt Lake Desert to the headwaters of the Humboldt River in Nevada. The land was bleak and barren; the water, bitter with alkali. Pasture was scarce when livestock needed it most. At the "Sinks" the Humboldt disappeared into a salty marsh; in the distance, the Sierras shimmered. The cattle strained to pull the wagons through deep sand. Bones of hundreds of oxen littered the trail. They reached the sparkling, chill water of the Truckee River, the outlet of Lake Tahoe, and followed the river into the mountains. In the gorge the oxen pulled the wagons up the boulder-strewn riverbed, and their hooves softened from continuous immersion and bruised on the rocks.

The mountain air was cool, moist, and scented with pine. The men hunted while the stock rested and grazed the lush meadows. On the way up to the pass, they rolled quietly through the forsaken ruins of the Donner camp, where snowbound pilgrims had been reduced to cannibalism. Donner Pass was the last obstacle; wagons were winched to the top with rope and tackle. The air warmed as the group descended the western slopes.

Sacramento, like Independence, was a boomtown. The riverfront bustled with steamboats and cargo; the streets, with exotic people—Chinese, Mexicans, Chileans, Irish, and Italians. Hammers banged, saws rang, and new businesses sprang up amid the throngs.

All the Alsup livestock survived the journey. Cattle prices were extremely high. The oxen, wagons, and gear were worth many times their value in Missouri; the cattle more than paid off the Alsup's expenses.

After training and conditioning the horses, they went on to San Francisco. Locke said later that they "cleaned out the competition." Their popcorn stock was unbeatable at certain distances. For awhile they settled in Sonoma County, north of San Francisco, and considered making it their home. Instead they chose to return to Booger County. The men rode back. The women and children, including fourteen-year-old Shelt, boarded a ship in San Francisco, sailed down the

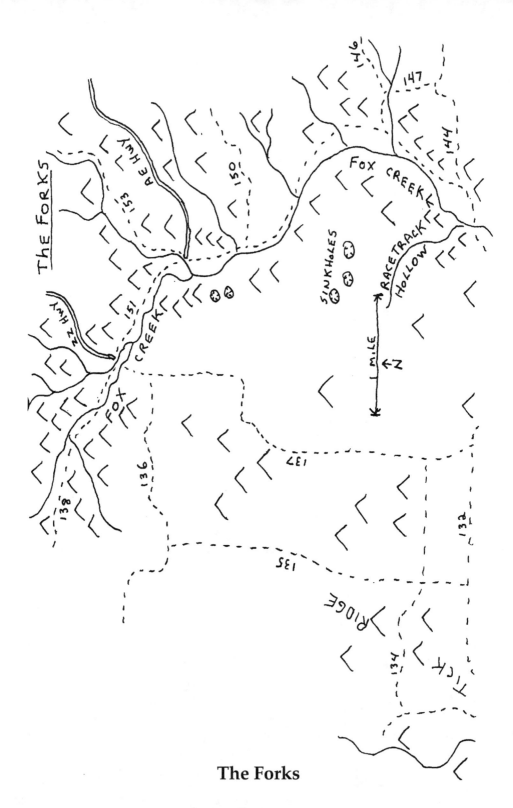

The Forks

West Coast to Panama City, and crossed the Isthmus by stagecoach. Another ship transported them to New Orleans, where they took a steamboat up the Mississippi to Ste. Genevieve. Patsy bought a team of oxen and a cart. Ironically, the worst part of the journey was Missouri's pothole-ridden roads, which grew progressively rougher as they approached Booger County.

We cross Hwy 76 at Coldspring. There is a Baptist church on the left. Locke and Patsy settled here when they returned from California. Their house was on the east side of the creek a few hundred yards north of 76, near a spring where a barn stands now.

Actually, they built two houses. Rebels burned the first. Only Patsy and the girls were home when the Rebels rode up. As the house burned Patsy tossed out valuables, only to see the Rebels throw them back onto the flames. Finally, Patsy, exhausted and exasperated, dragged her favorite chair into the yard and sat down. With the flames curling up behind her, she faced the Rebels and yelled that they'd have to kill her before IT would burn! Suddenly, the Alsup men and the militia rode up. They killed two of the Rebels, though, one lived long enough to dictate a letter to Martha Alsup for his mother in Arkansas. The Alsups buried the Rebels in their yard.

Locke and Patsy named this stream Clever Creek. In the dialect of the time, "clever" meant amiable, hospitable, and good-natured. Despite their often-violent ways, the Alsups are remembered as warm, generous neighbors.

After we cross 76 CR 237 becomes CR 125. A half-mile up Clever Creek turn right on CR 132, wind up a spring-fed side hollow and onto Tick Ridge. Go past CR 135 to CR 137 and turn left (north). This is open country with upland pastures and hayfields. The Christiansen Ranch owns much of it. Fine homes have been built on knobs overlooking the grasslands. CR 137 eventually drops down into the "Forks" of Fox Creek at the end of ZZ Hwy.

When the Alsups returned from California, they were one of the wealthiest families in Booger County. They acquired more and more land. Trouble started right away. The Neal family disputed the Alsup's claim to land in Racetrack Hollow. One Alsup and thirteen Neals were shot before the Neals were driven out. At the outset of the Civil War, there was an outstanding warrant for the arrest of Locke Alsup for the murder of John Gideon, but no one wanted to face Locke to serve it.

Seventeen-year-old Billy Fleetwood had begun courting Bill

Alsup's daughter, Nan. Though Billy was a pleasant lad, Bill disliked him. One day while Billy was visiting, Bill had his stepson, Drew Upshaw, pick a fight with Billy to run him off. But Billy whipped Drew. Angry and humiliated, Drew asked Bill for a pistol. No, Bill said, he'd take care of Billy himself. At the Fleetwood place Billy was expecting Drew and had his squirrel rifle in his hands. Bill rode up into the yard and shot Billy down. Eph, Billy's dad, grabbed his pistol and ran out of the house. Both men emptied their revolvers. Bill, firing from a plunging horse, missed all five shots. Bullets from Eph's gun tore into Bill's left arm, abdomen, and lung. The Alsups were tough men. Bill rode home; after several months of convalescence, he recovered.

During the Civil War the Alsups declared for the Union and joined the Republican Party, which held control through the Federal Army of Occupation. Martial law was in effect; Constitutional rights, suspended; elections, cancelled. The state government had been chased into Arkansas by Federal troops. The Provisional Governor appointed county positions. All men were required, under onerous penalty, to join the local militia, commanded by Captain Locke Alsup. The Alsups grew even more powerful with the Federal government behind them. They seized land and livestock from Rebels and decided who stayed in the county and who didn't.

They paid a price, though. Tom, severely wounded when a bullet passed between his ribs and hipbones, was sent home to die by an army surgeon. Patsy nursed him continuously and drew a silk cloth through his wound to allow the dirt and infection to drain. He recovered to live a normal life. Ben was captured and spent forty months imprisoned near Jonesboro; the warden, who hated him, made him work in harness alongside a blind mule. After the war Ben rode into Arkansas, hunted down, and killed the warden.

The official end to the war meant little in Douglas County, where fighting and trouble continued for years. Returning Confederates were banished. When the county seat was forcefully removed to Arno and then back to Vera Cruz, hard feelings arose between the eastern and western townships. Nightriders, including Locke Alsup, seized the county records and moved them to Ava, a "town" with one building. The county documents were destroyed when Ava burned. The eastern townships "seceded" and joined Howell County.

A man named John Hatfield moved into the county. Legend says he was chased out of Arkansas by a posse and escaped only because he'd stolen the best horse in the area. At first he got along well with the Alsups, but that soured when Hatfield gave up his lawless ways and married the widow Elizabeth Todd Davis. The Alsups wanted the Davis farm at Falling Spring; Ben and Shelt had murdered Isaac Davis, hoping to get it.

Trouble began with a small incident. Shelt's wife, Nancy, was picking apples with her sister-in-law, and Hatfield insultingly accused them of stealing. When the hot-tempered Shelt heard about the accusation, he rode over to the Davis place. Shelt's dog got into a terrible fight with Hatfield's dog as the men exchanged angry threats.

The Alsups offered $300 for the Davis farm, but the feisty Liz sent them away. The next morning as she was gathering eggs, Liz saw a group of armed Alsups riding up. She ran to the house and helped her husband fortify it. Hatfield was a formidable man in a gunfight, and when the Alsups rushed the house, they were driven back. Three of them died, and two were wounded. By noon, when Constable Brown Wyatt arrived, Hatfield was nearly out of ammunition. A truce was arranged. The Alsups promised to let Hatfield be taken to Hartville to stand trial for the murder of the Alsups killed that day. Hatfield was put on a horse, his hands tied to the saddle horn, and his feet tied under the horse's belly. But just up the road, the Alsups were waiting. They shot the horse; it fell heavily onto Hatfield. Then they shot Hatfield twenty-eight times.

Later, Liz attempted to appear before the Grand Jury to testify against the Alsups. At the time all county officials were sympathetic to the Alsups, and Locke was Presiding Judge. He took the widow to the courthouse door and kicked her down the steps. Shelt gave her a horse and buggy and escorted her to the county line. Locke's brother Ben claimed the Davis place.

Ride onto the pavement of ZZ Hwy. Noah Strunk built a gristmill here after the Civil War with an overshot water wheel and a race parallel to the creek. This area was known as Omo. Later, there was a store, blacksmith shop, post office, and gas station. Cross two highway bridges over the Forks of Fox Creek and turn right at CR 151. To the north the land rises dramatically to a sinkhole-pocked plateau near Norwood. Pioneer Eli Finch settled here before the Civil War. From Marshfield, Kentucky, he was a half Cherokee who raised blooded horses. Luticia, his wife, was nearly blind. She swept the floor by feeling for dirt with her bare feet, and she carried water from the spring with slow, sliding steps. Eli and Luticia raised eleven children. During the Civil War Eli served with the Federal Cavalry. Depredations by soldiers and bushwhackers forced Luticia and the children to move to the teeming refugee camp at Rolla. The oldest boy, Lonzo, was run over and killed by a car on the square in Mtn. Grove in 1914. A few years later their daughter-in-law Nannie Vaughan fell to her death from a circus Ferris wheel in Mtn. Grove; another son, Bowling, had perished during a typhoid epidemic in the 1890's.

Ride down the valley. CR 153 runs up the East Prong of Fox Creek toward Mtn. Grove. Notice the picturesque abandoned homestead on the west side of the valley. AE Hwy comes in on the left at the Glendale Church. After we round a bluff and cross a branch, CR 150 T's on the left. Look for a small streambed past a house on the left. The Alsups murdered Hatfield here. The valley bottoms widen. The soil is loose and fertile. Behind a prosperous farm is the Livingstone Cemetery, named for a family related to the Alsups. Where the road hugs a steep bluff, slow down. Listen for the sound of water. This is Falling Spring. Water seeps out of the strata along this hill. Imagine the weekly washday at a spring like this. Children gathered firewood as women boiled clothing in iron kettles. Laundry dried on trees and bushes while children played and folks picnicked. At the end of the hill, look for the ruins of buildings and cellars. This is the old Ben Alsup place that was taken by force from Liz Davis and John Hatfield.

Elizabeth "Liz" Marler was born at Falling Spring in 1855. People remember her as a "frolicking," self-confident woman who could dance the jig all night long and draw from the hip to shoot a bird on the wing. As a girl she would climb a tree, brace her feet together, and "ride" it to the ground before her brothers could chop it down. She boasted as a young woman that she could gallop a horse and change her baby's "nappin" without slowing down.

Liz and her husband, Civil War veteran Richard "Bud" Hodge, built a 16'x16' log and daub cabin on their two hundred acres nearby, with an earthen floor, a stone chimney, two doors, and no windows. Laboriously they cleared the land with axes, saws, and oxen. They planted peach, cherry, and apple trees, as well as, annual crops like corn, sorghum, wheat, and vegetables. They had nine children; Barney died soon after his second birthday.

Bud never liked farming. He studied law and served as a constable, deputy sheriff, justice of the peace, postmaster, and tax collector. Twice he was defeated for sheriff. The corncrib behind their house doubled as a jail. Bud "nailed" his prisoners in until the sheriff arrived from Ava.

Bud, like everyone else in the area, knew that Mrs. Getz and her daughter were "entertaining" gentlemen in their home for profit. He left them in peace. Others were offended and sent a committee to Prosecuting Attorney John Reed to demand that the ladies be brought to trial. Warrants for their arrest were sent to Constable Hodge. Unfortunately, the Getz's were keeping company with the formidable Frank Raney. Expecting trouble Bud deputized John Wood and his son Isaac. Prudently Hodge held the horses and sent the Woods in to make the arrests. Inside Raney protested, saying the ladies had done no harm. The angry argument ended when young Isaac put a fatal bullet through Raney's neck. A Coroner's Jury exonerated him.

Liz outlived Bud. In 1928 at the age of seventy-three, she struck a deal with Ava Ford salesman Harry Martin and traded $200 and three cows for a Model A. Though she drove it in the fields, she usually had one of her grandsons chauffeur her on the roads. One Sunday morning, on the way to church at Denlow, she died of a heart attack.

South of Falling Spring, Fox Creek Road rounds a steep, wooded hill on the left. Look and listen again for a spring trickling out of the rocks from a pipe. This is Lakey Spring, the home of pioneers Enos and Isabella Lakey. They built a cabin, worked these bottoms, and raised eleven children. The life they'd made for themselves was obliterated when the great flood of June 1, 1876, swept down the creek before dawn and washed away the cabin. Frantically Enos went into the roiling waters again and again in search of his family. He put Levi in a tree and Will on a pile of driftwood, but the next morning the bodies of Isabella and the four youngest children were found partly buried in flood debris. James Lakey was one of the survivors. His wife, Nancy Julian, and all their children except Myrtle died later when they ate poisonous mushrooms.

Beyond Lakey Spring Fox Creek Road hugs a forested hillside, passes between a house and barn, and comes out into a broad valley. We're back to the Sheeks Ranch. On the hillside above us, split by CR 140, are the ruins of an ambitious dairy operation. The road doglegs to the right and crosses Fox Creek on a concrete slab. Stop here. This is Racetrack Hollow. On the west side of the ford a gate enters a small field. Beyond is a steep, forested hill. At its base are two large boulders. One has a recent scar where Sheeks Ranch tried to doze it out. Before the Civil War these rocks were the starting line. The power pole out in the middle of the valley approximates the finish line. When the starting gun was fired, the horses, turned backwards to the finish, whirled and sprinted across the soft, sandy soil.

Large sums of money changed hands. Men were killed and terribly beaten over the races at Racetrack Hollow. Sheriff and Rebel leader, Preston Todd, owned this land before Bill and Locke Alsup claimed it. In 1859, when one of Locke's horses raced one of the Neal's, a group of upper Fox Creek men rode in and boasted they would "run old Locke Alsup and his boys off, and if any of them Woodses or Upshaws sided in with them, they'd get the same treatment." Thirteen injured upper-creek men were hauled home in wagons. Two of them died.

In 1884 John Douglass campaigned at Racetrack Hollow as the Republican candidate for assessor. As he worked his way through the crowd, bantered, and shook hands, an anti-Alsup Democrat confronted him with a club and said that some heads were about to be knocked. Jack Alsup stepped forward and asked the man to try knocking his head first; the Democrat dropped his club and left.

In the 1930's Faye and Buster Coble rented this field from Jess Cox. Jess had come here as a little boy before the Civil War with his mother and sister from Tennessee after his father had died suddenly. They traveled up the Tennessee to the Ohio, up the Mississippi to the Missouri, and then up the Osage as far as possible. They bought an oxcart, walked to Douglas County, and homesteaded on Dry Creek south of Norwood. Jess split rails for fences and broke the new ground with a heavy wooden plow drawn by seven pairs of yoked oxen. Though still a boy, Jess joined the Federal Army and fought many battles, including Pea Ridge and Prairie Grove. Jess married Locke and Patsy's daughter Martha in the Alsup cabin at Coldspring. He died in 1939.

Look south. You can see Hwy 76 winding down the slope in the distance. It's only a mile back to the cemetery. The road runs along the west side of the valley and passes under a low limestone bluff.

We've ridden twenty-three miles. While you cool down, take a walk around the cemetery. Next to the highway, in raised stone platforms, are the oldest graves. The inscriptions in the limestone monuments, eroded by decades of rain and frost, are nearly obliterated. Stroll along the fence to the lane and turn left; downhill in the fifth row, between a McCall and an Upshaw, are two old stones side by side: Captain Moses Locke Alsup 1813-1896. Further down by the tree, look for Tom's grave. Shelt has a double headstone and a cracked marble plaque set horizontally in the ground. He died in 1879 at age thirty-five. Notice that one of his children died that same March day. Beside him Nancy's stone reads "True Grit." These inscriptions hint at Booger County's most infamous incident. Bitterness over these deaths exists today.

Your back is stiff and your legs ache, but we've got to take another short ride to finish the Alsup story. Load the bikes and drive east on 76. At the top of the barren ridge, park at CR 245. Cycle down the hill to the stream branch and stop.

Locke and Patsy had nine children. Tom, their eldest, was born in Tennessee in 1836. He was a handsome man with blue eyes and light skin. Catherine Sweeten, his wife, was a spinner and weaver. They raised fine horses on their farm near Buckhart. Tom's prize mare, Brown Kate, sold for $1500, a huge sum then. On Election Day November 1884, Tom rode to Hebron to vote. On the way home someone waited in ambush. A bullet ended Tom's life. Morgan Riley was arrested and brought to this hollow to the home of Justice of the Peace Squire Williams and tried for murder. Riley was acquitted for lack of evidence. The Alsup clan believed that Henry Tetrick was involved in Tom's death.

Jack, the second born, also died suddenly. He had traveled to Mtn. Grove with a great deal of money. His body, minus the money, was found under the ice of Lake Lily. Foul play was suspected, but no arrests were made.

Burt was born at Falling Spring in 1850. Physically disabled from birth, he never served in the army or lived the violent life of his brothers. Nevertheless, two brothers named Branson murdered him for the fifteen dollars in his pocket, two miles south of Mtn. Grove near the Lone Star Cemetery. Cleverly the Bransons made the crime scene appear as though Burt's wagon crushed him when his horses had shied and overturned it. No one was arrested.

Patsy and Locke raised a tenth child, a boy named Wiley, at their home in Coldspring. Born in 1855, he was Locke's son by a slave whom Locke bought with her child, who was sold separately, at an auction in Ozark. Wiley was raised as a son and member of the family, though his Uncle Bill referred to him as "that nigger." When Wiley killed a man during a Hartville card game, he ran away to escape the law; no one saw him again.

Ride over a low ridge, across another intermittent stream, and pedal up the slope past an abandoned farmstead where Shelt and Nancy's cabin once stood. Stop at the crossroads. To the left is Vanzant, to the right Fox Creek. Straight ahead the road descends to cross Greasy Creek and continues on to Drury adjacent to the Dept. of Conservation's Shannon Ranch.

Shelt (James Shelton) was born in 1844, just old enough to participate in the Civil War. People remember him as redheaded and fiery-tempered though congenial and pleasant. From childhood Shelt had special gifts with horses. As an adult he raced his string of small, muscular bays. Little Easter, his prized mare, was the fastest horse in the county.

A man from Yellville, Arkansas, Doc Cantrell, brought a magnificent white mare into Douglas County. He proposed a match race between Shelt on Little Easter and himself on the white. The race, he said, would be one of a series of contests to be held at the Nave's Bend of the White River—a soft, flat bottomland field enclosed on three sides by the river. A thousand-dollar wager was agreed upon.

The Alsups were part of a big crowd on race day. Men from all over the Ozarks, former Rebels and Unionists, were united by a love for race horses. Camps lined the riverbank; liquor flowed freely, and betting was feverish. Shelt put down his thousand dollars.

The course was a half-mile. The horses were led to the starting line with their tails toward the finish. Landowner Ben Nave raised his pistol and fired. Nostrils flaring, the racers whirled and lunged; dirt flew. Cantrell had an early lead, but gradually Little Easter closed the gap. She surged in the last yards and won by twenty feet. Cantrell, visibly stunned, left the track. Jubilantly the Alsups shook hands and slapped each other's backs.

Cantrell had no intention of paying his bet. His thousand dollars was withdrawn. Shelt and all the Alsups were damned cheats, he declared. These sneaking, lying Yankees needed to be taught a lesson. An angry confrontation occurred at the Cantrell Place between the Alsups and Cantrell's liquored-up supporters. Hands nervously fingered holstered revolvers. Shelt, furious, wanted to fight, but cooler heads led him away.

On the trail back Shelt slipped away and rode south for retribution, but Cantrell and his friends waited in ambush with axe handles. Left for dead, Shelt limped home.

As his wounds healed Shelt burned for revenge. He and his kinsmen waited above a ford on Shoal Creek near the Cantrell farm. Young Jess Cox wanted the first shot, but when Cantrell and another man rode into the water, Jess froze. Shelt pulled the rifle from Jess's hands and knocked both men into the stream. As the riderless horses bolted into the farmyard, Cantrell's wife screamed. "Boys," Shelt said with a smile, "that's music to my ears."

Later, back in Booger County, the likeable Shelt was elected sheriff and collector in 1874 and again in 1876.

In Arkansas the friends and family of Doc Cantrell petitioned the Governor for justice. He then appealed to the Governor of Missouri to extradite Shelt Alsup. Strangely, Sheriff Alsup received warrants for his own arrest. When Shelt's second term expired, no one filed for sheriff. An outsider named Hardin Vickery stepped up; some called him Victory Hardin. From Illinois originally, he had served with the Kansas Cavalry along the Missouri border and had chased Quantrill and the James brothers. After the war he went to Texas and drove cattle. A few months after he moved to Ava, Vickery was surprised to be asked to run for sheriff. Soon after assuming office, Sheriff Vickery received a warrant for the arrest and extradition of Shelt Alsup for murder and other crimes and a letter from Governor Phelps demanding action. What kind of justice could a Unionist expect in Rebel Arkansas?

For Shelt's wife, Nancy Coats of Vera Cruz, there was heartache. First, Shelt was nearly killed. Then, their infant son died suddenly. Now, Shelt was a fugitive.

Again and again Victory and his deputies prowled the Clever/Fox Creek area and searched for Shelt. People were sullen and suspicious. The lawmen had a feeling of imminent danger. Once they nearly caught Shelt, but he escaped on horseback down a steep embankment near the 76 bridge over Fox Creek.

One evening someone came into the sheriff's office. Shelt, he said, was going to spend the night with Nancy and the kids. Sheriff Vickery called for a posse. Men from many families—Fleetwood, Pease, Dobbs, Tetrick, Clinkingbeard, and Kendall, most of whom had served with the Alsups in Co. H of the 46th Missouri Mounted Infantry—saddled their horses and loaded their weapons. Old grudges were about to be settled.

They rode through the night. Before dawn they left their horses at this crossroads and silently approached the Alsup cabin. When Shelt came out at daybreak to relieve himself, the cabin was surrounded. Victory stood up and called out to Shelt to avoid needless bloodshed and give himself up. But before Vickery had spoken three words, someone fired and knocked Shelt down. Instantly he leapt up and, with bullets whizzing past, he scrambled into the cabin. Suddenly, a scream rent the morning air. Nancy burst through the door, a bloody bundle clutched in her arms. Their five-year-old daughter had been shot. Nancy cursed and reviled the posse. Shelt's kinsmen would kill them all, she cried. The fight went on. Nancy sent her son out to fetch his father's horse, but he was captured.

By now an argument had started among the posse. The cabin had logs behind the boards, some claimed. No, others said, the structure was flimsy, and eventually a bullet would find its way to Shelt. Sheriff Vickery said he'd find out. Running from tree to tree, he snuck up to the cabin and hammered off a board with the butt of his pistol. Shelt's bullet passed through him. He fell, writhing in agony.

Bullets splintered the cabin as the posse fired and reloaded. Inside Shelt, bleeding profusely, grew weaker. Nancy stepped into the doorway; knowing the posse wouldn't shoot a woman, she lifted her skirt. Shelt aimed and fired beneath her legs. Then, unfortunately, a round misfired and a bullet lodged halfway up Shelt's rifle barrel; it was hopelessly jammed.

As the posse closed in, Nancy fought them off with an ax, but they pushed her aside and dragged the now helpless Shelt into the yard. The Alsups say Henry Tetrick stuck the end of his rifle barrel into Shelt's mouth and blew off the back of his head. As he chambered another round to further mutilate the body, Lafayette "Fate" Upshaw stuck his revolver into Tetrick's belly and said, "If you shoot him again, I'll put a hole through you."

The corpses of Sheriff Vickery and ex-Sheriff Alsup were thrown across horses and taken to Ava. Vickery was buried in an unmarked grave. The Alsups swore revenge. Though trouble continued for years, the Alsups endured, and their descendents still live in these hills.

Locke lived to be an old man. In the last years of his life, he left a legacy to the people of Booger County and anyone interested in horses. After the war the immigrants who came to take land under the Homestead Act were culturally "Yankees." Their preachers railed against dancing, drinking, gambling, and horse racing as "sins of the flesh." Realizing that the old settler ways were dying out, Locke no longer raised racehorses. Instead, he began to buy and breed "gaited" stock. While most horses have four gaits—walk, trot, canter, and gallop—a few can be trained and bred to have five. Trotting, the most efficient gait, is jarring for the rider, especially across rough terrain. Over years Locke developed a breed that could walk quickly with the front feet and trot with the hind feet at a smooth, swift pace. Across hilly country these horses could maintain eight-to-ten mph over long distances. Tall and muscular, the breed tended to be chestnut (reddish brown), calm, sure-footed, and easy to train. Their tough hooves and forefeet could withstand the Ozarks' punishing terrain. People called them Fox Trotters after the graceful steps of the dance, and today this registered breed is headquartered on Hwy 5 north of Ava. Now, as in Locke's time, they bring high prices.

Get some rest! Tomorrow we'll negotiate the rugged Devil's Hill region of the Mark Twain National Forest. We'll push our bikes up a boulder-strewn stream bed where long ago other travelers sought lost youth from the healing waters of a mineral spring.

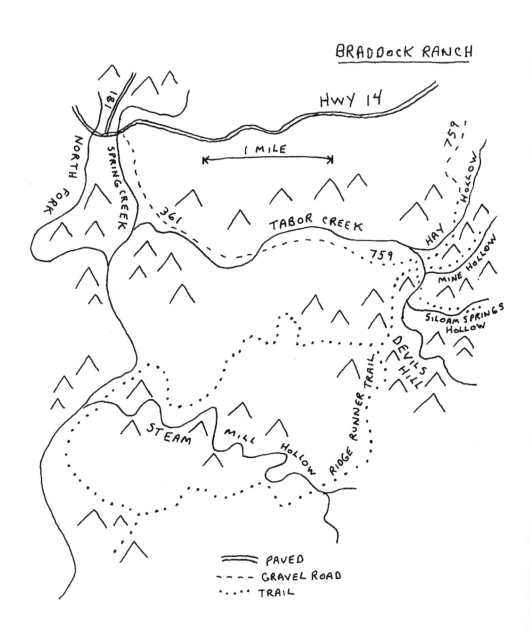

Braddock Ranch

Devil's Hill

Today's ride begins at Twin Bridges near the intersection of Hwys 14 and 181 in the southeast corner of the county, where the North Fork and its major tributary, Spring Creek, flow closely together. Beautifully engineered bridges span both streams. Twin Bridges Canoe and Campground is open during the summer, with cabins, campground, and store. When you rent one of their canoes, they will pick you up downstream and bring you back to your vehicle.

We're taking CR 361, the Tabor Creek Road, which begins just past the bridge over Spring Creek and runs first south, then east. Park along the county road wherever there is room. We'll be going through rugged, hilly country on rough tracks. In some places you'll have to walk.

At first the road parallels Spring Creek and passes a sand and gravel quarry. Look on the left for "Cathedral Rocks," a limestone alcove with twisting protrusions. Tabor Creek is on the right. A series of springs augment the creek near its confluence; however, Tabor is a dry or "losing stream." Though it drains a huge area and has many tributaries, water seldom flows in it. Sudden downpours can cause flash flooding.

After crossing the creek, we enter a small valley. Livestock graze the fields between farmsteads. At the Ledbetter Place the road narrows and becomes FS 759. All this land, including the bottomland field, is national forest. A mile up the road look on the right for the ruins of Braddock Ranch. The house and outbuildings were dozed out by the forest service when they acquired this 600-acre parcel in 1970. Only the lower portion of the once magnificent stone barn remains. Walnut and dogwood trees now grow within its walls. Originally, it had a tall arched roof. Loose hay was brought to the barn in a wagon pulled by a team of mules. A rail with a cable wheel and pulley hung from the upper beam. The hay was lifted into the barn loft and dumped. During the winter hay was forked down into feeders. The Braddocks milked by hand and sold cream in ten-gallon cans. Hundreds of baby calves were raised on the bottle and weaned onto grain. There were stalls for horses and mules. On the hillside above the barn a masonry building encloses a small cave and spring. Water was gravity piped to the house and barn. The forest service now utilizes the spring water for wildlife ponds on the edge of the meadows.

Walter Braddock was twenty-three when his parents, Elmer and Lena, bought this place in 1932. Though born in Oklahoma, he'd been raised on a cattle ranch in Montana. When he was still a boy, Walter spent his summers alone in the alpine meadows of the Rocky Mountains watching over sheep and cattle. The stockmen who hired him gave him boxes of bullets for his revolver and orders to shoot every coyote he saw. A gifted horseman, Walter earned his living catching, training, and selling wild horses.

Earlier this was called the Moore Place. Just up Tabor Creek, on Devil's Hill, a man named Shapely lived in the cave named after him. Shapely wanted a wife, approached Moore, and asked to "buy" his daughter. Moore refused, but Shapely persisted. One day Shapely told Moore that he was taking the daughter whether Moore liked it or not. Angry words were exchanged; Moore shot Shapely dead. The body lay in the yard for hours while the sheriff was brought from far-off Ava, and a coroner's jury convened. Moore was sent to the penitentiary in Jefferson City, where he died. Later, a giant named Taylor lived here. He was so tall, legend says, his feet dragged the ground as he rode.

Walter, Elmer, and a hired hand built this barn. With a team of mules and a steel-runnered "rock sled," they hauled in hundreds of loads of rocks. Notice how they painstakingly laid up a finished surface on both the outside and inside. While wrestling a heavy stone into position high on the wall, Walter injured his back. The Braddocks blamed the hired man for the injury that plagued Walter for life.

Back then all roads were dirt and gravel. Instead of going to town, people went to the local store, Johnson's, where Twin Bridges Canoe Rental is now. Upstream was the Big Spring Church and schoolhouse, the center of social life in the area. Here Walter met Ruby Carter. He walked her home from church one day and continued to court her for three years. In 1941 they married at the courthouse in West Plains. Walter was thirty-three; Ruby, twenty-three.

Ruby was raised "hardscrabble" on a farm two miles north of Twin Bridges. Her family came from South Dakota, where they'd truck-farmed. Perhaps her parents, Maude and Faye, hadn't realized how infertile and droughty that Ozark ridge top was when they bought it. Ruby was the youngest of six children. When she was six, her father complained of a splitting headache. A few hours later an aneurysm burst and killed him.

Maude had to manage as best she could. The Great Depression and Dust Bowl Drought brought low prices and meager crops. Shoes and clothing were expensive. The older boys, Eldon, then seventeen, and Ray, fifteen, worked the land with their mother. Occasionally, they hired out for fifty cents a day. The younger children cleaned, gardened, and hauled water. With diligence the Carters raised a big garden out of the shallow, acidic dirt.

Though Ruby felt self-conscious about her threadbare clothing, she completed all eight grades at the Big Spring one-room schoolhouse. An excellent student, she hoped to attend high school, which meant she'd have to board in town, but she was needed at home.

Here the soil was rich. Walter and Ruby raised a garden of corn, beans, Irish potatoes, sweet potatoes, squash, melons, and cabbages that was a neighborhood wonder. They pulled their manure spreader into the barn, shoveled it full, and then scattered it on the garden and fields. Using gravity flow from the spring they were immune to drought. Asparagus thrived because the Braddocks annually cleaned out the henhouse and layered manure thickly on the bed. Knowing that asparagus was salt tolerant, Ruby scattered rock salt to kill the grass and weeds.

Ruby canned, dried, and stored food either in the springhouse or in the barn, where the thick stone walls and the enormous pile of hay above kept the temperature at 54°F in the winter and 64°F in summer. In good years they harvested 150 bushels of corn to the acre when seventy-five was considered an excellent crop.

But farming in these bottoms is unpredictable. When local folks say the creek is "coming down," they mean the water is coming up. One year when it hadn't rained a drop here, heavy downpours further up Tabor Creek sent a flood that destroyed the Braddock's corn.

At first Ruby and Walter lived with Elmer and Lena. A few months later, they moved into the cabin they built in Mine Hollow near the ruins of an old lead operation. Ruby shot squirrels for supper with the Harrington Richardson .22 seven-shot revolver Walter had traded a wild horse for back in Montana. She baited steel traps with urine and trapped bobcats and foxes to supplement their income.

When Elmer died in 1946, Ruby and Walter moved back in to care for Lena. They "mechanized" in 1947 and bought a yellow military-style jeep to pull their horse-drawn equipment. But they still milked their Jersey cows by hand, morning and evening, seven days a week.

Ruby drove a six-mule team for the heavy farm work.

In 1954 Lena died. That summer was devastating; with no rain, temperatures reached 120°F. The REA strung a power line up the valley that year. Ruby and Walter wired the house and barn and bought a refrigerator and freezer.

We're at the bottom of a north slope known locally as a "frost pocket." Late spring and early autumn frosts are normal; fruit is nearly impossible to grow. Winter days are short and dark. On clear, still nights the arctic air "pools" in the hollows and freezes the ground. Ruby read -26°F one morning.

But the Braddocks had a snug house. Walter installed a coil of copper pipe in the wood cook stove and mounted a storage tank on the wall. By piping water from the spring, they had hot and cold running water when most of their neighbors still carried buckets. One morning, though, as Ruby was preparing breakfast, the water tank began to make strange noises. Ruby left the room just as the tank, its plumbing clogged with lime, exploded and sent scalding water across the kitchen.

Sadly, no children were born to give them companionship in the remote canyon. However, Walter brought an English shepherd pup home from a livestock sale in Willow Springs. They named the tiny bundle of brown and black fur Lucky; she could fit into the palm of Ruby's hand. Right away Walter, communicating with hand signals, taught her to herd chickens. Lucky became a consummate stock dog, by far the most valuable animal on the farm. She brought up the cows for milking. When they drove their cattle to rented pastureland, Ruby and Walter would follow the herd on their riding mules, Tom and Jerry, while Lucky kept the cattle in a tight group.

In the afternoons Ruby and Lucky hunted squirrels with a Mossberg .22 rifle. Deeply affectionate, Lucky spent hundreds of hours riding in the jeep draped across Ruby's lap. She also saved Walter's life. The Braddocks had hand-raised a Holstein bull. As a two-year-old, he became aggressive and unpredictable. While Walter was crossing the barn lot, the bull "snuck up" behind him, bellowed, charged, and knocked him down. Walter managed to scramble behind some machinery as the bull, nostrils flaring, closed in. Suddenly, like a miracle, Lucky sunk her teeth into the bull's hind leg. She tenaciously held on as he kicked and thrashed. Walter carried the injured dog to the house, and in a few days she was fine. Even when Lucky was old, half-blind, and crippled with arthritis, she went out with Ruby and

Walter and tried desperately to do her job. Eventually, though, Ruby had a neighbor put her down.

Walter bought a five-gaited sorrel filly named Minnie and spent hundreds of hours training her as a trail horse. He taught her to "shake hands." Strong, responsive, and a smooth ride, she gave the Braddocks two fine foals. Later on, when she wasn't being ridden or handled, she chased and attacked cattle and inflicted bloody, flesh-tearing bites. Reluctantly, Walter sold her.

One of their draught mares had a red mule foal that hated to get its feet wet. When there was water in Tabor Creek, the little mule would jump into the wagon bed and hitch a ride across.

Walter's chronic back pain had him in and out of doctors' offices. There were two traumatic sessions under the surgeon's knife. Cataracts impaired his vision. Ruby assumed all the driving and much of the mechanical work. When their New Idea hay loader arrived in boxes, Ruby spent days assembling and adjusting the 2100 parts.

The Braddocks lived frugally. The milk check and the sale of livestock were their only income. Every penny possible they put back into the ranch for fencing, fertilizer, crushed limestone, maintenance, and for upgrading their livestock. They built three silos next to the barn and later had a dozer dig a pit silo. In the summer a silage contractor came through the neighborhood with a crew and heavy machinery. When the Braddock's turn came, Ruby would spend the morning preparing a big noon dinner for the men. The chopped crops were packed in the silos, fermenting like sauerkraut into a fetid mess that cattle relished.

Five crops of light green, sweet-smelling alfalfa hay were cut each season. Later, a pernicious pest, *Phytonomus Murinus*, the alfalfa weevil, weakened their well-tended crop. Native to the Middle East, it suddenly appeared in Utah in 1904. Transported in loads of hay, the insect infested fields across the U.S. and somehow found this isolated farm. Thousands of adult weevils overwintered in the Braddock barn. Early in the spring, as the alfalfa made new growth, the female weevils punctured the alfalfa stems and laid tens of thousands of eggs. Ravenous grubs then gorged on the fresh leaves, crippled and stunted the plants' growth. The Braddocks cut the infested fields, took an inferior crop, and hoped for better hay on subsequent cuttings. Though they bought and sprayed insecticide, the weevils persisted.

Every ten years Ruby and Walter logged the place and used the money for a new vehicle. They bought a two-ton Chevy truck; in '53 they purchased a new Ford "Jubilee" tractor with a three-point hitch disk plow, a "laying out" plow, and a Dearborn sickle-bar mower. They'd never had a car, though they talked about traveling. In 1963 they bought a two-door Rambler. Whether bouncing over rough gravel roads or cruising on the highway, the Rambler was solid and dependable. They traveled west, camped in Idaho and Oregon, and saw the Rocky Mountains and the Pacific Ocean. The front seats folded flat and made a comfortable bed.

Let's ride further. The country ahead is rugged with forested canyons. Tabor Creek turns sharply to the south along the base of Devil's Hill. Three drainages come in from the north—Hay Hollow, Mine Hollow, and Siloam Springs Hollow. The Ridgerunner Trail follows the ridge between Hay and Mine Hollows. It crosses the bottoms and heads south toward Hammond Camp and Arkansas. A network of ATV trails makes it easy to get lost.

First, we'll ride into lower Hay Hollow, also known as Braddock Lakes. The trail to the left leads to a 4x4 road.

Walter Braddock had a dream. Here, amid the forested hills, he wanted to create a resort where hunters, fishermen, and outdoor lovers could enjoy the serenity of the Ozarks. Where a cluster of springs and seeps flowed out of the bedrock, Walter staked out his lakes. Eventually, he hired five different dozer operators to push up the clay embankments before he was satisfied that they would hold against flooding. He stocked the waters with bass, blue gill, crappie, and channel cat.

The Braddocks built cabins and a campground. "Snowbirds," retirees from the North, stopped with their trailers and RVs on the way to Florida and the Gulf Coast. Walter and Ruby charged a dollar a day to fish, and soon fishermen had worn a path around the lakes. A fun-loving crowd of deer hunters always packed the resort for opening day. The Braddocks sat around the campfires and listened good-naturedly to hunting yarns.

As Ruby and Walter aged, Braddock Lakes became too difficult for them to manage. They sold the farm and their modest herd of Hereford cattle and moved to West Plains. There, they invested part of their money in neglected houses. They "fixed them up." Because Walter's back was chronically injured, Ruby did most of the heavy work. She cut lumber with a circular saw; hung drywall, paneling, and trim; patched plaster; painted. Ultimately, when Walter's eyesight diminished, they retired.

The forest service converted Braddock Lakes to a YCC camp. Modeled loosely on the CCC, the YCC brought youth to the country to work. Groups of boys and girls came in alternate years. They cleared the Ridgerunner Trail. When funding for the program was terminated, the forest service tore down the buildings.

Unfortunately, the lakes were destroyed. Low bridges were built over the lake spillways. When torrential rain flooded Hay Hollow, logs and debris carried by the roaring current jammed up against the bridges, and floodwater cut through the dams. Today the emptied lakes are a scar on the landscape.

The next drainage is Mine Hollow. The trail once extended all the way through the hollow, but now it is choked with brush a half-mile ahead. The third hollow, Siloam Springs, is wild and overgrown. Push your bike up the usually dry, boulder-strewn streambed. Further up is a complex of unusual springs. Legend says that this drainage and its springs were sacred to the Native Americans, who believed the waters had the power to restore vitality. Long ago, when the Spanish invaded the New World looking for treasure, the Indians told them of a spring that could restore youth. Ponce de Leon wandered with his army in the forests of the southeastern U.S. in his search for a fountain of youth. He failed, but the legend persisted. Across North America mineral springs attracted people seeking revitalized health.

In 1817, when this region was a roadless wilderness, Elijah Fenton of Ste. Genevieve heard from trappers about a spring with curative powers. He made the difficult journey through tangled forests and brought his invalid wife to this hollow. After several months of drinking the waters, she rejuvenated. As the years passed, thousands came here to be healed.

In 1921 Florida entrepreneur N.O. Tate bought the springs and three hundred adjoining acres. He planned to build a fabulous hotel, spa, and resort. As work began on the four-story structure, the spring branch was dammed to create lakes; an electrical power plant and a telephone system were set up. But Tate overextended himself financially. Shortages of building material and skilled workers, in addition to the difficulty of delivering to the site, slowed construction. Springfield developer John Woodruff bought not only Tate's land but also an adjoining three hundred acres. An attorney turned promoter, Woodruff had built the Frisco Building, the Colonial Hotel, the Woodruff Building, and the Kentwood Arms Hotel in Springfield. He hired a plasterer from Italy to apply a stucco finish. The stucco was dashed with particles of marble, granite, and quartz that glistened brilliantly in the sunlight. Native oaks were felled and lumber milled on site. Skilled carpenters sanded, varnished, and fitted the interior. In the elaborate dining room all four walls were hand-painted in a blue-green landscape mural. Sparing no expense, furniture was purchased and shipped from Chicago. A massive fireplace dominated the main lobby.

Outside, the grounds were beautifully landscaped. Cottages were erected for those seeking a more secluded stay. A swimming pool was dug and poured. In the basement of the hotel, guests could soak in the healing mineral waters. They could take out saddle horses from the stable and ride on forested trails or paddle boats on the lake. Tennis courts were built. Guided fishing excursions on the North Fork were available.

In 1924 the nine-hole, two-thousand-yard golf course was completed with grass greens. The unique and challenging course had natural hazards. The "Punch Bowl" hole was 130 yards from tee to green with a seventy-five-foot elevation drop through numerous traps. A foursome of Springfield's top players established par at forty-two.

The Pinebrook Inn, though still under construction, opened August 8, 1923. Most guests came to West Plains on the Frisco Railroad. Twice daily the hotel's bus, referred to as the "jitney," a four-cylinder REO Speedwagon, ferried them back and forth over the tortuous gravel roads. There were fifty rooms at the hotel, twenty-five with private baths. Rates were $4/day/guest and up. Cottages with modern plumbing rented for $20/week.

Each spring had unique powers. Spring one, heavily iron laden, was stronger than most stomachs would tolerate. Spring two was only slightly more palatable. Spring three, "Chamomile Spring," was cathartic. Springs four through seven were solutions of magnesium and sodium salts advertised to revitalize "sluggish digestions" and "torpid excretions." But springs eight, nine, and ten were the most popular. Spring ten was used to treat arthritis and kidney disease.

Tate and Woodruff had hoped that the remoteness of Pinebrook Inn would attract patrons. They were wrong. As the years went by fewer and fewer guests arrived. By the late '20's the hotel was open only in summer. The primitive roads appalled guests in private vehicles. One woman said that the road from West Plains was so muddy that her husband had to tie ropes around the spoked wheels of their car to gain enough traction to get to the hotel. The "Golden Age" of

Pinebrook ended. The Great Depression brought its demise.

Desperate to make ends meet, the owners set up a bottling plant and sold the spring water as a tonic. However, the succession of dry years in the '30's caused the waters to diminish. Many times Woodruff sent workmen to dig further into the springs. Convinced that a larger channel could be opened up, he even used dynamite. Eventually, he conceded defeat and converted the hotel into a rest home before it faded into obscurity.

On the ridge above to the right is FS 774. Take the faint trail to it. If you miss the fork, just keep going. The trail will eventually reach the road. Stop for awhile at the Siloam Springs Cemetery and look at the venerable gravestones and wonderful view. Further on 774 ends where the pavement of T Hwy begins. On the left is the driveway to the Pinebrook Inn, now renovated and open for business as a bed and breakfast.

Yes, the old hotel is still standing. For a generation or more it sat vacant while most of the logged-off surrounding land was bought up by the forest service. In the late 1960's Gene and Shirley Mask, who had heard stories of the hotel's grand days, drove out from their home in West Plains to look at the crumbling resort. People told them it was haunted. Brush and weeds choked the grounds. Vandals had not only broken all the windows but had also torn out plumbing fixtures and had kicked holes in the walls. Owls, spiders, rats, bats, snakes, and flying squirrels made the hotel their home. The cottages were hopeless ruins, their porches and stairs rotted away.

Yet Gene knew that the Pinebrook was still structurally sound. He and Shirley were convinced that the building could be saved. A lover of the out-of-doors, Gene wanted to create a private hunting lodge. The hotel was currently part of a seventy-eight-acre parcel owned by an attorney who had acquired it in lieu of legal fees. The Masks bought it at a bargain price. At the time they owned and operated the movie theaters in West Plains. During the day they would leave their children, Clarissa, eight, and Travis, two, with Shirley's mother and work on the Pinebrook. In Springfield they purchased used windows, bathtubs, and sinks that matched the originals. Story by story, room by room, they remodeled. A dump truck hauled off the debris. During the remodeling Shirley discovered a loose panel inside a closet on the upper story. A secret door led to a hidden room. Amazingly, there was an alarm connected to the front desk. Most likely the secret room was a speakeasy and/or casino during the hotel's Prohibition heyday.

After two years the Masks moved in and occupied a small portion of the main floor. Gene put his Appaloosa horses to pasture on the grounds. He bought a bulldozer and pushed up a lake on the north end of the property. A professional taxidermist, Gene decorated the lobby with cougar, bobcat, deer, boar, fox, and bighorn sheep, most of which he'd collected himself. Soon after, some of the rooms were ready for guests.

Deer season was especially busy, but people came for quail, turkey, dove, rabbit, and squirrel. Gene kept coonhounds for guests who wanted to listen to the dogs track and "tree" under the starry sky. The price was $25/person/day and included guide service. The Masks enjoyed the business, but it wasn't always easy. Guests would arrive with brand new rifles and no idea how to use them. One man got lost in a forty-acre patch of woods completely surrounded by roads.

Most of the time the hotel was the Mask's private home. The kids had the entire building to play in. But disconcertingly, people were drawn to the famous old resort. There wasn't a feeling of privacy. Again and again strangers simply came in and wandered around, thinking the hotel was a public space. When family and friends came to visit, Gene would play hide-and-seek from the hidden room. While the searchers rushed about, Gene would hallo from time to time. No one ever found him. However, one day after the secret room hadn't been used for months, Shirley discovered neat stacks of clothing and food. Someone had been living there while they lived downstairs! They never saw anyone. In 1975 Gene and Shirley sold the Pinebrook and bought the truck stop at Hwys 14 and 63.

A few hundred yards up the pavement, where CR 103 runs south, are an abandoned church and some scattered dwellings. Once the thriving town of Siloam Springs stood here. In the years following the Civil War, demand for lumber attracted loggers to the stands of virgin pine. The town served the loggers and sawmills, and the mineral springs, owned by D.F. Martin, attracted tourists. Siloam Springs had two hotels, the Emerson and the Bottom, several stores, a bank, blacksmith shop, drugstore, jail, livery stable, tannery, and four newspapers: the <u>Review,</u> <u>Banner,</u> <u>Optic,</u> and <u>Siloam Springs Gossiper</u>.

The word Siloam comes from the Hebrew *Shiloah*, which means sending forth. In *John 9* Jesus heals a blind beggar by spitting into a handful of dust, anointing the man's eyelids with the mud, and telling him to wash in the Pool of Siloam, where his sight will be restored. When this town was founded, British archaeologist Charles Warren made "Siloam" a worldwide sensation. In the thirty-second chapter of 2 *Chronicles*, Hezekiah, King of Israel in the ninth century B.C., had feared that the Assyrians under King Sennacherib would invade and lay siege to Jerusalem. He ordered the spring of Gihon outside the city to be concealed and the water diverted into the city. Warren's excavations on the west side of old Jerusalem uncovered a long stairway with a pool at the bottom. An inscription carved in stone told how two crews of workmen, one from under the city, another from Gihon, tunneled toward one another and created an aqueduct from Gihon to the Pool of Siloam. The Bible says that an angel destroyed the Assyrian army. Sennacherib, returning home, was put to the sword by his own sons.

Eventually, the forests were cut, and the government gradually bought up the nearly worthless land. The tannery closed. The Pinebrook became derelict; when Foster's Store and Post Office, the last business, burned in 1967, Siloam Springs disappeared. The old site is now considered unsafe because its hidden wells and cisterns could trap the unwary.

Let's ride on. Our destination is the "Sinks," two dramatically steep-sided sinkholes separated by a narrow backbone ridge. One is dangerously precipitous, rocky, and overgrown; the other, larger, with bluffs and a peat bog that seems to tremble as you walk across it.

Douglas County has many sinkholes; some cover several acres. Over centuries rainwater flowed below the surface, dissolved the soft limestone, and created caves. When such a cave collapses, it forms a funnel-shaped sinkhole. Some sinks are spectacular with streams that abruptly disappear. The rich, moist soil that accumulates in them often supports large trees, such as the locally uncommon bur oak and shellbark hickory. Unusual plants, like rose mallow and orchid, are found in Booger County sinkholes.

Go south on CR 103 for two miles. Pass forest road 822 on the left and 778 on the right. Cross Tabor Creek again at the ford and pedal up a long, steep hill. The faint trail to the sinkholes is in some big pines and is easy to miss. The forest service bulldozed up a barricade to keep trucks out. We're now in Howell County (called "Howl County" by wags). Many of the people in this neighborhood belong to a pioneer family from Virginia named Collins.

The sinks are examples of *karst* geology. Long ago, Booger County was the bottom of a warm, shallow sea. Over millennia dissolved

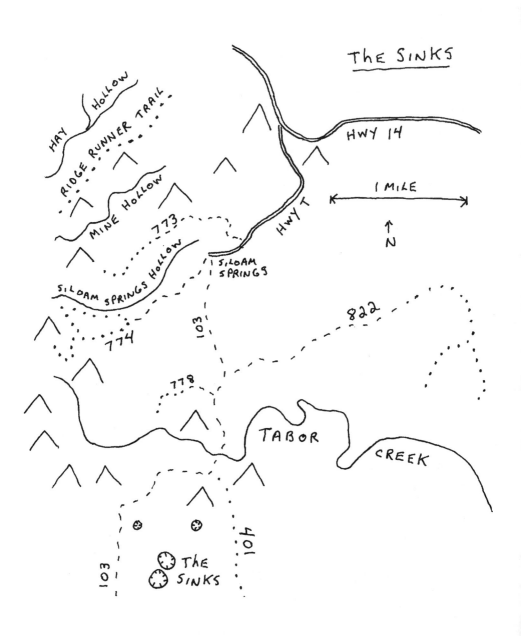

The Sinks

rock particles, shells, and the bones of sea creatures settled on the seafloor in layers hundreds of feet thick. Time and pressure hardened them into limestone. Sometimes sand washed into the sea to form the *roubidoux* sandstone that intersperses the limestone. Between these layers irregularly shaped deposits of chert (also known as "flint," "nodules," "lenses," or "stringers") formed when dissolved silica fell out of solution. As softer rock has washed away, chert has been left as fieldstone and as the gravel in our streambeds. Brittle, fine-grained, and resistant to weathering, Booger County chert comes in many colors and textures. Sometimes it is embedded with fossils and crystals. Lapidaries shape and polish the finer stones into semiprecious gems called "agate" and "jasper." The Native Americans learned to flake chert into surgically sharp-edged tools and weapons.

Long ago immense tectonic forces deep in the earth pushed magma upward, lifted the land, and created the dome-shaped Ozark Plateau. The uplift severely fractured the sedimentary rock and allowed billions of gallons of rainwater to seep into the cracks. The slight acidity of the rainwater gradually dissolved the soft rock and created the three-dimensional maze of underground conduits and streams which are part of our complex aquifer.

Starting in the 1960's, geologists began "mapping" the movement of groundwater in Douglas County by pouring dye into losing streams and sinkholes during heavy rain. Small carbon filters were placed in springs and later brought to laboratories to check for traces of dye. The results were surprising. Dye released into the upper drainage of the Gasconade River north of Mansfield, in Wright County, was recovered at both North Fork and Double Spring in Ozark County. The dye had traveled thirty-five miles and had passed completely under Douglas County! Another tracing on Dry Creek, south of Norwood, was recovered twenty-seven miles away at Hodgson Mill Spring, on the Bryant in Ozark County.

It's hard to believe, but the crystal-clear water we see pouring from a spring like Topaz actually carries tons of dissolved limestone out of the aquifer and into the Mississippi and the Gulf of Mexico. In the warm, shallow ocean it drops out of solution and settles as a thick paste on the seafloor. In time it will become limestone again. Well water is "hard" and forms a whitish mineral film that gradually becomes a crust on cooking pots; it clogs plumbing, water heaters, and coffee makers.

Our unusual geology in Booger County causes strange events. In

August 1993 a "cloudburst" sent a flash flood down Clifty Creek that covered the bottoms of Faye Coble's farm with water and debris. Water pressure forced a subterranean cavern to collapse in the middle of her hayfield. Faye had to build a fence around the dangerous, steep-sided twenty-five-foot sinkhole to keep livestock from falling into it. Around the same time, Faye began to have troubles with armadillos, a non-native species from the South. When her dog cornered one that was digging up a flowerbed, Faye picked it up and drowned it in her fishpond. It took a surprisingly long time to die, she said. The Cabool Enterprise picture of Faye holding the dead animal was the first armadillo that folks in Booger County had seen. Though she eliminated as many armadillos as possible, they continued to dig up her famous garden and fields. However, the new sinkhole was a deathtrap for them. The slow-witted, near-sighted creatures walked over the edge and tumbled to the bottom, unable to escape.

Further upstream, on the West Prong of Clifty Creek, an even more bizarre incident occurred on the old Joe Kennedy Place, the Micky Plummer Farm. In the summer of 1978 the Plummer's palomino gelding, Golden, was standing in the shade, stomping at pestering flies, when suddenly the ground gave way under him. He fell backwards and upside-down into a chamber fifty feet below and died. When people went down to explore, they found a strange skeleton with a long snout and big teeth. The bones created a local sensation. Stylishly-dressed Springfield TV newscaster Erin Hayes taped a story and climbed into the cave. The skeleton was identified as *Mylohyus Fossilis*, an Ice Age peccary, a type of pig thought to have become extinct 20,000 years ago. Perhaps, people speculate, there was another entrance to the cave. The peccary entered the shelter and was trapped when the other opening collapsed.

There's no point visiting the Sinks in the summer. Thick vegetation makes it impossible to appreciate their grandeur. But there are other reasons. Poison ivy grows everywhere—remember the adage "three leaves together warn a feller." Chiggers, *Eutrombicula Alfreddugesi* and *Euthrombicula Splendens*, the larval form of parasitic red mites 1/150th of an inch in diameter, infest the area. They crawl upward and burrow into the flesh of a person's waist or ankles. With sharp mouthparts they pierce the skin, inject tissue-dissolving saliva, and feed by sucking. Inflammation and intense itching can last for days. There are also ticks. The three species, the Lone Star, Dog, and Black each have three stages—adult, "yearling," and "seed" or nymph.

Adults climb onto a host, a dog for example; the female incises the skin and engorges herself as the male mates with her. She drops off and lays masses of eggs that hatch into seed ticks. They are the size of a grain of sand just large enough to see. Clusters of seed ticks climb onto a stem or blade of grass and infest whatever brushes against them. After a seed tick has taken a meal of blood, it drops off and metamorphoses into a yearling, which must again find a host to become an adult. A "mess" of seed ticks can ruin your day! Remove them with adhesive tape.

Local folks avoid sinkholes because they are a haven for snakes. Watch where you put your feet! Cottonmouths and timber rattlers are rare but potently venomous. Pygmy rattlers are common in some places. Ubiquitous, copperheads are difficult to see; their pinkish-tan and dark brown markings are perfect camouflage on a background of dry leaves. Where sunlight and shade dapple the forest litter, they are nigh invisible. Copperheads have yellow eyes with elliptical pupils. When they strike, they inject venom through hollow fangs that fold into the roof of their mouth. Though not aggressive, their bite is painful and causes a burning feeling and nausea. Throbbing and swelling begin in a few minutes. The bites are seldom fatal but are slow to heal and can leave a scar. Copperheads are called pit vipers because of their infrared-sensing facial pits. In complete darkness, silent, patiently coiled, they wait in ambush for warm-blooded quarry like mice; with blinding speed they strike, inject venom, and quickly recoil before prey can counterattack. The snake trails the wounded mouse and swallows it headfirst.

That's the end of today's ride. Go back the way we came to Twin Bridges. If you're still energetic, explore forest roads 401 or 822. It's possible to take a shortcut back if you ride to the end of FS 773 and walk through the forest to Mine Hollow.

Tomorrow we'll visit sparkling Bryant Creek and Booger County's most celebrated cave. Nearby are rock shelters used by Stone Age people at the end of the Ice Age. Have you heard of the "Cistercian Brotherhood?"

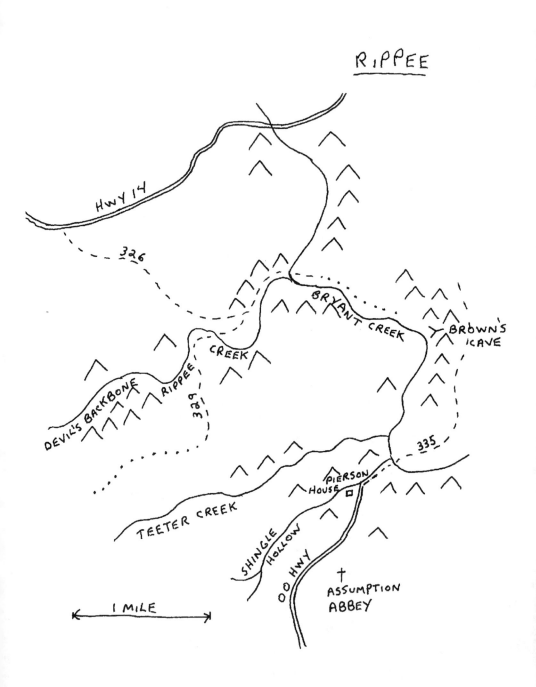

Rippee

Rippee

Booger County has many caves. Today we will visit its most famous, Brown's Cave. Park near the Dept. of Conservation's sign to Rippee Recreation Area at CR 326 and Hwy 14, twelve miles east of Ava. A two-mile ride downhill through fields and woods leads to a T in the road at the edge of a bottomland hayfield. The cave is to the left, but first go right, up the valley, and cross Rippee Creek to a picturesque horse ranch beneath colorful limestone bluffs. Turn around and ride past the picnic area, across Bryant Creek, and past the campground to the end of the road. Ahead is a big meadow planted with black walnut. Take the equestrian path across it, aiming for the bluffs on the other side. Stash your bike and continue on foot.

The spring-fed waters of Rippee Creek once powered a gristmill built by a mountain man named Sawyer and his Native American wife. During the Civil War the 10th Illinois Cavalry and the local militia constructed a fort to protect the mill but were unable to keep Colonel Burbridge's Confederate Rangers from burning it down. Later, Samson and Vandalia Rippee settled here. Sam was a carpenter, beekeeper, and farmer; Vandalia, a schoolteacher.

Much earlier, Native Americans had lived along Rippee and other streams in Douglas County. They left behind thousands of projectiles, including the famous 9500-year-old Scottsbluff point found along K Hwy. Collecting arrowheads is a favorite pastime of the locals, especially after rains on fresh-plowed ground expose new rock fragments.

As boys Herb Sanders and Howard Curry were avid Booger County artifact hunters. The old timers showed them prehistoric campsites along the streams, some of which covered several acres. They found not only arrowheads but also stone hoes, pottery shards, tomahawks, and stone tools. At the Ava library they learned that these artifacts belonged to people who had lived 1000-2000 years ago in settled villages who grew corn, beans, and squash and raised turkeys and dogs for meat. The favorable climate of eastern North America encouraged civilizations based on agriculture. Villages grew into towns with marketplaces, specialized workers, priests, and soldiers.

Along the Mississippi, just below the mouth of the Missouri River, Native American farmers planted seeds in the rich silt of the extensive floodplains. Cahokia, the largest city in the prehistoric United States, was a natural trading hub for waterborne commerce. Scores of flat-topped mounds crowned with wooden buildings were constructed with millions of man-hours of labor. The largest, Monks Mound at Cahokia Historic Site, is one hundred feet tall and covers fourteen acres. In the bustling marketplaces of Cahokia travelers from Booger County bartered for improved seeds, salt, tools, and weapons. Exotic trade goods from the coast and far-off Mexico were displayed. Many came as athletes or as spectators to the large playing fields built for a sport in which a heavy stone disc like a small tire was used. Gambling was popular.

The hard-running Native Americans would have covered the two hundred miles in just a few days. Along the way they would have passed the open pit mines near present-day Crescent, Missouri, in the Meramec River drainage, where workers had exposed massive deposits of tool-quality flint. They built fires, heated the rock, and then dowsed it with water to crack off workable chunks for trade. Other mines produced red ochre paint-stone, or hematite (iron oxide), crushed into a powder for body decoration and pottery.

Sanders and Curry talked about ancient people when they fished the Bryant. They agreed that their numerous artifacts were relatively modern. The real excitement in archaeology was excavating much older sites used by the Paleo-Indians at the end of the Ice Age. Could there be sites in Booger County? As their johnboat floated lazily under the towering bluffs, they looked for likely spots. They imagined a time of harsh climatic change with cycles of drought and heat alternating with brutally cold winters. Sanders and Curry searched for caves or rock shelters with a southern or eastern exposure and a year-round spring close by.

They started digging in 1950. Finding time wasn't easy; they were in their thirties with families and businesses. Howard was the dentist in Ava. Herb owned a bulldozing company and later erected large metal-framed buildings. Thursday was Doc's day off. They threw buckets, shovels, and a sifting screen in the pickup and headed for the Bryant.

Near Rippee they excavated the floor of a large overhang. Just below the surface they found arrowheads and pottery shards they were familiar with. Deeper down were layers of bone and worked stones new to them including, near the bottom, two 10,000-year-old Dalton points. Eureka! Booger County, with its many caves, was a natural migration route for ancient people who had passed through the area in waves.

Bertha Cave, at the mouth of Fox Creek, was a rich dig, but the shelter near Yates Cemetery was even better. A massive section of the "roof" had fallen in and had nearly blocked the entrance. As Doc and Herb slowly sifted through the dry soil, they realized that people had lived here both before and after the roof had collapsed. They dug up the skeleton of a small adult human whose teeth were nearly worn away, along with stone knives, bone needles, an awl fashioned from a deer bone, two heavy grooved tomahawks, plenty of pottery shards, and many mussel shells. Great numbers of bones—deer, bear, bison, raccoon, turkey, and small birds—were intermixed with the artifacts. At the lowest level they found arrowheads dated to 4000 B.C. Nearby, in a small shelter they unearthed the burial of a teenager interred in a sitting position with a dog and a large clay pot.

Near Swan Creek, on the west side of the county, Sanders and Curry explored an intriguing spot. They were investigating an ancient campsite near a spring when they discovered a cave that had purposely been sealed with black dirt long, long ago. Once it had seen heavy use. Though rich with human bones and artifacts, the cave was never thoroughly explored.

Sifting through dirt is slow, hard work. Because of the dust they carried the soil outside in buckets for sifting. After thirty years they had excavated only a few of the many promising sites. Their collection is a remarkable life's work. The oldest arrowhead, a 12,000-year-old Paleo point, was discovered by Herb one day at work. As he was standing beside a concrete chute, Herb glanced over at the moving concrete and saw the arrowhead among the aggregate fragments. Alas, the prize Curry and Sanders sought most eluded them, the Sandia-type point, which had been found in shelters in nearby counties mixed with the bones of extinct Ice Age animals.

As we walk toward the bluff, glance at the rock fragments underfoot and search for projectile points. Above us, in the vertical face of the limestone cliff, are the Ladder Caves. Notice the exuded mineralization. Brown's Cave is on the other side of the bluff. This is the private property of Assumption Abbey, a Trappist monastery. In 1950 Chicago journalist Joseph "Drew" Pierson gave this 3400-acre parcel to the Roman Catholic Order of the Cistercian Brotherhood. Pierson was a Methodist who wanted the land used for quiet reflection where hospitality would be extended to everyone. The land was ideal for solitude and hard work, the two tenets of Trappist life.

Father Vincent Daly, of New Mellery Abbey outside Dubuque, Iowa, was the first to arrive. Soon eleven monks were building the monastery and later adding wings for a novitiate, guestrooms, infirmary, and chapel. To support themselves they raised cattle and sheep and ran a grade A dairy. In 1960 they founded a thriving business, Trappist Concrete Products, which manufactured concrete blocks for building construction. Membership peaked in 1962. Following the edicts of Vatican Council II, disillusionment caused many to leave, including Dom Bruno Payant, the first Abbot. In addition to holding liturgy in English, the rule of silence was broken and a new set of monastic practices adopted.

The monks rise at 2:15 A.M. for prayer (vigils), then breakfast, prayer (lauds), and then Mass. They work through the morning. At midday there is prayer (sext) and lunch. Following the afternoon's work is prayer (vespers) and supper. At 7:30 P.M. the monks pray together (compline). Bedtime is at 8:00. Vows of poverty, chastity, and obedience rule their lives; they struggle for compassion toward their fellow humans and offer themselves to Christ. Many practice silence and do not eat meat. Some, after forty years of monastic life, become hermits, as did former Abbot Dom Robert, who lives in seclusion on the property.

Monasticism arose in the early Christian period. As Jesus wandered in the desert, men sought solitude, prayer, spiritual renewal, and union with Christ. St. Anthony of Thebes went alone into the Egyptian desert in 271 A.D. Others followed his example. By the Middle Ages monasticism was a powerful spiritual and political force. St. Robert of Molesme founded the Cistercian Brotherhood at Citeaux, France, in 1098. When the order was reorganized in 1664 at La Trappe, France, it became known as the Trappist Order. Assumption Abbey is one of about one hundred Cistercian monasteries worldwide.

The concrete block business has been sold. Today the small, quiet community of monks earns its living making and selling fruitcake. To order some or to make reservations to stay at the Abbey or to tour the grounds, call 417-683-5110.

Though Brown's Cave seems like a wild refuge deep in the forest, it's actually the most visited place in Douglas County. For many years the annual Brown's Cave Picnic was held in high summer; people came from miles around in wagons, on horseback, and later, in cars. On the flat ground below the cave, "stands" sold sodas, lemonade, hamburgers, and ice cream packed in tubs of ice. Square dancers swirled across a rough-sawn oak-board floor; kids swung far out over the Bryant on a thick rope hung from a limb. Foot races, swimming matches, and a ladies' jug-throwing contest were held. In election years candidates held forth. The adventuresome lit kerosene lanterns and explored far back into the cave. For years the cave was the destination for Ava High School's "senior sneak day."

Brown's Cave has a sinister side. In his confession Edward Perry wrote that he and his uncle, Will Yost, plotted the robbery and grisly murder of the Sawyer family here. On Saturday May 23, 1896, someone reported to the sheriff's office in Ava that clouds of flies and a revolting stench were emanating from the Sawyer house. When Deputy W.B. Singleton broke open the door, nauseous fumes of putrefying flesh sickened him. A black, bloated head protruded from under the bed. Two other corpses, grotesquely stiffened in pools of dried blood, were further under the bed. A coroner's jury dragged the fetid bodies into the yard for examination. Their heads had been battered in by a blunt instrument, and their throats had been cut. Evidence suggested that the Sawyers had been killed in the barn. The house had been ransacked; the wagon and team were missing. A newcomer, Edward Perry, the Sawyer's hired hand, was immediately suspected. A $300 reward was posted for his capture.

When Perry turned himself in and confessed, the county was electrified. Will Yost was arrested. That night an unruly mob gathered in the streets. Heavily armed men rode around the square and threatened to break down the jail door and lynch the prisoners. Prosecuting Attorney, E.H. Farnsworth, faced the angry crowd and told them to go home and allow the court to do its duty. Trustworthy men were deputized to protect the jail.

Two days later the trial was held with Judge Evans presiding. Farnsworth used Perry's confession to make the state's case. Greed, he said, was the motive. Mr. Sawyer received a pension and kept money in the house. Late at night, while Ed Perry hid in the barn, Will Yost knocked on the Sawyer's door. Earnest, their twenty-five-year-old son, asked, "Who's there? What do you want?" "A sick horse is making a racket in the barn," Yost replied. Earnest lit a lamp and walked to the barn. When he stooped to examine the horse, Yost struck him with a piece of pipe. Perry rushed in, and both of them pounded Earnest's head, caving in his skull. Unexpectedly, Mr. and Mrs. Sawyer came into the barn, asking, "What's going on here?" The murderers attacked with their pipes. Yost went to the house for a butcher knife to make sure the victims were dead.

Perry's lawyer, L.O. Hailey, pleaded for mercy, but it took the jury only twenty minutes to find Perry guilty. Judge Evans sentenced him to death by hanging.

A festive crowd of three thousand attended the execution on the Ava square. Hotels and restaurants did a brisk business. There were only a few liquored-up rowdies. Perry seemed calm and unconcerned as he mounted the gallows. "Good people of Douglas County: This perhaps will be the last time you will ever see me in life, but I hope to meet you hereafter. May God bless you is my prayer." Sheriff Johnson handcuffed Perry's hands behind his back, tied his legs, pulled a black hood over his head, and adjusted the noose. Unfortunately, when the trap sprung, Perry's neck didn't break. As the dangling Perry slowly strangled, the attending physicians periodically checked his pulse.

Will Yost was granted a change of venue to Howell County and was acquitted. Perry's confession was the only evidence against him.

Look out from the cave and imagine the great flood of June 1, 1876, when the Bryant rose twenty-five feet nearly to the cave. Homes, crops, livestock, and people were swept away.

The cave gets its name from pioneer settler Tom Brown. A Virginian born in 1812, he moved to Indiana and married into the Davis family. When his wife died young, he brought his infant twin daughters, Julia and Margaret, by oxcart to the Davis farm at Falling Spring on Fox Creek. He left the girls with their grandparents and looked for a place to homestead. When he made camp for the night below the cave, the ground was thick with broken arrowheads and flakes of worked stone.

Tom was a blacksmith. He lived in the cave while he cut logs and hauled in foundation stones. The neighbors gathered and helped "raise" a shop and a cabin for Tom and the girls. In 1846 he married Mary "Polly" Burden. They had seven children. Tom was also a Methodist minister; people called him Parson Brown. The cave was his church. Though a Southerner, Tom believed slavery was evil, and secretly as a "conductor" on the Underground Railroad, he used the cave to hide fugitive slaves.

During the Civil War Tom, then fifty-two, as required by law, joined Co. H, the local militia led by Locke Alsup. He died in 1896 and is buried at Yates Cemetery further down the Bryant.

Earlier, in the 1830's, another family from Virginia, the Fleetwoods, lived in the cave. Isaac, Adam, and James were hunters, trappers, and traders in pelts who came here via Indiana. Adam, legend says, was a fugitive wanted in connection with a counterfeiting ring. A large extended family or clan, the Fleetwoods had an "open door" tradition. Their cabins had members of different households living together in a way that was confusing to visitors. The Fleetwoods also baffled genealogists and census takers. They were Unionists and enemies of the Alsups.

The entrance to Brown's Cave is large and imposing. Cool, vibrating air flows past as you come to a "stump" stalagmite near the edge of darkness. There are beautiful caves in Booger County with colorful formations, but Brown's Cave isn't one of them. It is a pit of muck. A small stream meanders through slippery mounds of viscous, clinging clay. Turn off your light, wait a minute, and then try to find your way. The darkness is disorienting.

Years ago two boys snuck off to explore the cave. Their lantern went out, and they were trapped. Family members and neighbors searched for hours before someone suggested looking inside the cave. Supposedly, there is a "hole" high up on the north wall near the entrance that leads all the way to Fox Creek. Further back, according to J.E. Curry, a dangerous side passageway leads through the "devil's gulch" and narrow crevices to an inner room with "beautiful stalactites and stalagmites."

Let's head back through Rippee and up the hill to Hwy 14. Since this was a short ride, why not take the trail to Yates Cemetery, considered by many the most beautiful place in Booger County? In a small valley above the Bryant, the cemetery is circled with imposing bluffs. Sanders and Curry dug in the natural rock shelters set in these bluffs. Tom Brown and many Fleetwoods are buried there.

Park at Hwy 14 and CR 341. The junction is about midway between C Hwy and Hwy 95 on Hwy 14. A rough gravel road runs along a mostly forested ridge top for three miles and then drops steeply to the cemetery. Explore the side roads off 341 for a longer ride.

Tomorrow we'll follow the 1818 route of prospector Henry Schoolcraft along the North Fork. Henry hoped to find a bonanza in Booger County.

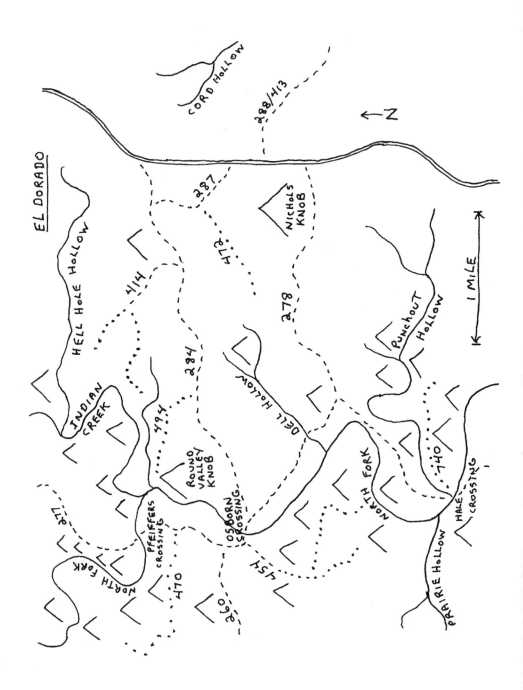

El Dorado

El Dorado on the North Fork

The North Fork bottoms deep in the Mark Twain National Forest are the destination of today's ride. Along the way we will explore a section of the Ridgerunner Trail. Fortunately, there's only one grueling uphill. Mature oak-pine forest intersperses small pastures and hayfields. Wildlife is abundant; trophy whitetail bucks and long-bearded tom turkeys watch warily from the thickets.

Park at the junction of Hwy 181 and CR 284 three miles south of Blue Buck. Look at the map. There are three river crossings: Hale and Osborn below the mouth of Indian Creek and Pfeiffer's above. Notice the forest service roads that branch off the county roads. Officially all of them are dead ends, but some continue on as ATV trails. Why not explore?

Except during hunting season it's unusual to see anyone here. Most of the land belongs to the Forest Service; its master plan, the Topaz Project, includes the reestablishment of native flora, as well as, clearcutting. Near the highway cedars have been cut for glade restoration. Further on we'll see big clearcuts and "seed tree" plots, which are clearcuts with a few big pines left standing. Eventually, much of the oak-hickory forest will be replaced with native pine. Some land will be dozed, disked, and machine planted.

Head down CR 284 past CR 287. You can fly down the long, gradual slope. Look for the quaint ruins of a log cabin on the left. FS 414, on the right, meanders along the flat ridge top between Hell Hole and Clough Hollows. The right fork ends at a dramatic backbone ridge, the wildest, most rugged part of Booger County. Continue further on CR 284 for a mile; FS 494 winds back to the base of Round Valley Knob. You'll hear the river before you see it. Osborn Crossing is a popular canoe launch for the float to Twin Bridges; in the high water of late spring and early summer, the area can be a tourist zoo. But back in November 1818 when Henry Schoolcraft, the first person to write about Booger County, passed through, it was wilderness. An unlikely prospector, the straitlaced New Yorker thought he could find El Dorado on the North Fork drainage.

At the time Missouri was much in the news. St. Louis was the world's foremost fur market. Trappers, traders, and Native Americans exchanged pelts for goods or squandered hard-earned dollars among the saloons, brothels, and slave pens along the riverfront. In mid channel Bloody Island, notorious as the site of murders and criminal activity, rose forlornly from the mud, a no-man's-land outside the jurisdiction of both Missouri and Illinois. Cargo was loaded onto steamboats for faraway Santa Fe, where cloth, tools, guns, and luxury goods could be traded for Spanish gold and silver. Huge profits were possible, but many lost their lives on the high plains to the Comanche, Kiowa, Cheyenne, and Arapaho before they could enjoy them.

Just a few years before Schoolcraft's journey, the most powerful earthquake in U.S. history shook southeastern Missouri along the New Madrid Fault. The Mississippi River ran backwards, and church bells rang in Philadelphia. Over the winter of 1811-1812 hundreds of powerful aftershocks liquefied the soil in low-lying areas and swallowed forests, houses, livestock, and entire families. "Sand boils" poured out of the ground like lava and covered many acres. Terrified refugees fled north across the winter landscape. In Washington, Missouri was about to be admitted to the Union as a slave state. Emotions ran high as Northern and Southern legislators acrimoniously debated the details of the Missouri Compromise.

Schoolcraft grew up in western New York. Minerals fascinated him; at Middlebury College he studied geology, chemistry, and mineralogy in preparation for his inheritance of his family's glass manufacturing business. Unfortunately, new methods of glassmaking made his father Lawrence's Ontario Glassworks obsolete, and bankruptcy closed the factory.

As a geologist, Henry came to Missouri to make his fortune. Years earlier the French had discovered lead southwest of St. Louis, and American miners and engineers had greatly expanded the diggings. They built smelters, found new deposits, and reaped great profits. No one realized at the time, however, that a geological anomaly deep in the earth, the Viburnum Trend, was the richest lead belt in the world.

Henry headed west to Pittsburgh with his savings and floated down the Ohio on flatboats and keelboats to the Mississippi and St. Louis. On foot he reached teeming Mine à Burton, later called Potosi. The town was surrounded by acres of tailings, collapsed tunnels, dangerous open pits, and rubbish heaps. Schoolcraft surveyed smelters and talked with engineers. He met another young New Yorker, Levi Pettibone; they decided to strike out on their own for a fabulous lode that awaited them somewhere in the Ozark wilderness.

Enthusiastically, they never stopped to consider that it was November, and winter would soon settle in. There were no roads, not even trails. How would their packhorse subsist on last season's frost-withered grass? Neither of them was an outdoorsman, yet romantically they saw themselves "living off the land." They barely knew how to build a fire, cook over it, butcher game, or care for the horse. Foolishly they bought a pair of smooth bore, muzzle-loading "fowling pieces," and every boy they met snickered at the puny weapons. Repeatedly they were warned about the formidable Osage who jealously protected their Ozark territory.

Wilderness began just outside town. The guide they'd hired rode off after a deer and vanished. Day after day they walked further into primeval forest past present-day Salem, Houston, and just west of Cabool into the North Fork drainage along Panther Creek. Wildlife was everywhere—elk, bison, bear, turkey, deer, prairie chickens, wolves, and cougars. Four bears were in a tree. Shaking with excitement, Henry and Levi rammed extra powder and ball into their little shotguns, but their shots had no effect on the bears. Pettibone fell and badly sprained his ankle. The horse had to carry him, as well as, the gear.

Ride across the river; a quarter-mile further, turn right on CR 277. Explore FS 470 that winds uphill and into Jim Coble Hollow. Just before Pfeiffer's Crossing look for a faint trail that leads to the mouth of Indian Creek.

The crystal-clear water of the North Fork amazed Schoolcraft and Pettibone. A multitude of springs "welled up" along the banks and streambed. The land looked different then: the woods, scrub, and pasture we now see were savannas of prairie grass with scattered trees and groves of pine. The glades, where bedrock lies near the surface, were nearly treeless and extended for miles. Schoolcraft called them "barrens." Fires set by the Native Americans to flush game kept the glades open. The creek bottoms, now mostly hayfields, were then riparian forest tangled with cane, vines, and brush. Big pines and oaks covered the moist slopes; the uncleared land absorbed more rain than it does today and released it at springs. The North Fork was more powerful. The holes were deeper; floods, less common.

Other prospectors followed Schoolcraft. On the old Tom Reed Place near Ann is an old mine, a wicked-looking vertical shaft, on a hillside terraced with limestone bedrock. Back in the 1920's, when Jewell Loomis attended the nearby Shady Grove one-room schoolhouse, the kids would throw stones into it. No one knows who dug the mine or what was found. Recently, after a steer fell into it, Tom's grandson Kevin Reed filled it in.

As they followed the North Fork south, Schoolcraft examined chunks of stone and pieces of gravel for mineral-rich rock. He particularly searched for galena (lead sulfide), a soft, dull gray rock, and "Rosin Jack" (zinc sulfide or sphalerite), a resinous stone with a high red, brown, black, or tan luster on freshly-broken surfaces. Ruby red crystals are sometimes imbedded in Rosin Jack. Both are crushed and removed from limestone by gravity separation or froth flotation and smelted into ingots. Schoolcraft "discovered" Topaz and named it Elkhorn Spring for the massive elk antlers he found there.

Booger County was a hunter's dream. Schoolcraft and Pettibone rammed powder and ball into their fowling pieces and fired repeatedly at game, but nothing fell. Instead of living off the land, they depended on their meager supplies of corn meal, flour, and sugar.

At the mouth of Indian Creek, disaster struck. The clear water's depth was difficult to judge, and at a seemingly shallow spot, the horse plunged into deep water. Frantically, the men pulled at the bridle, but it was too late. Their food was spoiled; most of the gunpowder, ruined. The men spent a miserable night on the riverbank drying gear by the campfire. Pettibone hobbled around the makeshift camp; his ankle was again inflamed.

Schoolcraft didn't realize that their camp at Round Valley was a traditional Osage campsite. The Osage were big people—six feet or taller—handsome and robust. Washington Irving called them "the finest looking Indians." They towered over Whites whom they considered foul and uncouth. The Osage bathed regularly and dressed well. The men shaved their eyebrows and heads and left a narrow strip of hair that they "roached up" and decorated to match their ear ornaments, tattoos, and bracelets. The women dyed their long hair red for bravery and dressed colorfully; they wore makeup, perfume, and tattoos and bejeweled themselves with beads and mirrors.

Family, tradition, ceremony, and the natural world of changing seasons were the focus of the Osage religion. They called themselves the "Children of the Middle Water," where sky, land, and water meet, and also, the "Children of the Sun," the manifestation of their deity, Wah´ Kon-tah. Once the universe was *ga-ni-tha*, chaos. Wah´ Kon-tah created the earth and sky. The Children floated down from the stars. Some stretched their arms like golden eagles and perched in a red oak tree; they became the *Tzi-sho*, the Sky People. Everyone else became the *Hunkah*, or Earth People. Their doors faced east to greet the dawn. In the morning light they chanted to their father, Wah´ Kontah, who had given them the Ozarks. The bones of their ancestors were interred in the hills. They felt it their duty to defend their home.

Part of the year they lived in permanent towns along the tributaries of the lower Missouri. A wide road divided the nine clans of the Sky People and the fifteen clans of the Earth People, who were subdivided into Land People and Water People. Each clan was represented by an animal spirit totem: bear, bison, eagle, etc. The households of the chiefs stood at the center of the village. The Sky Chief maintained peace and gave sanctuary to anyone who felt threatened. When one of the Children committed a crime, the Sky Chief met with the families involved to arrange a reparative peace gift and a ceremonial smoking of the peace pipe to renew the sacred bond of brotherhood. If the truce was broken, the Sky Chief could banish individuals or families from the tribe. Occasionally, the Sky Chief spared the life of a captive and made that person one of the Children.

The Earth Chief made war.

Aggressive, the Children traveled long distances to raid the Comanche, Caddo, Pawnee, Cheyenne, Sac and Fox, and others. Lances, bows, tomahawks, and stone knives were later augmented with pistols, muskets, and sabers. The scalps of enemies adorned their shields. Killing enemies and stealing their property was a virtue; death in battle, a supreme honor, rewarded by a rich and happy afterlife. Europeans were amazed at the Osages' stoic ability to withstand pain and wounds.

Anthropologists call the Osage a "flexible culture" because they opportunistically adapted ideas and technology from other peoples. Early on they acquired horses and European tools, and as shrewd traders, they bargained for the best prices with St. Louis fur merchants. What they couldn't barter for, they took by force.

Marriages were arranged in secret negotiations between families of different clans. During four days of celebration and feasting, gifts would pass from the boy's family to the girl's, sealing the union. The girl now lived among her in-laws. Sometimes, a man would take a second wife, his wife's younger sister or his brother's widow. Divorce was possible only if both parties agreed and the marriage gifts were returned.

Children were pampered. Aunts, uncles, cousins, grandparents, and clan-folk were responsible for child rearing. Men taught boys to hunt, fabricate tools and weapons, and the arts of war; women instructed girls in farming, gathering, and handicrafts. Example, not punishment, was the Osage way. Whites considered Osage children spoiled brats; the European custom of beating children deeply offended the Osage and reinforced their contempt for Whites. As adults the Osage were a proud, self-confident, outgoing people who stood erect and walked with graceful dignity.

Men, women, boys, and girls played a vigorous sport similar to field hockey, using a hide ball stuffed with bison hair. Everyone loved the moccasin game. Two teams sat opposite one another with four moccasins placed side-by-side between them. A rock or piece of bone was put in one moccasin. Amid chanting and drumming the moccasins were moved to confuse the other team, who had to guess which moccasin held the object. Sometimes, precious possessions—horses, jewelry, fine clothing—were wagered.

In spring the women planted corn, beans, and squash in the fertile river bottoms. After weeding and thinning the fields, the tribe dispersed in groups of about one hundred to live as hunter/gatherers in the Ozarks. Here at Round Valley they laid out temporary camps in concentric circles of igloo-shaped huts of saplings and thatch. A larger, oblong, ceremonial building stood at the center. While the men hunted or made tools tipped with surgically-sharp stone points, the women handcrafted beautiful clothing, sturdy footwear, and household goods and foraged for nuts, fruits, roots, and edible plants. In September the Children returned to harvest their crops and then left again for the autumn hunt. They overwintered in their towns in sturdy, arched communal buildings 100'x20'x10' tall and lived on stored food and local game.

In 1673 a French expedition in search of a route from Canada to the Pacific Ocean descended the Mississippi from the Great Lakes. Jacques Marquette, a Catholic priest, claimed the vast Mississippi Valley for the King of France. Soon, the Osage and the French were uneasy allies and business partners. Rivers were the only practical means of transportation; with French weapons and trade goods the Children controlled commerce on the lower Missouri River and became the dominant tribe in the region. The French encouraged them to raid other tribes for slaves destined for the sugar cane fields of the West Indies. Yet the French could never trust the Osage. One day they were generous, convivial hosts; the next, vicious river pirates.

Nevertheless, when the French garrison at Fort Duquesne (Pittsburgh) was threatened in 1755, two hundred Osage warriors ascended the Ohio to help ambush and destroy the Anglo/American army of Edward Braddock and George Washington.

In 1803 Napoleon sold the Louisiana Territory to the Jefferson administration for fifteen million dollars. Simultaneously, displaced eastern tribes, such as the Shawnee, Delaware, Creek, and Cherokee, crossed the Mississippi into Osage territory. Burned villages, massacres, raids, and retaliation followed. Soon, White settlers were clearing land in the Ozarks.

When Schoolcraft passed through, the Osage were trying to avoid war with the Americans. Whites were captured, stripped of their belongings, forced to work as slaves, and then turned loose to return to the fringe settlements as best they could. Time was running out for the mighty tribe. Here along the North Fork, the Bryant, and their tributaries, beaver were once found in terrific numbers. European hatters had discovered that felted beaver fur made superb hats, not only warm and waterproof but also durable and good-looking. Beaver hats became the height of men's fashion; their great expense, a symbol of elite status. Demand soared. A man with a set of traps and knowledge of beaver behavior could make a small fortune in a season. Beavers had a fatal weakness: excretions from another beaver's musk glands are not only irresistible but also easily used as bait by the trappers who would almost exterminate them.

As trappers and traders advanced into the Ozarks, they brought diseases to which the Osage had no natural immunity. Childhood illnesses, such as measles, mumps, and chicken pox, killed young adults; smallpox decimated villages. In 1826 the Osage ceded all of Douglas County west of the North Fork to the Shawnee. When White settlers arrived in Booger County in the 1830's and 40's, only a small band of friendly Piankashaw gardened, hunted, and gathered along Beaver Creek.

Weakened after years of war and disease, the Osage migrated to a 50x125-mile reservation in southeastern Kansas, a harsh country of hot, dry summers and winter blizzards. Bison hunting became the focus of their lives. They drove the animals into rivers and lanced them from boats or herded them into hidden corrals for killing. The meat was smoked or jerked; the skins, sold. Osage entrepreneurs took guns, liquor, and trade goods onto the Great Plains and exchanged them for livestock, especially horses, stolen in Texas and Mexico by the Comanche and Kiowa. Bands of Osage opportunistically looted weak or poorly organized parties of traders and immigrants along the Santa Fe Trail.

Following the election of Abraham Lincoln the Children, like the United States, divided. Confederate Indian agent Albert Pike convinced some that his government could protect them from their enemies and White squatters and would not interfere with tribal matters. They joined Cherokee Stand Watie's Rebel Army. Others became part of the Federal 9th Kansas Infantry or the Indian Brigade. Military discipline, drills, regulations, and uniforms were distasteful to the individualistic Osage warriors; most of them deserted.

After the war the government opened Kansas to White settlement and moved the Children to a new reservation north of present-day Tulsa, Oklahoma. The bison disappeared. Plagues of grasshoppers and years of drought forced the Osage onto the government dole. Indian agents pressured them to wear European-style clothing, to speak English, and to become Christian farmers and stockmen. Though missionaries rarely converted full-blooded Osage, many joined the Native American Church, which used peyote cactus in a communion ceremony similar to bread and wine. Principle Chief and spiritual leader, Fred Lookout, was a "roadman" or ceremonial head of the church.

Federal bureaucrats denigrated the Children as lazy, insolent, ungrateful "blanket Indians." Washington decided to "tame" the Osage by placing the youth in military boarding schools, where they marched to and from class and field work, spoke English only, and received Christian doctrine. Many were "hard cases" who resisted discipline and authority.

At the turn of the twentieth century oil speculator Henry Foster discovered vast petroleum deposits beneath the Osage reservation. Soon, hundreds of natural gas and oil wells made the Children "the richest people in the world." The Osage Allotment Act of 1906 distributed revenue, known as "Headrights," equally among the Osage. By 1925 a family of five had an income of $66,000, then a fabulous sum. Scores of luxury Pierce Arrows bounced over the dusty reservation roads. Wealth brought problems: alcoholism, crime, drugs. Every kind of con man appeared.

The Osage were a male dominant society. A council of the twenty-four clan leaders held supreme power. Chieftainship was passed from father to son. Venerable warriors known as "Little Old Men" presided over the ceremonies, games, story telling, prayers, and dances that were the core of Osage culture. When the government replaced the clan leaders with an elected fifteen-member tribal council, only men were given the vote. In the 1920's two sisters, Corine and Leona Gerhard, appealed to the Bureau of Indian Affairs for their right to vote. Traditionalists thwarted petitions for women's suffrage until 1941. When America went to war in Europe, Fred Lookout broke tradition and allowed young women entering the armed forces to participate in name changing ceremonies for departing warriors. In 1976 Camille Pangburn became the first female council member.

The Children are a unique and talented people. Army Air Force Major General Clarence Tinker reorganized U.S. air power after Pearl Harbor until his death at the Battle of Midway. Angela Gorman, Eagle Maiden, was a diva with the New York Opera. John Joseph Mathews, the "Osage Renaissance Man," attended reservation schools, the University of Oklahoma, and then rejected a Rhodes Scholarship; he studied at Oxford at his own expense. Later, he lived reclusively in the small stone house that he built in a copse of blackjacks. As a tribal councilman he tried to mitigate the divisions among his people: men/women, full/part blood, traditionalists/progressives, bureaucracy/tribe. Two sisters, Maria and Marjorie Tallchief, became prima ballerinas. Maria was called "the finest American-born classic ballerina the 20th century has produced." She performed with the New York Ballet Company and the American Ballet Theatre. Later, she directed the Lyric Opera Ballet of Chicago and taught advanced dance. Marjorie danced with the Grand Ballet de Monte Carlo in Europe.

Before we ride on, stop and look at Pfeiffer's Crossing. Be careful! When water runs for awhile across a low-water bridge, the bridge develops a layer of insidiously slick green slime. You and your bike could end up like my wife, Janet, who, when she tried to walk through the turbulent current on that algae, slid, hollering, into the downstream pool. All we could see was her bobbling blue helmet until she grabbed a tree limb and clambered ashore, shivering in the chill November breeze. Ride back across Osborn's ford and turn right on CR 260. Pass the dairy. This rarely-traveled road hugs the east side of a beautiful river valley. At the top of a steep hill CR 260 T's into CR 275. Turn right and stop at the top of the knife ridge to enjoy the spectacular view of the North Fork bottoms on the right and serpentine Punchout Hollow on the left. Ahead the road spans the river over Hale's Crossing to W Hwy via Smith Ridge. We turn east and pass south of Nichols Knob to Hwy 181. Turn north (left). Be alert on the pavement; these narrow, winding roads have no shoulder; folks drive fast.

Turn right on CR 288/FS 413. No one lives here. The road dead-ends at the Ridgerunner Trail. To the left the trail descends into wild Cord Hollow; to the right it's relatively level, but you'll have to hop logs. When you've finished exploring, go back to 181 and north to CR 287. If you're still strong, check out FS 472 on the left. Turn right on CR 284, and soon you'll be back to the vehicles.

What happened to Schoolcraft and Pettibone? For days they struggled south toward Arkansas, sometimes on upland savannas, occasionally, lost in the cane and brush thickets along the North Fork. Schoolcraft unsuccessfully fired the last of the gunpowder; they had to eat acorns as the weather turned cold with icy rain. Foolishly, they led the horse into a bog. After hours of exhausting digging, they rescued him.

Weary and hungry, they reached the confluence of the North Fork and the White River. Moored on the riverbank was a sleek, freshly-painted three-ton keelboat out of Pittsburgh. The floating trading post exchanged whiskey, corn, flour, salt, coffee, and hardware for pelts, "bear-bacon," beeswax, and honey. Prices were exorbitant. Schoolcraft and Pettibone shared a tiny cabin with a group of boisterous hunters, some on the lam from authorities back East. Vulgar and greasy, they talked incessantly about their hunting prowess and their dogs that they loved more than their wives and children. Their outright agnosticism deeply offended the pious Schoolcraft. As night fell a bonfire was lit and the whiskey broken out. A temperance man, Schoolcraft was an unwilling witness to the riotous brawl. All night the hunters drank, danced, sang, fought, and vomited until they fell in sprawling heaps. Schoolcraft and Pettibone rejoiced when dawn broke, and they could move on.

They traded the starved horse for a canoe and paddled downstream to Batesville, a cluster of one-room cabins. The explorers parted company. Pettibone began the long walk back to St. Louis; Schoolcraft journeyed east. He became an Indian agent, scholar, and obscure author and died penniless at age seventy-two.

Let's head back to our vehicles. In the next chapter we'll explore the center of the county and look for the "lost" county seat, Vera Cruz, the scene of a hard-fought Civil War battle.

Finding Vera Cruz

What happened during the Civil War in Booger County? No one seems to know; people speak of skirmishes and bushwhackers. Back then there was only one town in the county, the village of Redbud, or Vera Cruz. But where was Vera Cruz? One spring day my wife, Janet, and I took today's route to find it.

Go south on Hwy C from Skyline School, which is at the junction of C and 76, to the first gravel road on the right, CR 232, and park. We'll cycle about twenty miles, out and back, over infrequently-graded dirt roads through a hilly, sparsely-populated area. Expect potholes, "washboarding," and loose rocks.

At first we descend a long ridge top with Wilson Hollow on the left and Bluegrass Hollow on the right. A half-mile into the ride you'll see the ruins of an old sawmill and the entrance to Chapel in the Woods. After two miles we reach beautiful Wilson Hollow with hayfields, brushy fencerows, and wooded slopes. At the intersection turn right, downstream. The road fords the creek several times as it meanders through the bottom. We cross the Bryant on a concrete "low water" bridge. Just past the bridge on the right is a gate to a lane that leads upstream. The lane is a remnant of the Vera Cruz Road, the pre-Civil War wagon route shown on old maps.

Half a mile further on another concrete bridge spans Hunter Creek, the Bryant's main tributary. Turn right onto the pavement of AB Hwy and into the Dept. of Conservation's Vera Cruz picnic area. A magnificent limestone bluff overlooks a pool known locally as the "Millpond." James and Margaret Wilson came here by oxcart in the early 1840's. They built a gristmill and sawmill to harness the power of Hunter Creek. James became the local magistrate while this was part of Ozark County. Later, the Wilson's granddaughter Massey and her husband, Josiah Elliott, owned the mill known then as Elliott's Mill Yard. Unfortunately, the great flood of June 1, 1876, took out the mill along with 120,000 bd. ft. of lumber awaiting shipment to Springfield and hundreds of bushels of grain.

Ride south down the creek bottom on CR 223. This area floods periodically, and the sand gets too deep to ride through. Ahead, looming over what present-day maps call Vera Cruz, is a brooding bald knob. Below it another concrete bridge spans the Bryant at a small

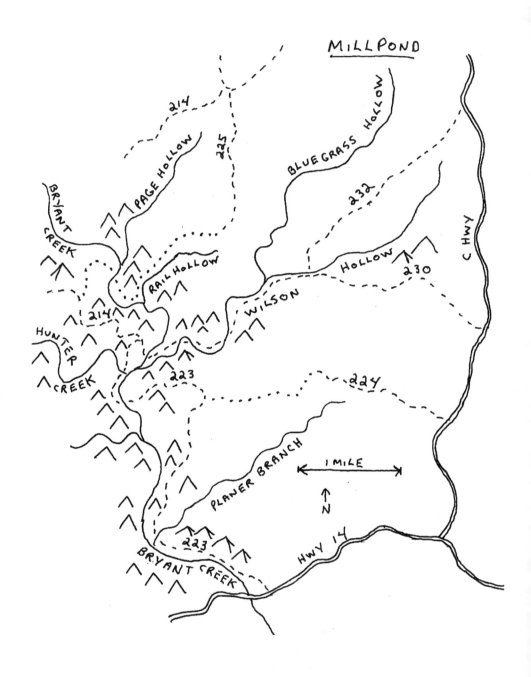

Millpond

Dept. of Conservation campground. The cluster of buildings is Camp Joy, a Baptist summer camp. Pass a picturesque old log church on the left, a cemetery on the right, and start up a long, treacherous hill. This ascent is perhaps the most difficult in Douglas County; only the fittest riders make it to the top.

Riding is level and easy, however, on the ridge. If you're feeling strong, take CR 224, the "Closed on the 4th of July" Road on the left, four miles out and back, through a stunted forest of blackjack, post oak, and cedar, to C Hwy. From the ridge CR 223 drops down into lower Planer Hollow and follows the sparkling Bryant beneath imposing bluffs. Turn around at Hwy 14. Stop at the millpond to cool off.

But where was Vera Cruz? Wilson's millpond didn't look like a town site. Camp Joy is too new. I made several phone calls. No one knew anything about Vera Cruz. Someone suggested contacting the local school bus driver, sheepherder, and musician, Kip Smith. Yes, Kip said, Old Vera Cruz is farther up the Bryant. Call Jack Vineyard; he can answer all your questions.

I arranged to ride to Jack's home, a converted barn on the Bryant near Rail Hollow. The area is steep and heavily forested. Though slowed by a stroke and nearly eighty, Jack was informative and a gracious host.

Jack has the speech patterns of an out-of-stater but is a native Ozarker. His mother and father, Grace and Logan, were farm kids from Reynolds County who went to St. Louis to seek their fortune. Logan got a good job at the Fischer Body factory. He died tragically when Jack was a little boy and left Grace destitute. Jack spent the next nine years at the Baptist orphanage in north St. Louis County.

Eventually, Jack was reunited with Grace when she found a job among kinfolk in Mesa, Arizona. The town was predominantly Mormon. Though Jack would receive two college degrees, he never finished high school. He was drafted in his senior year after Pearl Harbor was bombed.

The army sent him to the newly created 75th Infantry Division at Fort Leonard Wood, Missouri, known locally as "Fort Lost in the Woods." They were on maneuvers in Tennessee when Jack received orders to ship out as an infantry replacement. In a bewildering rush, a series of trains took him to New York City. He boarded the stripped-down luxury liner, *Isle de France,* along with 11,000 other soldiers and 1,000 nurses. Steaming unescorted at high speed on a zigzag course, the great ship sped down the coast and across the central Atlantic to land at Preswick, Scotland.

Jack reported to the 9th Infantry, which had taken heavy casualties in North Africa. Late on the afternoon of D-day, the 9th landed on the invasion beach at Normandy.

The Germans had pulled back into the more defensible "hedgerow" country behind the beaches. Over scores of generations, Norman farmers had cleared the rocks from their small fields, piling them up in fencerows that became overgrown with brush. Every day Jack and his companions would attack across the patchwork of little fields. The Germans, though pounded with artillery and bombs, waited grimly to rake the advancing American infantry with rifle, machine-gun, and mortar fire.

Jack carried a Browning automatic rifle, or BAR, a powerful, clumsy weapon with a strong kickback. One day a German bullet shattered the bones in his face. Jack spent two years in hospitals. When he returned home, he went to college on the GI Bill and became a teacher and school administrator.

Jack married Viola and became a Mormon. In the spring of 1957, after a falling out with the school board, Jack and Viola packed their six children into their new Ford station wagon. Loaded with a tent-trailer and camping gear, they set off to travel around America.

The Vineyards came to Mtn. Grove and asked about a place to camp. Someone suggested Bryant Creek. The kids loved the forested hills and the swimming hole with its rope swing. An elderly gentleman offered to sell 550 acres that were bisected by the Bryant. Jack and Viola, after much debate, bought the place for $13/acre. They returned to Arizona to raise their family and to pay off the Missouri farm.

Years later they retired to Douglas County. The house on the property, on the Brushy Knob side of the creek, had burned down, so they decided to convert the old barn into a house. Amateur archaeologist and local historian Herb Sanders was hired to bulldoze a new road and a level building site. Before he started his engine, Herb said, "You know what you're destroying here, don't you? This is Old Vera Cruz, the lost county seat."

Jack altered his plans to save as much of the town site as possible. Fascinated, he studied the history of Vera Cruz, and he discovered that a Civil War battle, Clark's Mill, had been fought in his front yard. Eventually, after months of research, Jack wrote a book, <u>The Battle of</u>

Clark's Mill. Two hundred copies were printed.

A Civil War buff asked Jack to host a re-enactment of the battle on his property. Over the weekend of November 12-13, 1994, two hundred fifty Rebels and fifty Federals charged and skirmished in the meadow below the house. A period dress ball took place Saturday night. The re-enactors were delighted to fire live rounds. A shack was set up on the hillside as a target for the cannons. Jack displayed the copies of his book and sold them all. Now, he has only one copy. Recently, Jack has been working to have Old Vera Cruz designated an historic site.

Bryant Creek is a natural north-south route for travel. An Osage path along the creek was widened into a wagon road that ran from Hartville, the seat of Wright County, south to Rockbridge, the seat of Ozark County. The village of Redbud was established where the Old Salt Road from Springfield joined the Bryant Creek Road. Another lane ran northeast up Rail Hollow from Redbud to Houston, the seat of Texas County. A post office was established at Redbud in 1848. Nine years later, when Douglas County was established, Redbud became the county seat, with a primitive log cabin for a courthouse. In 1859 the post office moved from Robert Hicks' to Jeremiah Coats' farm. Jeremiah called his place Vera Cruz, after the Mexican city occupied by the U.S. forces during the Mexican War.

Numerous springs well up at Old Vera Cruz, including a boiling spring that percolates out of white sand. A gristmill, Clark's Mill, and a sawmill utilized the abundant waterpower.

During the Civil War both Federal and Rebel units used the Vera Cruz Road. The 10th Illinois Cavalry built two forts there, but the forts were captured and destroyed by rebel Missourians. Booger County became a razed no man's land where soldiers, bushwhackers, and brigands preyed upon everyone. Martial law was in effect; civil liberties, terminated. Men were required, under severe penalty, to join the militia. The Alsups and their allies eventually controlled the militia and used it to further their ambitions.

The postwar years were tumultuous. There were two Republican political factions, the pro-Alsups and the anti-Alsups. Animosity grew between the east-enders and the west-enders. For a time the eastern townships seceded into Howell County.

A group of west-enders plotted to move the county seat to Beaver Creek. Late one night a posse broke into the Vera Cruz Courthouse, stole the records, and re-established the county seat at Arno. Later, a

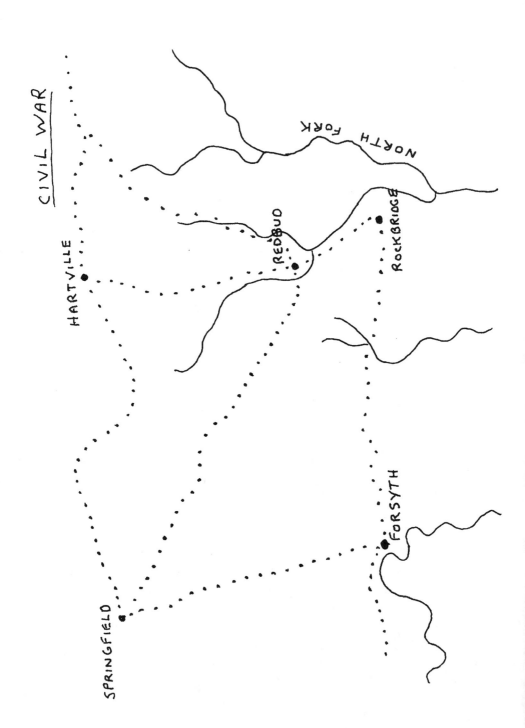

Civil War Roads

group from Vera Cruz recaptured the records in a midnight raid and brought them back.

In 1871 Locke Alsup, siding with the west-enders, shifted the county seat again. Three "commissioners" burglarized the Vera Cruz Courthouse, took the records, and locked them up in Ava. With a daytime population of three, a nighttime population of zero, and one building, Ava was not yet a town. A few nights later, someone, presumably a Vera Cruzan, burned the new "courthouse" and destroyed the documents. Nevertheless, Ava remained the county seat, much to the disgust of the east-enders who, to this day, feel isolated from county business.

At two A.M. on the night of June 1, 1876, a freak cataclysmic cloudburst struck central Douglas County. People called it a "waterspout." Rainwater cascaded down roofs and hillsides. The Bryant and its tributaries—Clever, Tarbutton, Dry, Hunter, and Fox Creeks—raged. At Vera Cruz the Bryant rose twenty-five feet in twenty-five minutes. Survivors spoke of an "immense rumbling" sound like a locomotive that became louder and more intense as it approached. A wall of water and uprooted trees struck with relentless force, tore buildings off their foundations, carried off crops, livestock, and entire families. At daylight corpses, human and animal, were tangled among the flood debris.

Vera Cruz became a ghost town overgrown with tangled brush. The road, however, with its many creek-crossings, was traveled until the early 1930's.

The chapter ahead tells the story of the Civil War in Douglas County. To understand what happened here, readers will hear the larger story of the Civil War in Missouri. I was lucky to have Jack's manuscripts to study. At the library in Rolla I met research librarian Donna Reed, whose family had come as war refugees from Vera Cruz. To my surprise, I found that my former college professor, Michael Fellman, had written the definitive work on the guerilla conflict in Missouri, <u>Inside War</u>.

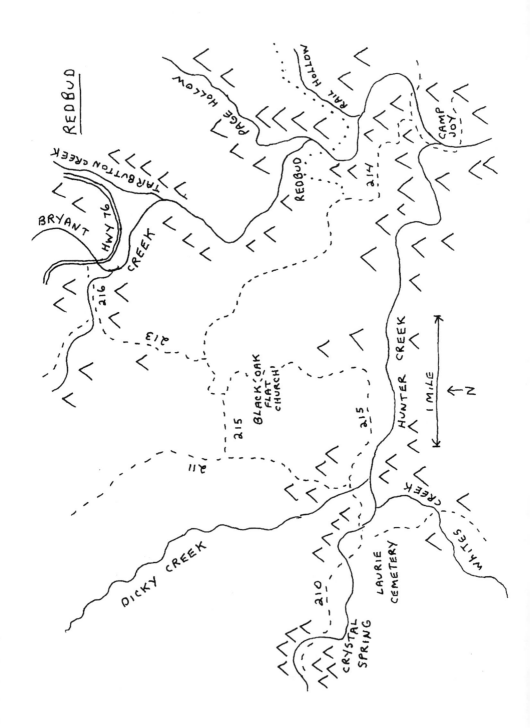

Redbud

Uncivil War

The center of Booger County, near the confluence of Bryant and Hunter Creeks, is a mosaic of pastures, woods, and overgrown fencerows. Though the ridge tops are relatively flat and rolling, the hollows are deep with meandering, spring-fed streams. Surprisingly, few people live in this picturesque part of the county.

During the Civil War Rebel cavalry passed this way to raid Federal positions. We'll ride by Old Vera Cruz, headquarters for the local militia. In 1862 the 10th Illinois Cavalry built two forts there only to have them captured and burned by the Confederate Rangers. That same year a large Federal army marched across the county on its way to subdue northeast Arkansas.

Park at the junction of Hwy 76 and CR 216, just west of the bridge over Bryant Creek, twelve miles east of Ava. Take the gravel road up brushy Camp Creek Hollow less than a mile to CR 213. Turn left up a side hollow and gradually climb onto the ridge top. To the right in the distance is an imposing arched barn. Turn right onto CR 214 at the T. Just past a house turn left onto CR 215. The road winds for a half-mile to the Black Oak Flat Church. We're on the Old Salt Road that ran down Hunter Creek, then climbed over the ridge, down to Old Vera Cruz, and avoided the rugged terrain further down Hunter Creek.

As we drop down into the lush Hunter Creek bottoms, look at the winding road ahead. Imagine how it looked in the spring of 1862 as Samuel Curtis' veteran Federal Army of the Southwest, fresh from their decisive victory at Pea Ridge, crowded the road for miles. Sunlight glinted off thousands of polished musket barrels. Infantry regiments snaked along the road with heavy knapsacks and blanket rolls tied diagonally across their shoulders. Officers armed with sabers and pistols rode ahead. Flags fluttered over the undulating mass of blue-clad men as dust billowed from dozens of mule-drawn wagons and horse-drawn artillery.

In sparsely settled Douglas County, the army had to be resupplied en route by slow-moving oxcarts from the railroad fortress at Rolla. Rations were monotonous: beans, beef from the slaughter herd, coffee, and "hardtack," a plain flour and water biscuit three inches square and half an inch thick. General Curtis expected his men to "live off the land," to simply steal what they needed from the local people. "I leave nothing for man or brute in the country passed over by my army," Curtis wrote. Missouri was in a state of rebellion; Curtis felt that her citizens had forfeited their rights and property and had caused this war. Now, by God, they would pay for it![1]

By stripping the land bare, the general not only fed his troops but also left behind a region that could not supply Rebel forces. That a family claimed to be Unionist meant nothing to the hungry soldiers. "Devastation, horrid to contemplate, marks every section of the country…the army has passed," wrote an Illinois soldier; "An air of sickening desolation is everywhere visible…No country ever was, or ever can be, worse devastated and laid waste than that which has been occupied, and marched over, by the Federal Army." [2] An Arkansas man reported, "Everything which could be eaten by hungry horses or men has been devoured…almost everything which could not be eaten was destroyed." [3]

Yet discipline was harsh in the Federal Army. Officers expected unquestioning obedience. The men were marched mercilessly, flogged, executed, hung by their thumbs, "bucked and gagged," forced to carry knapsacks filled with rocks, locked in sweatboxes, and close-order drilled for hours. The soldiers were expected to perform like well-oiled machinery.

Keep cycling along the creek. CR 211 comes down the hill on the right. Cross the bridge to the end of VV Hwy and turn right. We're now on CR 210. Numerous springs and creeks feed into Hunter Creek; even in drought years it flows abundantly. Rounding a ridge on the right, we pass prosperous looking Crystal Springs fish farm with its many small lakes. A half-mile further on, beneath a massive, blue-gray limestone bluff, there is another spring. Stop and rest awhile in the shade. Two miles further, at the end of FF Hwy, is the confluence of Hunter and Turkey Creeks. Either turn around here, or, if you want a longer ride, head up Turkey Creek on CR 209 and loop back on CR 207 and CR 206, an extra nine miles.

Go back the way we came past Black Oak Flat or use steep, rugged CR 211. Don't go back toward Hwy 76 on CR 213. Continue on CR 214. As we wind through fields and woods, the ridge narrows dramatically with drop-offs to the left and right into Bryant and Hunter Creeks. Just past a white house, a driveway goes downhill to the left. "Vineyard" reads the mailbox. This is the road to Old Vera Cruz. If you call Jack, perhaps you can visit the town site, cemetery, and battlefield. Turn around and go back to the parking area. Beyond Jack's mailbox CR 214 plunges down one of the longest, steepest hills in the county to Wilson's Mill at the confluence of Hunter and the Bryant.

We've had a long ride today across magnificent countryside. It's hard to believe, but right where we parked is the site of the 1864 Battle of Vera Cruz, where an unknown Rebel force routed the local militia, Co. H of the 46th Missouri Mounted Infantry. Why did the young men of Douglas County lose their lives at this lonely spot in a battle virtually forgotten? What made Missourians willing to kill each other? Why was Douglas County, this most rural and isolated of counties, so devastated by the war? While we rest from the ride, I'll try to answer these questions. What you learned in school about Bull Run, Gettysburg, and Appomattox has little to do with Missouri. To tell the story of the Civil War in Booger County, I'll first have to talk about the war in Missouri.

In 1860 Douglas had been a county for just three years. Census takers counted 2500 people who lived primitively on farmsteads scattered along the richest creek bottoms. There were no towns; the county seat, Vera Cruz, was just a village of small houses. Across the county there were only a few mills, stores, and blacksmith shops. The people were Evangelical Christians with a love for family; these early residents wanted to peacefully raise children, livestock, and crops. Most were ardent Unionists who deeply believed in the ideals of the American Revolution; however, the majority were from Tennessee, North Carolina, Kentucky, and Virginia and had kin and cultural ties to the South. Northerners, whom they considered foreign, were often disliked. They believed the North and South could reach another compromise that would preserve the Union.

Missouri was booming economically. St. Louis was a fast-growing city whose population had more than doubled in the last ten years. Hundreds of miles of railroads had just been built; steamboats carried people and cargo up and down the Mississippi and the Missouri. Each year thousands of emigrants assembled at Independence for the overland journey to California and Oregon. Farms supplied cash crops; new mines, industries, and banks were established with Eastern capital. The state had strong economic ties with far-off Chicago, Pittsburgh, Cincinnati, and New Orleans, and people talked excitedly about the prospect of a transcontinental railroad across Missouri.

Though tied economically with the North, Missouri was a slave state with 115,000 people held in legal bondage, often under cruel and brutal conditions. Slavery was concentrated on hemp and tobacco farms along the Missouri River. Only a few families owned more than twenty slaves; statewide, one family in eight owned between three and five slaves. Though the 1860 census showed no slaves in Douglas County, family histories speak of slave ownership. Three runaway slaves were captured and sold at auction in Vera Cruz by Sheriff Robert Hicks. One brought $600; another, $585.

Missouri's own army of citizen-soldiers, the Missouri State Guard, protected life and property. Many feared slave revolt. Graphic tales of the bloody insurrection on the Caribbean Island of Hispaniola, as well as, the Turner rebellion in Virginia filled newspapers. People imagined desperate slaves, inspired by the Abolitionist Yankees, slipping into their homes at night to cut throats. Brown's Cave on the Bryant was a "stop" on the Underground Railroad for fugitive slaves.

Ironically, the first test of the State Guard came out of the Northeast. The area around Palmyra, New York, became filled with religious fervor, revivals, and competing sects. Religious historians call the area "the burnt over district" because of its intense spiritual ferment. Eleven-year-old Joseph Smith, bewildered by the confusion of theologies, wandered in the forest, where God and Jesus appeared, and said his life would be a prophecy. Later, an angel named Morani gave Joseph inscribed golden plates that he translated from "Reformed Egyptian" into the Book of Mormon. The plates revealed that God had led a group of Israelites into North America in 600 B.C. The Native Americans were God's chosen people, and Joseph was the latter day prophet sent to restore God's Church in America. He founded the Church of Latter Day Saints among a few family members. Miraculously, the church grew rapidly and spread worldwide.

Joseph moved his followers to Ohio. When his bank failed, a suit filed by non-Mormons against Smith for debts caused internal dissent; he was tar and feathered. Joseph commanded that a New Jerusalem be built in western Missouri near Kansas City, on the edge of Indian Territory: the new Zion.

From the start the Missourians and Mormons did not mix. The Mormons' anti-slavery views were antithetical to those of their neighbors. As a voting block the Mormons could control local politics, and while fair and honest among themselves, the Saints acquired a reputation for unscrupulous business dealings with outsiders, whom they called "Gentiles." Tensions rose; arms were stockpiled. A secret Mormon vigilante society, the Danites, formed to violently enforce religious orthodoxy among the sect, committed crimes against Gentiles. Fights escalated into killings, reprisals, and executions. Governor Liliburn Boggs mobilized the State Guard and issued the Mormon Extermination Order: "The Mormons must be treated as enemies and must be exterminated or driven from the state…their outrages are beyond all description." In a climactic battle at the Mormon town of Far West, Smith and most of his "ringleaders" were captured, tried, and sentenced to death, but at the last moment, they were pardoned.

The Mormons were pushed into Illinois, where they established a "capital" at Nauvoo above the Mississippi River. Thousands of new converts arrived, and trouble began. Soon war broke out, and after pitched battles the Illinois State Militia drove the Saints west into the wilderness.

Peace was short-lived in Missouri. When expansionist President Polk realized that Mexico was weak from internal strife, he provoked a border incident, declared war, and began to seize Mexican territory. The Missouri State Guard mustered to conquer California and the Southwest. Ironically, they fought alongside their enemies, the Mormons, now allies of the Polk administration and the American Army.

Meanwhile in Washington, tensions between the North and South grew progressively bitter. The compromises that had maintained political balance were swept away by the Kansas/Nebraska Act that granted the territories the right to choose to be either a free or slave state. Amid the bickering South Carolina Representative, Preston Brooks, attacked Massachusetts Senator Sumner with his gold-headed cane and left him unconscious and bleeding on the Senate floor.

Although Kansas had previously legally belonged to various Native American tribes, settler families from Missouri had taken land along the rich valleys and had sometimes defended their "claims" with violence. Like settlers here in Douglas County, they were originally from Virginia or the Carolinas and had moved west, through Kentucky and Tennessee, across Missouri, and into Kansas. They thought of themselves as Southerners and believed deeply in home, God, family, honor, and private property. Northerners, especially Yankee Northeasterners, whom they considered "sour faced," sanctimonious hypocrites, were greatly disliked. In their churches Missouri preachers held that the Bible authorized slavery; those who opposed it refuted God's plan.

Missouri slaveholders, convinced that Missouri was surrounded by hostile free states, organized armed bands that crossed the border to vote Kansas a slave state. Though most of the votes were fraudulent, the election was a landslide for pro-slavery. The Missouri-controlled legislature convened and passed a slave code; it imposed the death penalty for anyone who aided fugitive slaves and required all voters to swear to uphold the new slave laws.

Across the North and Northeast there was immediate outrage. Meetings were held; anti-slavery societies, formed. Thirty-five-hundred clergymen sent a petition to President Pierce, and debates raged in Congress. Out of the foment the Republican Party was established. A powerful religious-based organization, the New England Immigrant Aid Society, incorporated in Massachusetts to help settle free-soil families in Kansas by subsidizing rail and steamboat costs. Agents of the Society laid out towns, farms, and roads. As the emigrants traveled west, church groups met them at train stations and sang "Onward Christian Soldiers." Preachers delivered sermons of praise to the free-soilers while they denounced slavery as an abomination and those who practiced it, evil. Ironically, though the company's leadership included Quakers and pacifists, hundreds of new Sharps breechloading rifles were secretly shipped into Kansas.

In Topeka a convention of free-soilers created a second Kansas government. Chaos followed with arrests, murders, panic, and confusion. The U.S. Army tried desperately to maintain order. Along the river bottoms, Missouri settlers and free-soilers, who formerly lived peaceably as neighbors, formed antagonistic communities. Disputes over land claims, water rights, and grazing led to tavern shouting matches and street fights. Towns were sacked; farms, burned; families, murdered.

Strange characters were attracted by the violence. People called them "Jayhawkers." James Montgomery was a small, black-bearded Campbellite preacher from Ohio who sat astride his horse and quoted Scripture while his men killed, burned, and looted the homes of Missourians. As they rode away, they left men hanging from trees. "Doc" Jennison was a dandified, swivel-eyed dentist from Ohio whose vigilante company swept across the land, stole wagonloads of loot and herds of livestock, and sold them "out of Missouri by Jennison." Free-soil Governor John Ingalls called Jennison's raiders God's "band of destroying angels."

A fifty-five-year-old tanner turned visionary minister settled with his many sons along a Kansas valley. Rail thin and dressed in tattered clothing, his gray-blue eyes glowed luminously from a wild tangle of hair and beard. His name was John Brown, and he believed, literally, that he was the "Sword of God." Armed with lances and sabers, his family would approach a Southerner's cabin late at night, call out the men folk, chop off their hands, and then stab, bludgeon, and hack them to death while Brown shouted, "Blood for blood, eye for eye!" Missouri Governor Stewart offered a $3000 reward for Brown's capture; Kansas Abolitionists posted signs that offered twenty-five cents for Stewart's capture.

Lionized by the Northern press, Brown became a cult hero. In a daring surprise attack, Brown and his congregation of zealots seized the Federal arsenal at Harpers Ferry, Virginia, and called for an apocalyptic slave rebellion. The South's worst nightmare was at hand! U.S. Marines under Colonel Robert E. Lee retook the arsenal, building by building, with bayonets. Though severely wounded, Brown survived. At a sensational trial that was headline news, Brown defended himself eloquently and polarized the nation. To Northerners he was a martyr; for Southerners, a demon. Emerson said that the gallows were his cross.

The Eastern press throughout the Kansas/Missouri border war was virulently anti-Missouri and described Missourians as "white trash," "border ruffians," and "Pukes" who spit tobacco juice and guzzled whiskey. Free-soilers, on the other hand, the press depicted as the chosen people who carried Anglo Saxon Protestantism into a wilderness inhabited by barbarians. As God had aided the Israelites against the Philistines, so, too, would He aid the Kansans to banish the Missouri Pukes.

Gradually, the Southerners were pushed out of Kansas. By 1860 Jayhawker bands raided Missouri's western counties. Governor Stewart shipped rifles to his embattled citizens and mobilized the State Guard, which spent the summer futilely chasing phantom Jayhawkers.

In eastern Missouri there was conflict also. Tens of thousands of Germans, many of them Catholic, had moved into the St. Louis area and had made it the largest "foreign" city in the United States. Antagonism sparked rioting; a secret political society, the Know-Nothings, anti-foreign, anti-Catholic, anti-Negro, and pro-temperance, tried to exclude the Germans politically. In response Wide-Awake clubs formed in the German community to secretly gather arms and train recruits. The Wide-Awakes constituted a solid voting block for the new Republican Party. Frank Blair, a stern-faced Marylander with a drooping mustache and a goatee, became their Congressman. An anti-slavery slave owner, Blair, like Lincoln, advocated the "Colonization Plan." He envisioned the seizure of Central America by the U.S. Army and Navy and then the removal of slaves to form a colony, which would exchange raw materials for finished U.S. goods.

At the 1860 Republican convention in Chicago when, after two ballots, William Seward of New York seemed ready to carry the nomination, Blair threw the Missouri delegation to Lincoln and gave him victory. In return Lincoln presented Blair with two Cabinet posts, one for his brother Montgomery, and another for his ally, St. Louis lawyer Edward Bates.

But Lincoln was not favored to win the election. Stephen Douglas, the moderate Democratic Senator also from Illinois, looked like the next President. With victory almost assured, the Democrats bitterly split, and John Breckenridge became a pro-slavery candidate. John Ball of Tennessee, running for the centrist Constitution Party, made up of remnants of the Whig and American Parties, also diverted crucial votes from Douglas. Missouri was the only state Douglas carried. Lincoln won the election with less than 40% of the votes.

Lincoln received only 10% of the votes in Missouri, nearly all of them cast by Germans. In his campaign swing through Kansas, Lincoln had given inflammatory speeches that invoked the ghost of John Brown and infuriated Missourians. Both of Missouri's senators, James Green and Trusten Polk, were pro-slavery. The new governor, Claib Jackson, had campaigned as a pro-Union Douglas Democrat but was actually strongly pro-slavery and pro-Southern; like most Missourians, Jackson wanted the state to become neutral. Twice a widower, he successively married all three daughters of wealthy Dr. John Sappington, the manufacturer of quinine pills.

As the Confederacy formed, a special election was held to select delegates to decide a single question: should Missouri remain in the Union or join the seceded states? These delegates voted nearly four to one for the Union, though Douglas County's Preston Todd voted for secession.

St. Louis was a powder keg. The city was rife with rumors, plots, and hysteria. The mayor ordered all taverns closed. The Germans, financed by railroad magnate John Forbes, were well armed and trained; across town the State Guardsmen gathered to drill under their beloved ex-Governor, Sterling "Pap" Price. When Lincoln called on the states for volunteers, Governor Jackson declared that Missouri would not furnish a single man in an unholy war.

At the calm center of the storm was U.S. Army General William Harney, a handsome aristocrat and veteran Indian fighter who had married into a prominent St. Louis family. He believed that bloodshed could be avoided and some sort of compromise reached. But in early May Congressman Frank Blair and U.S. Army Captain Nathaniel Lyon staged a coup d'etat. Blair crossed the Mississippi and secretly telegraphed his brother in Washington, who had General Harney recalled to Washington for "conferences." Lyon, a slender redhead with intense blue eyes and a history of mental instability, was a Connecticut-born Abolitionist who had served under Harney in Kansas, where he had developed an abiding hatred for Missourians. Considered a fanatical zealot by his fellow officers, Lyon was said to foam at the mouth during mess hall debates. He demanded extreme discipline from his troops. He kicked and abused his men and left them bound and gagged on the parade ground; others, he tied up with honey poured over their heads to draw insects.

With Harney gone Lyon and Blair assembled the German militia and surrounded the State Guardsmen at their camp in St. Louis. After a dramatic standoff, the Guardsmen surrendered to avoid bloodshed and were disarmed and marched to a makeshift prison. Along the route crowds of angry citizens shouted insults. The Germans fired indiscriminately into the mob, killed dozens, and wounded hundreds. Running for his life was the redheaded, well-dressed president of the St. Louis Street Railroad, William Tecumseh Sherman, who would later infamously burn a swath from Atlanta to Savannah with his Union Army. Seated on his wagon, an unlit cigar in his mouth, failed farmer turned firewood vendor, Ulysses Grant, watched the slaughter impassively. Though unsuited for civilian life, he was a paramount equestrian and a military genius. Quirks of fortune would lead him from a commission in the Illinois Militia to the command of the Army of the Potomac and into the White House.

St. Louis seethed. The legislature appropriated two million dollars to raise and equip a state army, restore order, and "punish" the Germans. General Harney returned the day after the massacre and threatened Lyon with court martial. Still hoping to avoid war and keep Missouri in the Union, the general met with Governor Jackson and worked out an agreement. Jackson promised not to raise a state army or to aid Rebels. Harney assured him that Missouri would remain neutral and that her citizens would not be forced to fight against the South. The German regiments were ordered out of St. Louis.

But the conspirators struck again! Blair telegraphed Washington and had Harney relieved of command and Captain Lyon promoted to general!

A final conference was held at the Planter's house in St. Louis between Governor Jackson, State Guard General Price, Lyon, and Blair. Jackson and Price pled for neutrality and peace. After hours of deadlocked exchanges, Lyon stood up and proclaimed that he would see every man, woman and child in the state dead and buried before Missouri became neutral. "This means war," he declared, and strode out of the room.[4]

Jackson and Price boarded a train for Jefferson City. They cut telegraph wires and burned bridges behind them. Lyon commandeered railroads and steamboats and requisitioned private property as he gathered an army to conquer Missouri. He commissioned rural and town men to form local militias. In Hannibal riverboat pilot Samuel Clemens, later known as Mark Twain, joined the Ralls County Rangers to protect his community from the "Dutch" (Germans).

With a flotilla of steamboats Lyon advanced up the Missouri River. He chased the State Government out of Jefferson City and routed the State Guard at Lexington. Many young men's romantic illusions about the glory of war were shattered as Totten's Regular Army Artillerists methodically slaughtered their ranks with exploding canister rounds.

The long, lumbering wagon train of the fugitive State Government, loaded down with legislators, clerks, the state records, pots, pans, furniture, wives, and children, trudged out of the State Capital. Governor Jackson was hard pressed to feed and care for everyone. Eventually, he established a temporary capital at Cowskin Prairie in the far Southwest, where Missouri, Arkansas, and Indian Territory cornered.

Military units from Kansas, Iowa, and Illinois moved into the state. Along the western border Indiana politician, Jim Lane, the "Grim Chieftain" of the Jayhawkers, launched a massive raid into Missouri. He told his "ragged, half-armed, diseased, mutinous rabble" of men to clean out "everything disloyal from a Shanghai rooster to a Durham cow."[5] His troops sacked Osceola and murdered its men folk. With wagonloads of loot, the drunken Jayhawkers drove out of the ruins.

Hundreds of men from across the state rushed to follow Pap Price as he patched together his defeated State Guard and marched toward Springfield. In Douglas County Preston Todd (b. 1817 Russell County, VA) and John Heard of Prairie Hollow joined Mc Bride's Texas County State Guard and followed Price. Others, like prominent mill owner James Wilson (b. 1799 Jefferson County, KY), James Sullivan (b. 1831 Indiana), and Bill Ross (b. 1846 Missouri), signed up with Lyon's army. Though most of the men stayed at home and hoped the war would soon end, a pro-Union militia formed under John Sevier Upshaw of Denlow, while the pro-Missouri men gathered around former sheriff Preston Todd of Falling Spring.

Lyon sought to end the "rebellion" by surrounding and capturing the State Government. In Rolla trains arrived loaded with German troops who scattered the locals before they, too, headed toward Springfield. Behind them engineers and convict laborers began to transform Rolla into a military staging and warehousing center to support the Federal Army.

Though a thousand of Pap's men were unarmed, and many others carried ineffective shotguns, squirrel rifles, or antique flintlocks, he had a plan, too. Southern reinforcements had arrived: the Pelican Rifles from Louisiana; a motley brigade of butternut-clad Arkansas infantry; a Texan battalion under flamboyant, long-haired Ben McCulloch, an ex-Texas Ranger and Mexican War hero who wore a white planter's hat and a velvet frock coat. Price hoped to surround and decisively defeat Lyon's army, which now occupied Springfield, and then systematically recapture the state.

As Price's army advanced, Lyon received orders from General Fremont, now in overall command, to fall back; his officers advised withdrawal. Provisions were low; Jeff Thompson's "swamp rats" had captured needed wagon trains of supplies from Rolla. In addition, men whose three-month enlistments had expired were leaving. Pro-Union families packed their wagons and fled up the Rolla Road.

When night fell the Federal drummers sounded "Fall In." Lyon's army, with horses' hooves padded and artillery wheels wrapped in blankets, marched silently south toward the Rebel encampment along Wilson's Creek. Though heavily outnumbered, Lyon was confident that a surprise attack would send the "mob" into panicked flight. Fortuitously it rained most of the night. The Federal Army, undetected, dug in on the ridge above the Rebel camp. Their artillery fired at first light. Wagons splintered; fires started; shrapnel dismembered men, while others ran in terrified circles.

Nevertheless, the Southern officers gradually restored order and moved their men up the slope toward the Federal battle line. The August morning was miserably sultry; the slaughter, grotesque. Because uniforms were not standardized, in the smoke and confusion "friendly" units exchanged volleys. The Southerners charged repeatedly into massed rifle fire and grapeshot. A German regiment overran the Rebel camp and looted it, but in a sudden counterattack the Arkansas infantry killed dozens of them.

By noon the Federals were forced back. A bullet tore through Lyon's chest and knocked him, lifeless, from his horse. Sensing victory the Southerners whooped Indian war cries and pressed forward until the Federal Army retreated toward Springfield. The Rebel cavalry harassed the withdrawing Unionists across hills strewn with bodies. One in four became a casualty. Man-for-man Wilson's Creek was the bloodiest battle of the Civil War.

Demoralized, the Federal Army limped the rugged one-hundred-ten miles to Rolla on a road clogged with refugees and disordered groups of soldiers. There was little food and much rain, mud, and misery. The State Guard was too exhausted to chase them. Price's men found enough rifles lying on the ground to equip every man. Pap reorganized his men and marched north. Along the way hundreds set down their axes and plows to help drive the "furriners" from Missouri. They captured an entire Union army at Lexington and bagged hundreds of horses, thousands of muskets, and much-needed artillery.

Meanwhile in St. Louis, amid a beehive of military activity, the "Great Pathfinder," John C. Fremont, now known as the "Presence," took command. As a young officer during the Mexican War, Fremont was arrested for insubordination and found guilty of mutiny by a military court. Though discharged in disgrace, political strings were pulled, and a presidential pardon returned him to the Army. Imperious, vain, and ambitious, he was the Republican Presidential Candidate in 1856. In St. Louis the Presence ruled like a viceroy from the Brant Mansion on Choteau Avenue. Bands played as colorfully-uniformed regiments marched the streets. Resplendent West Pointers and foreign officers surrounded him, including the dashing Hungarian, Charles Zagoni, Commander of the Presence's personal guard. Fremont's wife, the vivacious and politically astute Jessie, daughter of Thomas Hart Benton, Missouri's powerful first Senator, rode through the streets in a magnificent carriage and hosted elaborate balls in the mansion.

Along the city's riverfront ironclad gunboats were under construction. Vast industrial resources from the North were unloaded and shipped to Federal garrisons. Fremont declared martial law. The U.S. Army had the power of life and death and the authority to requisition private property. Without trial citizens were imprisoned; their belongings, confiscated. The Presence created a military-backed "Provisional Government." Subsequently, Missouri had two governments. In Douglas County officials were appointed by the military government, not elected.

But the Fremonts had strong enemies. Frank Blair's criticisms were so scathing that Fremont jailed him; Fremont's subordinate generals thwarted his orders and were openly insolent. Then summarily, without consulting Lincoln, the Presence issued an Emancipation Proclamation that freed the slaves of Southern sympathizers. Immediately, he became a hero in Northern newspapers. Enraged, Lincoln, who was trying desperately to hold slave-owning Maryland and Kentucky in the Union, looked for a way to replace Fremont.

Fremont ordered his army to advance toward Springfield and the victory that would bring him eternal fame. "On to New Orleans," his soldiers shouted as he rode by; beside him on a pony, his ten-year-old son, John Charles II, was dressed like his father in full panoply and glittering brass. Most of Fremont's men were ordinary farm boys from Illinois, Iowa, or Kansas who were raised to be honest, hardworking, and God-fearing. They were told to assume that all Missourians, unless they were German, were "secesh." Originally short for secessionist, the word was now a derogatory term that meant ignorant, dirty, lazy, and degenerate. As they marched the men "foraged" (a euphemism for stealing from the local people). Vilifying the Missouri country folk helped them to rationalize their thievery. Dan Holmes, an Illinois soldier, wrote his sister that when "we come to secesh houses we take the horses and property, burn the house, we clean them out."[6] Another soldier, E.T. McLane, wrote his cousin Sam, "[we] confiscate everything…secesh cattle, hogs, sheep, poultry, cabbages, potatoes, honey and molasses."[7] Families had worked for years to build rail fences to keep livestock out of the crops. Whenever the Federal Army passed, the troops broke down the fences and set them ablaze. E.T. McLane boasted that every night we "burn miles of fence." Another soldier, David Garver, wrote his sister that they had torched miles of fences and had destroyed whole farms. He believed the Missourians deserved punishment because they caused the war. The soldiers' contempt included Missouri regiments of the Federal Army, whom they considered clownish, motley, and unprofessional. [8]

Fremont's army converged on Springfield, the temporary state capital, in several columns. Major Zagoni led a surprise cavalry charge that routed the few Guardsmen blocking the road and sent the Rebels fleeing south. The Stars and Stripes were raised over the courthouse, and exultant victory parades wound through town. In the midst of the celebration, a courier arrived with Lincoln's order to relieve Fremont of command. The bands hushed, and the leaderless Federal Army once again withdrew toward Rolla; hundreds of Northern-sympathizing refugees, many of them barefoot, hungry, homeless, and thinly clothed, followed. The State Guard advanced to the Missouri River, captured steamboats, and ferried Southern recruits from northern Missouri.

It was November 1861. Reluctantly, Missouri became the twelfth Confederate State. With the crops in many men from Douglas County—Coble, Collins, Dobbs, Rippee, Robinett, Coats, Fleetwood, Hopper, Wood, and Alsup, among others—said farewell to their families and traveled to Rolla to join Co. E of Phelps Regiment for a six-month enlistment. Colonel Phelps (b. 1814 Hartford, CT) had no military experience. An Eastern-educated lawyer turned politician, he was Southwest Missouri's Congressman when the war began. The men were organized into "messes" of eight-to-ten and issued uniforms, rifles, haversacks, canteens, pans, and kettles. Thankfully, with the weather turning cold, they were given conical Sibley tents with a small stove in the middle. The men slept, feet to the fire, packed in like the wedges of a pie. They camped beneath the massive, diamond-shaped earthen walls of Ft. Wyman [on the hill south and east of present-day Wal-Mart] that was erected to protect the railhead and supply depot.

The region's trees had been cut to build the fort and to create clear lines of fire; the windswept site was miserably cold, forlorn, and muddy. The men were drilled for hours in companies and as a regiment until they mastered *oblique, flank, echelon, hollow-square,* and other complex movements. They practiced capturing cannon. With loaded muskets and fixed bayonets they "timed" the firing intervals of batteries by advancing in a series of rushes and falling flat whenever the battery was fired. When they were close enough to the cannons, they fired a mass volley and charged ahead with whoops and yells to bayonet the cannoneers.

Whenever payday came, a seedy-looking fellow parked his wagon in a nearby wooded hollow and sold peach brandy. Soon a well-worn path led there from Phelps Regiment. At first the privates worried that their officers might discourage drinking, but then they saw the officers, too, queued up, canteens in hand.

The interminable winter of '61-'62 set in with snow and freezing rain. The ground froze and thawed into a deep clay muck that stuck to everything. Lice infested the soldiers. Sanitation and hygiene were primitive; sickness, especially the debilitating "soldier's disease," diarrhea, made men vulnerable to lethal pneumonia. Sad volleys were fired over many graves. The short winter days went by in the familiar routine of drill, work details, and guard duty.

Fifty-seven-year-old Samuel Curtis, their new general, arrived with his wife and daughter, who reported to the hospital as nurses. Curtis was a big man with a calm, fastidious demeanor. A West Pointer and Mexican War veteran, he had resigned his commission and worked as a railroad engineer and later as the city engineer of St. Louis. When Unionist sympathizers told him that many of the State Guardsmen had gone home and that the despondent Pap Price was drinking too much, Curtis decided to attack. He knew the difficulties of supply for a winter campaign; the two-and-a-half ton ox-drawn wagons from Rolla only made two-mph through the mud. On the other hand, Curtis knew that his army was better equipped than Price's. In January 1862 the Army of the Southwest slung their knapsacks and trekked toward Springfield.

Inclement weather, mired wagons, and Rebel ambushes were not the only factors that hampered Curtis' army. Curtis had been promoted over the German Franz Sigel, now second in command. Pervasive anti-German prejudice, Sigel felt, had denied him his right to lead. Short, slightly built, myopic, and egocentric, Sigel was immensely popular in the German American community, as well as, well connected politically. Though a master of parade ground drill, he was inept and indecisive on the battlefield. Sigel ignored Curtis' orders and openly challenged his leadership. The deep rift between the generals spread throughout the Army, which was half foreign-born.

Curtis drove his men hard and hoped to attack before Pap could receive reinforcements. The Big Piney River was up. The men waded across the waist-deep ford despite freezing temperatures; often they marched in darkness. As they approached Springfield, the State Guard withdrew toward the Southwest. Curtis pushed on after Price. Supplies grew scarce the further they got from Rolla. The men simply took what they wanted from the country folk; they smashed down doors, looted root cellars, corncribs, henhouses, and barns and left families destitute.

The weather turned bitterly cold as the Federals tramped through Cassville and into Arkansas. They passed piles of discarded Rebel equipment, dead horses and mules. Most afternoons Price's rearguard set up ambushes followed by running skirmishes; the delays clogged the road with troops and slowed the Federal advance. Nevertheless, Curtis continued his offensive and sacked Fayetteville, Arkansas.

Price retreated to Ben McCulloch's Confederate Army winter quarters at Cross Hollows, Arkansas. The two generals immediately quarreled over command. Price believed his rank, Major General of the Missouri State Guard, was higher than McCulloch's. McCulloch, who had a low opinion of Missourians and doubted their loyalty to the Confederacy, answered that his commission in the Confederate Army held higher status. Unable to agree they torched everything they couldn't carry off and retreated into the rugged Boston Mountains.

Cross Hollows was still ablaze when the Federal Army arrived. Curtis had the fires put out and settled in to reorganize and rest from the long march. He wrote a sentimental letter to his brother that exulted about bird songs and the joy of living close to nature. Yet he was deep in hostile territory. Guerrillas and Rebel cavalry preyed upon the supply trains. His hungry men soon "cleaned out" Cross Hollows, and Curtis ordered Phelps Regiment to march east to Huntsville, Arkansas, where they hoisted the Stars and Stripes over the courthouse and established a military government.

Meanwhile out of the West, a third Southern army arrived to reinforce Price and McCulloch, the Five Nations of the Indian Territory. The Cherokee were the most numerous. Their portly leader, John Ross, seventy-two, wore a frock coat and stovepipe hat and rode in a fine carriage. Immensely wealthy, his plantation mansion, Park Hill, was luxuriously furnished. Over a hundred slaves worked his land. Yet Ross was married to Mary Stapler, a Quaker Abolitionist from Wilmington, Delaware. Daniel McIntosh, an ordained Baptist minister who curled his long hair and sported a flamboyant mustache and goatee, guided the Creeks. He delivered sermons in praise of slavery and the Southern way of life. Douglas Cooper, a hard-drinking Mississippian, led the Choctaws and Chickasaws; pompous John Jumper, six hundred Seminole warriors.

Confederate agent Albert Pike, with gifts and promises of money, had induced the tribesmen onto the battlefield. A fat man with flowing hair, an enormous beard, and rumpled clothes, Pike was a native Bostonian, an impoverished Harvard dropout, and a gifted linguist. He spoke the various tribal languages, as well as, French, Spanish, Greek, Latin, and Sanskrit. Pike became rich as an Arkansas journalist and lawyer. Though outwardly calm, he was a crack shot and easily insulted; Pike settled his disputes on the dueling field. He arrived at the Confederate camp dressed as a Sioux warrior. But the tribesman were an army in name only. They were untrained, undisciplined, and armed with a variety of weapons. Many of them hated Southern whites as much as Yankees.

The quarreling between Price and McCulloch ended suddenly with the arrival of Earl Van Dorn, sent by Jefferson Davis to take command. Van Dorn, a hotheaded nephew of Andrew Jackson and a neighbor of Jefferson Davis, loved weapons, fine horses, and other men's wives. Within a year he would be dead at the hands of a cuckolded husband. He halted the retreating Southerners and spoke to them like Napoleon: "Soldiers! Behold your leader. The blast of war is sounding in your ears. To arms!" [9] Van Dorn planned to encircle and destroy Curtis, push north to liberate Missouri, and capture St. Louis. He had no interest in logistics, reconnaissance, or organization. Speed and surprise, he stubbornly believed, won battles. Not once did he pause to consider the weakened condition of his men and horses, nor did he worry that his units were untrained, poorly armed, and led by politicians.

Bandy-legged Phil Sheridan reported to General Curtis that the Southern Army was advancing aggressively. (Later, Sheridan would lay waste to the Shenandoah Valley, rise to great rank in the post war Army, and preside over the genocide of the Native Americans.) Curtis burned everything that couldn't be carried and withdrew to Pea Ridge. The men dug in cannon, prepared trenches, *abatis*, and interlocked fields of fire.

A courier on a frothing horse galloped into Huntsville with orders for Phelps Regiment to rejoin the Federal Army by forced march. They traveled forty-five miles over snow-covered roads at quick-time with five minutes rest every hour. Rations were short—a half cracker and a lump of sugar. They started at 3 A.M. and walked until the following night. Some men gave out, but most rejoined the Federal Army stiff, sore, and hungry.

At dusk March 6, 1862, Van Dorn's Army reached the Federal fortifications. They had marched fifty-five miles and had eaten no food. During the night the Federals could see hundreds of Southern campfires twinkling. It was a ruse. Only a few men tended the fires. Van Dorn marched his exhausted men all night in a half-circle around Curtis, and when the sun rose, the Southern Army was in line of battle across the road to Rolla. The Federal Army was cut off.

The battle began in confusion. Phelps Regiment advanced into woods filled with the rattle of musketry. Across a ravine the brush swarmed with Southerners. Cannons roared as bullets and grapeshot whizzed through the air. Furiously, the Federals loaded, aimed, and fired. Left and right men fell. James Coats of Fox Creek was wounded in the leg; Ben Robinett, run over by a runaway wagon.

Phelps Regiment fixed bayonets and charged. Officers shouted and waved swords. A sheet of flames met them. E Company's Captain Adams was severely wounded in both legs. Phelps Regiment was repulsed with great loss. As cannon were brought forward to blast the Southerners, officers again exhorted the men. With a tremendous roar they charged; suddenly, the Southerners were running for their lives.

Van Dorn's strategy had backfired. Foolishly, he had divided his forces. Worse, he had forgotten to order the ammunition train to resupply the Army and had left entire regiments without the means to fight. Now the Federal Army blocked their retreat. Panic and disorganization spread. McCulloch was dead; Price, badly wounded. Bodies lay in heaps. Some of them had been scalped. The Germans killed prisoners, and the proud Southern Army became a mob and fled in every direction. Tribesmen sacked Confederate wagon trains and slaughtered men who only hours ago were their allies. Leaderless men formed gangs of "bushwhackers" that would terrorize the region for years. Many disheartened men, however, simply walked the dangerous routes home, finished with war.

The State Guard somehow remained intact and withdrew to the east. Hereafter Price was referred to as "Old Skeedad" (skedaddle) among the Federal troops. A diminutive, wealthy, slave-owning rope manufacturer from Waverly, J.O. Shelby, commanded Pap's cavalry. He covered the retreat, held back the Federals, and gained time to recoup men, livestock, and equipment. Fond of quoting romantic poetry, Shelby called his cavalrymen "Highlanders." At the Mississippi Price received orders to cross the river and join the Confederate Army. Many of those who marched with him into the Deep South were killed in the carnage at Shiloh, Corinth, Vicksburg, and other battlefields; others died of disease.

Unopposed, the Federals held all of Missouri and northern Arkansas; at Federal headquarters in St. Louis, Unionists rejoiced. Grim W.T. Sherman scoffed at them. Price and the State Guard will be back, he said, as sure as death and taxes.

The enlistments of the Booger County soldiers expired. Strangely, though, they returned home with the Army. Curtis crossed the county, camped near present-day Ava, then at Vera Cruz, and marched south along the North Fork on his way to Batesville.

The 10th Illinois Cavalry was sent to pacify this part of southern Missouri. With its headquarters at Marshfield, small detachments were stationed at intervals to suppress bushwhackers and to train the local militia. Captain Hiram Barstow's Companies C and M were ordered to occupy Vera Cruz, a cluster of houses, two sawmills, a courthouse, gristmill, blacksmith shop, and general store. Located at the juncture of the Vera Cruz Road that extended from Hartville to Rockbridge and the Old Salt Road that ran up Hunter Creek to Springfield, Vera Cruz was an overnight stop for travelers and teamsters. Barstow's orders were to keep the roads open to commerce, to suppress Rebel recruiting and organizing, and to make soldiers of the local militia, which had elected John Coats their Captain. Provisional Governor Gamble issued General Order #19, which required every able-bodied man to report, with a gun and a horse, for duty to the local Federal commander. Non-compliers faced arrest, fines, and imprisonment. They built two forts, one near the village and another by the gristmill. Other forts were constructed at Rippee and at Rome.

In Arkansas the defeated Confederates reorganized. Thomas Hindman, the new commander, was from a family of politicians. Dapper and only 5'1", he dressed in ruffled shirts, patent leather boots, and rose-colored kid gloves. He had killed a man in a duel, had written a sentimental novel, and had served in Congress. Though unpopular in Arkansas, he trained a new army of rounded-up deserters and conscripts. Hindman believed that low level, hit and run warfare would force Federal commanders to guard railways, bridges, mills, and mines or risk having them destroyed. He sent officers north into Missouri to set up guerrilla units and to find recruits for the South.

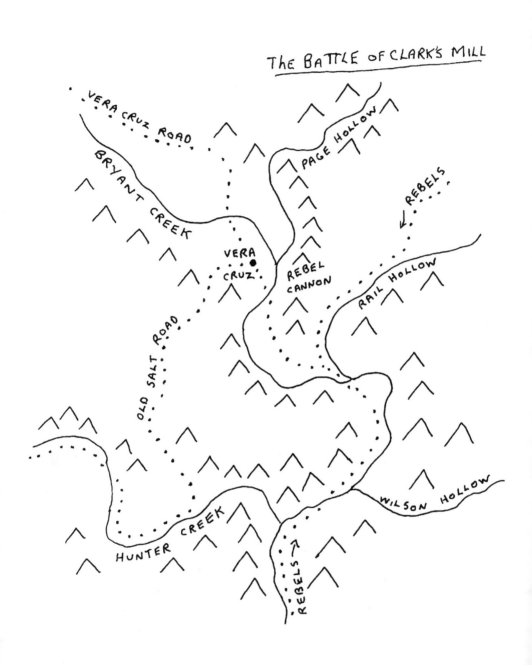

The Battle of Clark's Mill

He opened lead, gunpowder, rifle, leather, and clothing factories.

In Richmond the Confederate Congress passed the Partisan Ranger Act. Under it Shelby's Cavalry and other Missouri units were transferred to Arkansas for raids into Missouri. John Marmaduke, Claib Jackson's nephew and a member of the powerful Sappington family, would lead the Rangers. A handsome, though nearsighted, six-foot West Point graduate, Marmaduke wore a mustache and beard and brushed his long hair into a dandy's curl at his collar. When Marmaduke's men fought the Federals to a standstill at Prairie Grove near Fayetteville, Colonel Slayback, his chief of staff, rode out between the lines and challenged any man to meet him in single combat. Immediately, Lt. Thomas Willhite rode proudly out from the Federal lines and exchanged pistol shots with Slayback, only to crumple, lifeless, in his saddle. As twilight fell so, too, did many "champions."

Marmaduke ordered a regiment of Rangers under Colonels John Burbridge and Colton Green to raid north from their winter quarters on the big bend of the White River near Yellville. Along the way the local folk cheered as they passed. Most of the troops were hardened veterans from central Missouri. Like most Missourians, though, they felt little loyalty to the Confederacy, the Deep South, or plantation culture.

Late in the afternoon of 6 November '62 the Rangers appeared suddenly at Rockbridge, the seat of Ozark County. The local militia ran for the hills as the Confederates razed the gristmill and newly built blockhouse and set up camp near the flames.

Meanwhile in Vera Cruz, Captain Barstow received a report of Rebel troops near Gainesville and sent a patrol under Sergeant George Taylor to investigate. The day before one man had been captured and another killed in a skirmish with guerrillas near Coldspring. Another patrol of twenty men, under Lt. McClure, reconnoitered toward Denlow. Barstow then led eighteen men down the Vera Cruz Road straight into the advancing Rangers and fought a running skirmish near Bertha; several men and horses were killed and wounded. Barstow fell back to Vera Cruz and sent messengers to recall the patrols. When a scout reported that Rebels were moving toward town from Falling Spring, Barstow prepared a line of battle on Bryant Creek, where his cannon had clear lines of fire.

The Rangers left camp before daylight. Colonel Green moved the cannon and a battalion up Fox and Clever Creeks and cautiously approached Vera Cruz from the east. Undetected, they set up the artillery on the bluff above the village. At 11 A.M. November 7th Confederate cannons fired their first volleys and splintered the courthouse. The town folk fled. Several Federals were wounded when heavy shells penetrated the log and earth blockhouse walls. Old George Davis, the blacksmith, saw a cannonball crash through the side of his cabin. County officials gathered up the records and headed west up the Old Salt Road to Rome as Federal cannons answered back. Burbridge and the rest of the regiment came up the Vera Cruz Road. Skirmishes began as the Rangers probed the Federal line. While the fighting progressed, Burbridge sent units around the Federal position. Soon Vera Cruz was surrounded.

Late in the afternoon a Ranger captain rode out under a white flag to meet Captain Barstow. If you surrender, he said, everyone will be paroled and allowed to leave unharmed. Nearly out of cannon shells, Barstow accepted, and the Federal troops stacked their arms. Exultant Rangers swarmed in to gather up equipment and livestock. At last light, however, a shot rang out. County Commissioner William Martin had left his prized blooded mare behind when he escaped with the county documents, and a Rebel trooper, Pat Hunt, requisitioned her. In an angry exchange followed by a scuffle, Hunt shot and killed Judge Martin. Burbridge placed Hunt under guard for a later court martial.

In the darkness the Federals, stripped of their possessions, marched toward Marshfield. Three days later, exhausted, footsore, cold, and hungry, Captain Hiram Barstow and his men reported to Colonel Dudley Wickersham. Later, a review board found Barstow negligent and dismissed him from service, disgraced.

The Rangers rested for a day and a night at Vera Cruz. They burned the mill, courthouse, and forts. The mill and fort at Rome were attacked and razed the following day; the militia scattered. (Later, their captain would tell an amusing story of how the horses "spooked" and bolted.) The Unionists hurriedly took the county records back to Vera Cruz.

A week later Burbridge suddenly appeared in Wright County. A Federal wagon train en route from Houston to Hartville was unhitching to camp for the night along Beaver Creek when the Rangers rode in from three sides. The surprised guards and teamsters surrendered after a brief fight. Burbridge looted everything that could be easily carried; the rest, he set ablaze.

Across southern Missouri Ranger groups successfully raided isolated and vulnerable Federal detachments. In January 1863 Marmaduke made a daring strike on Springfield. After house-to-house street fighting, the Rangers drove the Federals into their blockhouses. Cattle, horses, and wagonloads of supplies were gathered from Federal sympathizers. Marmaduke's men pushed east with overwhelming Federal forces in pursuit.

Another column of Rangers, including Colonels Burbridge and Green, was ordered to ride north from Pocahontas, Arkansas, and rendezvous with Marmaduke in south central-Missouri. Months of hard campaigning had weakened the men and their mounts. Marmaduke wrote that they were "indifferently armed and equipped, thinly clad, many without shoes and horses…or cooking utensils…The horses are worn by continuous service of many months…unshod, very poor and unfit for any service."[10] Commanded by Colonel Joseph Porter, the three under-strength regiments had to cross one hundred forty miles of rugged country that had been stripped of provisions by Curtis' Federal Army. Nevertheless, they captured many infamous Unionists and Jayhawkers as they rode north up Bryant Creek, through Vera Cruz, and the charred ruins of the Federal forts.

Burbridge went ahead to Hartville, seat of Wright County and a Federal strongpoint on the upper Gasconade River. In a surprise attack he captured thirty-five militiamen, two Federal soldiers, Unionist civilians, and two hundred rifles. Unfortunately, there were few supplies and little food or fodder. They burned the fort. The following day Burbridge attacked Marshfield, the seat of Webster County. He took fifty militiamen and torched the blockhouse. Marmaduke and Porter joined him on January 10th.

Meanwhile, a Federal brigade of Illinois, Iowa, Michigan, and Missouri troops marched west from Houston, Missouri, to block Marmaduke while other Federal forces converged from Springfield and further north. Well armed and equipped, their cavalry were mounted on strong horses. Expecting a Rebel attack, they dug in at Hartville. With Burbridge again in the lead, Marmaduke's unsuspecting small army rode into the waiting Federals without sending scouts ahead. The Rebels advanced into a blackjack thicket on the edge of town; suddenly, the hidden Federal infantry rose up and fired a volley into them at close range. Burbridge's men panicked and fled. Increasing numbers of Rebels converged on Hartville and assaulted the Federals. Artillery shells ripped through the lines as men loaded and fired. Colonel Porter was knocked from his saddle by an artillery round. Colonel Emmett McDonald took a canister shell in the chest; he bled to death on the frozen ground. Both sides raised truce flags to retrieve their casualties. Fearing they would be surrounded, the Federals retreated and abandoned many wounded stragglers. Rebel horses were unfit to pursue them. Death tolls and descriptions vary widely; both sides claimed victory. Historians believe that Marmaduke's raid was a success because Federal troops were withdrawn from Arkansas and the Indian Territory to protect southern Missouri; consequently, Lincoln relieved General Curtis of command. Certainly, the Unionists were given a scare and the Southerners, renewed hope. Colonel Shelby wrote in his report of the Battle of Hartville:

> *I heard the cannons shivering crash*
> *As when the whirlwind rends the ash.*
> *I heard the muskets deadly clang*
> *As if a thousand anvils rang.*[11]

With the Federals closing in, Marmaduke rode south along the North Fork to camp at Round Valley, where Indian Creek flows in. He paroled his prisoners, who began the long walk to Houston, and marched his troops to Batesville, Arkansas. It "was a long and trying journey," Marmaduke wrote, "over rough roads, through rain and snow and icy mountain streams," across "a country laid waste by the Federals furnishing neither food for man or horse…At least two hundred of the command abandoned their horses on the roadside to die and waded many a weary mile through the snow and deep mud, some barefoot, yet they encountered every danger willingly and endured all fatigues cheerfully."[12]

Though the Ranger raids were a nuisance, the Federals were firmly in control of Missouri. They had vast industrial resources and powerful armies. The worst fears of Missourians were realized; they were controlled by "furriners." The hated Republicans dominated politically. Under Lincoln's amnesty program many State Guardsmen swore an oath, posted a $1000 bond, and signed up with their local militia. Nevertheless, guerrilla bands formed spontaneously in response to outrages by Federal troops. The guerrillas razed bridges, derailed trains, sabotaged telegraph lines, ambushed Federal patrols, and terrorized Unionist citizens.

Unfortunately, the Federal commanders were as callous and brutal as they were inept; many were concerned solely with furthering their careers. Most were "hawks" who felt that only progressively harsher measures would subdue Missouri. A deep schism, begun by the rift between Fremont and Frank Blair, developed between the Radicals, who were bent on vengeance, and the Conservatives, who hoped for eventual reconciliation. Conservative leaders, such as Provisional Governor Gamble and President Lincoln, believed that ordinary men and women wanted peace. The Radicals thought that Missourians were intrinsically evil. Curtis wanted to sack and level towns and drive off citizens. Total war would end the war.

Scholarly Henry "Old Brains" Halleck took over after Fremont was relieved. With owl eyes, a bald, bulging forehead, and a receding chin, Halleck took pride in the enormous volumes of orders and proclamations issued from his St. Louis headquarters. "Those who are not for us," he wrote, "will be regarded as against us…We are at war with those who were brothers, friends, neighbors. They are now enemies."[13] His General Order #32 declared that "insurgent rebels…will be arrested…and suffer death." Furthermore, all property, real and personal, would be confiscated. Local commanders must show "the severity of military power." "Every man who enlists" as a guerrilla, said his General Order #100, "forfeits his life and becomes an outlaw." General Order #30 proclaimed that the "strictest punishments" would be given to those who spied for and aided Rebels. Old Brains issued General Order #1, which replaced the civilian court system with military tribunals and the local sheriffs with provost marshals. Thousands were arrested; the courts bogged down, and the jails teemed with prisoners. Every week hundreds were sent to the notoriously crowded and filthy makeshift prisons in St. Louis, where nearly half of them died of disease.

When Old Brains became Supreme Commander in Washington, John Schofield, a brilliant West Pointer, took his place in St. Louis. At the outbreak of the war, Schofield was on leave of absence from the army and was teaching at Washington University. Plump and pious, with long, thin, elegant whiskers, he fought with Lyon at Wilson's Creek and had urged him not to attack. When Schofield took command in the spring of '63, the Mississippi was flooding. Grant's army, laying siege to Vicksburg from the swamps, was decimated by disease and in desperate need of men. Schofield's job, while still prosecuting the war in Missouri, Arkansas, and the Indian Territories, was to transfer thousands of men by steamboat to Grant. Nearly all of the out-of-state troops and many Missouri units headed into the Deep South.

Schofield was widely unpopular. Though an aggressive and competent commander, he was a Conservative. The Radicals continually thwarted his orders and plotted against him. They called him "Skowfield" behind his back, referred to him as a traitor, and sent a delegation to Lincoln to demand his removal. Despite Schofield's conservative beliefs, however, he issued General Order #96 which established military control of the press. "Copperhead" newspapers like the Chicago Times, the Cincinnati Enquirer, and the New York World were illegal to possess. Schofield also used the order to silence the radical St. Louis Democrat and the German language Westlicke Post. The St. Louis Herald was shut down as was the Cape Girardeau Eagle, the Hannibal Evening News, and the Columbia Standard. The Lexington Expositor had its presses seized. The Independence Border Star and California News were ransacked and demolished by Federal troops. "All persons [the order read] who publish facts calculated to embarrass or weaken the military authorities…shall be punished by fine and imprisonment."

Schofield's enemies included General Thomas Ewing, a Radical leader with a protruding lower lip and a close-cropped beard like that of his brother-in-law, W.T. Sherman. From a politically prominent Ohio family, Ewing had served as Chief Justice of the Kansas Supreme Court. His General Order #11 depopulated a large portion of western Missouri by ordering "all persons deported from Bates, Cass, Jackson, and northern Vernon counties." Twenty thousand people became refugees when their homes were looted and torched by Kansas troops. Ewing arrested the wives, mothers, and sisters of guerrillas and incarcerated them in a dilapidated three-story building converted into a prison. Filthy and crowded, sanitation and hygiene were impossible. One day it collapsed; dozens of women were crushed and maimed. A large crowd gathered behind the guards and listened to their screams.

Ewing's General Order #10 established "banishing." "The wives and children of known guerrillas," it read, will be "removed out of this district and the state of Missouri forthwith." With little money and few possessions, families were forced out of their homes and mercilessly left to live or die. His General Order #35 allowed provost marshals to banish families even if "no specific acts of disloyalty can be proven."

The barbarous General John McNeil commanded northern Missouri; his provost marshal, William "the beast" Strachan, believed that guerrillas were "not only enemies of our country but of Christianity and civilization and even our race, and the only remedy for the disease is to kill...We are fighting a battle for the world, for humanity, for civilization, for religion, for the honor of our forefathers...What is war? Is it anything but retaliation?"[14] When prominent Unionist Andrew Alleman was abducted, McNeil issued the Palmyra Decree which instructed Strachan to seize and shoot ten random hostages. Overnight McNeil became a Radical hero.

General John Pope was another Radical champion. A Kentucky born civil engineer, he was thirty-nine when war broke out. His corpulent body dressed in grandiose braid, he was insecure, boastful, and arrogant. Some called him a "loud-mouthed braggart." Historians ponder whether he was mad, a cruel tyrant, or hopelessly inept. He felt that Missouri could be taxed into submission, and under his General Order #32, whenever there was a guerrilla attack, he imposed a levy on the nearest town for damages. He withdrew his troops from their positions guarding the railroad and told the local people that they would now be responsible for defending it. If Federal troops were needed, the locals would have to pay for their services. When guerrillas shot up a train in Marion County, and the county seat failed to pay up, Pope told his men to seize whatever they needed from merchants and citizens. The 2nd Kansas and the 16th Illinois went on a rampage of looting, burning, and vandalism. Drunken soldiers ran the trains and shot men at work in the fields. They filled boxcars with stolen horses and cattle and shipped them into Illinois. Railroad agent J.T.K. Hayward wrote angrily to Secretary of War Stanton that Federal troops take "everything they want, entering and searching houses and stealing...committing rapes on the negroes and no punishment or none of any account has been meted out to them."[15] Pope was promoted, given an army in Virginia, then humiliated by Jackson at Second Manassas.

Pope's system of levies became institutionalized. Communities were fined $5000 when a soldier was killed, $1000 when one was wounded. Other fines were assessed at the whim of the local commander. With so much money changing hands so quickly, graft and corruption became rampant. General Order #24 directed that property would be seized and sold whenever levies were not promptly paid. Vast quantities of household goods were offered at public auction from a huge warehouse in St. Louis. Some Federal officers became rich dealing in confiscated goods. Lt. Colonel Daniel Anthony of the 7th Kansas Cavalry was one of them. "Come out here," he wrote his brother-in-law back East, "and speculate in cattle...horses and mules...there is a good chance to buy cheap...There is money in it to anyone who will attend to it...I would advise you to come out and try it."[16]

Soon a complex system of permits, licenses, and passports was created to control business, trade, and travel. Boats had to be licensed and inspected. Railroads and stagecoaches needed cargo permits, and people had to buy passes to travel. No one could do business without purchasing a permit. General Order #24 directed that "disloyal" persons could not raise crops, buy or sell goods, or engage in commerce. In some towns the local commander closed all the businesses. Disloyalty was ambiguous and often based on unproven suspicions or a commander's lust for revenge.

Strict military censorship kept the war in Missouri a secret. Few knew or cared about Missouri's agonies. Late at night in the White House Abraham Lincoln pored over reports and sat in deep melancholy, his soul racked by guilt and compassion. The endless, gruesome details aged him noticeably. He spoke of innate human evil and the need for Christian charity and forbearance.

The struggle between the Radical and Conservative factions of the Republican Party reached its zenith in the election of 1864. With the electorate carefully restricted and corruption at the polls, the Radicals swept into power, winning eight of the nine congressional seats. Lincoln carried the state, however, buoyed by the soldiers' votes.

War dragged on as Missouri seethed, tortured by violence on a Biblical scale. Federal generals had drawn a line in the sand. The guerrillas were desperate young men who roamed the countryside in temporary bands and suddenly attacked those they considered enemies. Robbery, arson, and murder were their tools; they believed they were defending their families and homes from Yankee invaders and the traitorous militia. Romantically they saw themselves as paladins on a quest for justice. Strangely, the most infamous guerrilla was a thin, handsome, polite, and soft-spoken schoolteacher from Ohio with reddish hair and pale blue eyes. When William Quantrill moved to Kansas, he was caught up in the violence. As bands of young men formed in response to Jayhawker outrages, his charisma made him a leader. Men admired his skill with a pistol, his incredible horsemanship, and his amoral, cold-blooded willingness to take life. He was deeply attached to his horse, Charley, and to his wife, Kate.

For years Lawrence, Kansas, was the base for Jayhawker raids into Missouri and a transshipment point for stolen property. In August 1863, as Lee's army tried to rebuild from the carnage at Gettysburg and New York City still smoldered from the Draft Riots, Quantrill led a band of savage young men toward Lawrence. They had seen their homes burned, their families banished, kinfolk and friends summarily shot. Now they sought a terrible vengeance.

At dawn on a hot, dusty day, they struck. The town of two thousand was completely surprised. Quantrill's orders were to "kill every man big enough to carry a gun." They galloped in like a tide and enveloped the town from several directions. Some carried lists of men to be executed and homes to be razed. There was mayhem, an orgy of murder and looting, amid the smoke and shrieks. Men were chased like rabbits and gunned down in front of their horrified families.

The massacre shocked the nation in banner headlines. Revenge-seeking Jayhawkers plunged into Missouri and destroyed everything. For hundreds of square miles only blackened chimneys remained. Colonel Bazel Lazear, the Federal commander at Lexington, wrote that his heart was "sicken[ed] to see what I have seen...a desolate country and men and women and children, some of them almost naked. Some on foot and some in old wagons. Oh God."[17]

Slowly Quantrill's men were hunted down, band by band, man by man. Federal troops combed the woods until they flushed the guerrillas. The chase was on. "We had quite a hunt last night," Illinois cavalryman Sardius Smith wrote in his diary. "We are getting quite hardened to this kind of thing and I can go into a house with a pistol in my hand, with a smile on my face, speak politely to the ladies, ask where the men are in order that I may shoot them."[18] An Iowa cavalryman wrote for the Keokuk <u>Weekly Gate City</u> that "hunting rebels is as interesting as deer hunting."[19]

The abhorrent cycle of violence continued. Mutilation of corpses was commonplace. As cadavers hung from trees with signs attached to them, men cut souvenirs: scalps, ears, noses, and fingers; they wore necklaces of bones and teeth.

Surprisingly, despite the chaos there was a chivalrous code on both sides against harming white women. Men had been raised to believe they were the protectors of women. Rape was rare and carried a stigma. However, symbolic rape, where soldiers exposed themselves to women and desecrated the marriage bed, was common. Their romantic code did not extend to women of color, who were raped and abused with impunity.

The people of Douglas County were caught up in the longest, most widespread, and destructive war in North America. This part of Missouri was known as the "burned over" zone where, historians believe, 100,000 people abandoned their farms and became refugees. Large sections reverted to wilderness. Some families, the Alsups for example, were Unionists and thought that only naked fear of authority would make their Rebel neighbors submit. In a letter to Federal officials in St. Louis signed by seven of his neighbors, G.O. Yeiser of Mexico, Missouri, wrote that to "bargain...persuade and talk soft to traitors is like...trying to make water run uphill. Disarm them entirely...Let them feel the force and power of the Government." If "some innocent must suffer," so be it.[20] However, despite their weaknesses the Southern folk resisted the Federal invaders, and many Unionists, including the Alsups, would pay when their farms were raided. Eventually, pro-Southern families like the Todds paid an even higher price when they were driven out.

People learned to live by lying. They professed to be loyal Unionists to Federal troops and Rebel sympathizers when questioned by guerrillas. Federal authorities would tell suspected sympathizers to prove their loyalty by making a list of disloyal neighbors. Federal provost agents impersonating guerrillas would ride into farmsteads, coax people into disloyalty, and arrest them. Likewise, guerrillas commonly dressed as Federal troops to fool soldiers and civilians alike. Suspects by the hundreds were marched out of Douglas and surrounding counties to Rolla, where Ft. Wyman had been converted into a prison. Most were then sent in boxcars to the fetid, jammed Gratiot Street Prison in St. Louis. Horrified Union surgeon George Rex wrote despairingly to his superiors in 1864 that "disease, evil [overcrowding] still continues unabated" with "no hopes" to decrease the death rate. Many prisoners in the "insufficiently ventilated quarters" were held on "very trivial charges" that would not be "sustained" in court.[21]

By the summer of 1864 the overwhelming industrial productivity and manpower of the North were wearing down the South. Sherman, outside Atlanta, planned his "March to the Sea." Lee's army slowly deteriorated in trench warfare around Petersburg. The Confederate high command needed to divert men and materials from Grant and Sherman. Missouri, they knew, was thinly garrisoned and vulnerable. Pap Price was ordered to take his remaining men on a desperate offensive. He was to cross the Mississippi, gather up the meager Confederate forces in Arkansas, and advance aggressively into Missouri. It was hoped his attack would divert enough Union attention and resources for a Confederate resurgence in the East. A secret pro-Southern organization, the Knights of the Golden Circle, promised Price that Missouri would rise up, and thousands of men would join his army. St. Louis would fall, they claimed.

Pap marched north from Pocahontas, Arkansas, across the eastern Ozarks. Cancer killed Claib Jackson. Thomas Reynolds, the second Confederate Governor of Missouri, traveled from the Missouri "State Capital" at Marshall, Texas, to join the offensive. Erudite and urbane, he rode in a carriage and in the evenings worked on the triumphant address that he would deliver in Jefferson City. Though ragged and poorly armed, Price's men were determined to expel the "damn Dutch" and recapture their birthright. There was no line of supply, no hope for reinforcement. They would take what they needed from Unionist families. While the Rangers under Shelby and Marmaduke raided on a broad front, Price's army converged on the railhead at Pilot Knob in the mineral-rich St. Francis Mountains. A strong Federal garrison stood watch at Fort Davidson, a heptagonal earthwork with nine-foot walls and a deep moat. Cannon barrels protruded from its walls and overlooked clear fields of fire. The hated General Ewing was in command with orders to hold out as long as possible. In St. Louis the Federals gathered every available man.

The fort is impregnable, Price's officers told him. Go around it, they said, or haul cannon up the mountainside and lob shells inside until they surrender. When the men heard that Ewing, author of General Order #11, was in the fort, they rose up and hollered. Price ordered an attack. His men surged forward in four solid ranks, whooping and yelling. The Federals held their fire until the attackers were in easy rifle range. Grapeshot and canister rounds tore through the ranks; mass volley fire cut them down in bloody heaps. They reached the moat. With nowhere to hide and no way up the walls, the men were driven back. They regrouped and attacked again and again.

As darkness fell the fields around the fort were strewn with hundreds of corpses: arms flung out, eyes vacant, mouths wide open. Late that night the Federals silently marched out of the fort through the sleeping Rebel lines and headed toward Rolla. The last Federals lit a fuse. Before dawn a tremendous explosion that destroyed the fort awakened the Rebel Army.

Price pushed north toward the Missouri River. Young men eager to fight joined him. Across the state guerrilla bands attacked and robbed wagon trains, railroads, stage lines, and banks. The homes and farms of Unionists provided Price's army of ragamuffins with plentiful supplies. Some towns welcomed them with cheers; entire militia companies switched sides to join him. Soon thousands of poorly-armed, untrained recruits marched with Price. He knew they would be nearly worthless in battle.

The carnage at Fort Davidson had broken Pap's spirit. Over the years he'd led so many ardent men to their graves. Perhaps he realized how hopeless the campaign was. He no longer rode Bucephalus, his gray warhorse; instead, he lay on a piece of carpet in an ambulance and drank heavily.

Meanwhile, three Federal armies converged on Price as he marched west past heavily fortified Jefferson City. His old enemy, Curtis, marched toward him from Kansas, another behind him from St. Louis, and yet another parallel and south of him. This was the moment the Federals had dreamed of. They had the Missouri Rebels surrounded hundreds of miles from their base south of the Arkansas River.

The fight began. The Missourians pushed the Kansas army back while they held off the other armies. They were finally cornered near Kansas City. It was late October 1864. Price rose to lead his men. After a spectacular battle they broke through and started south as Federal cavalry harried the rear guard. Repeatedly, the Missouri cavalry took a stand on a creek bank, only to be overwhelmed and thrown back in confusion. The dead and wounded littered the frost-browned grass. Price burned his wagons and destroyed everything that couldn't be carried; in a cold rain the men were force-marched sixty-one miles. They left behind cannons, guns, clothing, dead horses and mules.

The Federals caught up with the exhausted remnants of Price's army near Carthage and sent them limping into Arkansas past the Pea Ridge Battlefield. Men deserted by the hundreds. When the road south was blocked, they detoured west onto the prairies of the Indian Territory. With only acorns and scraps of horsemeat, men perished by the dozens. "We have endured more than is recorded of any soldiers in the Annals of History," Private J.H.P. Baker wrote in his journal, "and yet half is not felt or told."[22] Price's army was like the children of Israel, he wrote, wandering in the wilderness. The men cursed Price as they left the dead behind for the wolves. When Price reached the Confederate lines at Laynesville, Arkansas, he'd marched fifteen hundred miles, fought forty-three battles, lost all his cannon and most of his men.

Organized resistance to Federal authority in Missouri was over. Only a few guerrillas remained to be hunted down. Ironically, though Price's offensive was a holocaust that crushed forever the hopes of Southerners in Missouri, it managed to tie up thousands of Federal troops and perhaps give the dying Confederacy extra weeks of dwindling life.

What little is known about the Civil War in Booger County has been handed down, mostly orally, by surviving families. During the summer of Price's offensive, the Booger County militia had been reorganized as Co. H of the 46th Mo. Mounted Infantry, commanded by Locke Alsup. More a political than military unit, it would ensure Republican/Alsup dominance in the post war years and a haven from conscription in the regular army. Co. H very likely "politically cleansed" the county by driving out the remaining pro-Southern families. On the afternoon of November 3, 1864, thirty men of Co. H were resting and cooking supper on a rise overlooking the Vera Cruz Road near the [current] Hwy 76 bridge over Bryant Creek. A boy named Johnson Burris was tending three large kettles of beans over a fire while the men were drinking coffee; someone ran in and declared that two Rebels had just come around the bend riding south. The men jumped on their horses and, with a yell, galloped to intercept them. It was great sport. A wild chase was on, with Ben Alsup and Spence Collins on fast horses swiftly overtaking the fleeing Rebels.

Suddenly, a regiment of Rebels, a remnant of Price's shattered army on its way south to safety, came around the bend. They quickly formed a line of battle and fired a volley into the oncoming men of Booger County. Ben's horse went down. Spence tumbled from his saddle, mortally wounded. Nick Coble was killed, so were John Bevis, Robert Martin, and a boy named Yarberry. Everyone scattered into the brush and rode hard to get out of rifle range. Tom Alsup, mounted on his racehorse Big Jim, saw Ben hiding behind a tree with a Rebel closing in on him. Ignoring bullets, Tom galloped in and shot the Rebel as Ben jumped on behind him.

Though his horse was wounded, Bill Coats rode hard until it dropped dead near the mouth of Tarbutton Creek. Then he ran along the east side of the creek with two mounted Rebels after him. "Stop, you Yankee SOB," one of them yelled, "or we'll blow you in two."[23] Bill put his hands in the air, but when the Rebels dismounted to go through a split-rail fence, Bill ducked into the brush; he left behind his heavy boots in order to run faster.

Johnson Burris and another lad were still tending the beans when the Rebels marched up. They teased the boys, ate beans, and made camp.

During the night Locke gathered his men. They rode down Bryant Creek in small groups and positioned themselves on bluffs overlooking the road. As the Southerners marched south the following day, Co. H sniped at them. The militia fired on the Rebels at the mouth of Hunter Creek and again at the bluffs on the east side of the creek north of Hwy 14. At the "boat hole crossing" at Hwy 14, they shot two Rebels. One of them was taken in by a local family, nursed back to health, and eventually returned to his Shannon County, Missouri home.

Lafe Gentry, the youngest of the five children of Lafayette and Docey [Abner], was born early in 1862. In 1861 Lafayette left to fight and never returned. Born in Keytesville, the Chariton County seat and Sterling Price's hometown, Lafayette may have lost his life serving under Price. Cholera took Docey just after Lafe was born, and fifteen-year-old Nancy, the eldest, took her siblings to Rolla.

Hundreds of refugees poured into Rolla's railhead fortress. On dilapidated carts pulled by scrawny cattle, they carried their pathetic possessions. Many had been burned out by rival neighbors; some, robbed en route. Dirty, raggedly-dressed children swarmed around the wagons. The fortunate found work at the depot unloading hay, grain, food, clothing, and munitions from boxcars into warehouses and wagon trains. Others built fortifications or tended the hundreds of prisoners in the crowded jails. Lucky refugees were given houses seized from "disloyal" citizens. After registering with the commissary officer, each refugee received half a soldier's ration of hardtack, beans, and coffee. As measles, typhoid, dysentery, and pneumonia periodically swept through the overcrowded town, carpenters built hundreds of child-sized coffins. The Rolla refugees were hated and feared by Federal troops. "They are as dastardly a set of cowards as ever lived," wrote an Iowa soldier. "Missouri's present race is not worth preserving. Let them starve and die and quickly cover them over with sod."[24]

Lafe returned to Booger County after the war. Later, he married

Lizzie Spangler and fathered fourteen children. They homesteaded in Pleasant Valley, near the "Chicken Brisket" community on the upper Clifty drainage south of Mountain Grove, an area of extensive orchards. Lizzie was a master quilter who worked in the Butterfly pattern with the lock stitch of love. Because he had never seen his father, Lafe was thought to possess divine powers. He was called upon, through prayer and faith, to "lay hands" on the ill, staunch the flow of blood, and remove warts. He was also asked to "witch" for water.

Daniel and Mary Beard Hull owned a farm, tannery, and cabinet shop in Middle Brook, Virginia. In 1858, with their eight children, they made a three-month journey west in a Conestoga wagon that Daniel had built himself. Eventually, they settled on a thousand-acre farm south of Mountain Grove, where they built a house. Raids by bushwhackers forced them to move to Rolla for protection. Daniel died there. When Mary returned, everything—house, buildings, fences—was destroyed. Their grandson, Richard Denny, practiced medicine in Mountain Grove for forty-four years.

James Martin joined the Federal Army in July of 1861 and served under Grant and Sherman at Shiloh, Vicksburg, and Chattanooga. Outside Atlanta James was wounded; his unit, surrounded and captured. Railroad hog cars and exhausting forced marches brought them to Andersonville Prison, where guards took their valuables and much of their clothing. Thousands of men crowded the open pen; they were nearly naked, emaciated, dirty, and bug-ridden. Dying men lay groaning on the sandy soil "alive" with lice and maggots. A sluggish, contaminated stream was the only source of water. Yellow fever, "sand fever," dysentery, and other diseases haunted the prison. Every morning at eight a drum beat called the prisoners to bring corpses to the dead gate. One August morning 127 bodies were delivered for burial. A piece of cornbread, a few cups of congealed rice, and an occasional leathery strip of "salt mule" were the meager rations. James developed scurvy, became "moon blind," and lost his night vision. When winter blew in from the North, James and two friends huddled under one thin blanket. After the war he was taken to the U.S. hospital at Annapolis, Maryland.

James and Polly Turner came to Booger County from North Carolina via Tennessee and Indiana and settled near Arno. Their son, William, organized and led the local militia. He was shot by a pro-Southerner, and the Turners were forced to move.

Bill Smith was only two in 1861 when his parents, William and Nancy, migrated with a wagon train from Tennessee, through Indiana, into Missouri. William was impressed into the Federal Army in Rolla while Nancy, who had just given birth to Rachel, continued on and homesteaded on Beaver Creek. She never saw William again.

Elijah Sanders, a mill owner, enlisted with the Confederate Army at Yellville, Arkansas, early in the war. His mill and farm were ravaged and torched by cutthroats and thieves, and his wife, Margaret, joined other refugees and fled toward Rolla with four children. Along the way Federal soldiers stole their livestock. Somehow, however, Margaret fed her children and held out. For four years she heard nothing from Elijah. After the war Margaret and Elijah reunited; determined to start a new life for themselves, they settled near Rome, built a mill and farm, and had five more children.

Sterling Shipley, born in McMinn County, Tennessee, in 1831, was a wagon-wright and preacher who had a farm along Spring Creek north of Twin Bridges. He served with the Missouri State Guard throughout the war as a private. After the war the hostility of his neighbors forced him to move to Arkansas.

The Mankin family moved to Booger County in 1842 from Rutherford County, Tennessee. Slave owners, the war split the family. Jessie, the father, and William served with Price, while the other sons, James and Illy, became Federal soldiers. Following the war Jessie and William were despised by their Unionist neighbors and moved to Arkansas. So bitter were the personal feelings within the family that the two sides never spoke again.

James "Bushy" Wood and his son Dennis fought on opposite sides during the war. James served in the Union while Dennis joined the Rebel forces and became a Federal prisoner at Vicksburg. Both survived the conflict and are buried at Penner Cemetery.

Jeremiah "Early" Heard was born in 1816 in Dunlap, Tennessee, and became one of the first settlers along Prairie Hollow south of Vanzant. He was pro-Missouri (i.e. pro-Southern). His oldest son, John, fought with Price. Though Early's daughter Polly was married to James Coats, a prominent Vera Cruz Unionist, the Heards were driven out of Booger County by hostile neighbors and Jayhawkers.

The Todds were the most prominent pro-Southern family in Booger County. Preston (b. 1817 Russell County, Virginia), along with his father, Thomas, and a large extended family, settled along Fox Creek north of Falling Spring. Thomas was kicked to death by a horse in 1846; Preston was twice elected sheriff and was a delegate to the Missouri State Convention in 1861. He owned Racetrack Hollow and was "no stranger to conflict." A friend and ally of Sterling Price, he served in various Missouri/Confederate units throughout the war. His son Thomas died a Confederate soldier. After the war the Todds and their kin were forced out of the county into Arkansas. Preston, father of ten, lived until 1900.

Preston's sister Liz (b. 1821) married Isaac Davis in Indiana. Isaac won the fine farm just south of Falling Spring (remnants of it are still visible) from Ben Alsup's son-in-law, Tom Livingston, in a horse race. The Alsups, though, were determined to have it back. Ben and Shelt killed Isaac as he was carrying a bucket of corn to his hogs and claimed he was carrying the corn to Rebels hiding in the woods. They tried to force Liz to marry one of them, but she refused and married a man named Hatfield. After heated arguments and a gunfight, the Alsups ambushed and killed Hatfield. Soon, they violently drove Liz out of the county.

Joseph Lyons (b. 1810 Cincinnati, Ohio) established a mill on Beaver Creek in the early 1840's and built a fine house with the first glass windows in the region. They had to be carefully hauled by oxcart from Rolla. The mill was three-stories: corn was ground on the first, wheat on the second, and spinning wheels and a carding machine operated on the third. The stone buhrs were imported from France. In July of 1862 Joseph was accused of "giving aid and comfort to the enemies of the United States and did fail, neglect, and refuse to take the oath of allegiance." He was arrested and imprisoned at Lexington. After Joseph's release both sides mistrusted him. Jim Hellen, a pro-Southern neighbor, shot Joseph to death in the mill yard. His wife, Sarah, was left to care for eleven children.

Lewis Maxey (b. 1843 Tennessee) settled near Ann [the intersection of AD and EE]. Lewis didn't want to be part of the war, but attacks by bushwhackers and threats by the militia forced him to join the Federal Army. He was captured and imprisoned at Andersonville.

Newt Smallwood (b. 1844 Ducktown, Tennessee) and his wife, Sarah, settled on a farm near Topaz. He joined the Federal Army at age twenty and was captured at Athens, Tennessee, and confined at Andersonville. After the war he was a county judge and state representative.

William Thomas of Clinton Township spent three years under Sherman as an infantryman. He contracted fever in South Carolina, ironically his family's former state, which left him permanently debilitated.

Winfield White (b. 1843 Ashland County, Ohio) farmed near Twin Bridges. While serving with the Federal Army, he was wounded at Stone River, Tennessee.

James Sullivan (b. 1831 Indiana) fought under Lyon at Wilson's Creek. Later, he was discharged because of "chronic diarrhea and exposure and hardship during battle."

A large extended family, the Collinses, migrated into southeastern Booger County from North Carolina in the early 1830's. Spencer died at the battle of Vera Cruz. His cousin Cornelius was a Federal soldier; plagued by an abdominal illness that he had contracted during the war, Cornelius died at age fifty-two. One branch of the Collins family moved to Arkansas by covered wagon to be "neutral." The men, however, were given the choice of either joining the Rebel Army or death.

In April 1863 Luke and Witt Marler drove a load of corn to Jackson's Mill on Beaver Creek. That afternoon, while they waited for their corn, bushwhackers suddenly attacked the mill. Running for his life, Witt was shot dead in the creek. Luke jumped on the unhitched team and escaped as the bushwhackers looted the mill. Because bushwhackers didn't kill women, Luke's wife, Nancy, and her sister Elizabeth later returned for Witt's body.

Jesse B. James (b. 1803 Virginia) came to the Topaz area in the 1840's with his extended family. He had a gristmill along the North Fork. In the summer of 1862 a band of pro-Southerners came through to drive out Unionists. Jesse and a Mr. Brown were captured, tried for providing grain to the Federals, found guilty, and hung. His family took him down, dressed him in his best clothes, and buried him where he died. Jesse was a well-respected member of the community.

Eighty-year-old Jesse Huffman was working his crops with a mule when he was captured by Rebels who forced him to guide them into Arkansas. His wife, Elizabeth, waited in a small cabin for two months until he returned.

Irvin King, his father, John King, two of his brothers, a Keaton, and two Ritters were killed in a skirmish with Rebels along Prairie Creek.

James Woods (b. 1816 Tennessee) was an early pioneer along Fox Creek and a militiaman. He and Bill Dobbs were playing cards near a spring when two neighbors mistook them for bushwhackers and fired at them; James was killed.

James Robertson came to Booger County with his parents, Malaca and Sarah, and extended family by oxcart in 1855. They had been forced off their land near Chattanooga because of their sympathy for the Cherokee, who were being removed. At age nineteen James walked from the family farm southeast of Ava to Rolla to enlist. He was at Shiloh, Vicksburg, Lookout Mountain, Chickamauga, and the March to the Sea. Strangely, at Chickamauga he fought on the old family farm he'd left eight years before. Discharged at New Orleans, he rode a barge to St. Louis and walked home. For safety he walked at night and hid in the brush during the day. James married Catherine Ooley soon after his return. They raised eight children.

The official end to the war had little effect in Booger County. The vindictive killing and plundering continued. Sylvester Freeman had served with the Missouri State Guard throughout the war. Unionists shot him as he walked home north of Ava. He was buried on the spot.

Though Lee surrendered at Appomattox on April 9, 1865, further west the war went on. In mid May the Governors of Arkansas, Louisiana, Texas, and Missouri met with their generals. The hawks threatened to stage a coup to prolong the war. Some wanted to move out onto the plains to join the wild tribes' fight against the Federals. Governor Reynolds angrily refused to sign the compromise agreement. By June 1st the last Confederate units laid down their arms. The desperate and starving pro-Southern Cherokee forces under Stand Watie, outlawed by their people, their property expropriated by the government, surrendered on June 23, 1865.

The Missouri Partisan Rangers under Shelby never surrendered. While Federal troops were disarming their fellow Rebels, they rode south. At the Rio Grande they lowered their battle flag into the river and watched the brown current carry it away. They crossed the river and turned their backs on America. Some became mercenaries for the French under Maximilian in his ill-fated war against Juarez. Others went to Brazil or British Honduras.

William Quantrill fought on, knowing his enemies would never let him live. Dressed as Federal Cavalrymen, his small band cantered east to kill Abe Lincoln. Booth shot Lincoln as they were crossing Kentucky. "Here's to the death of Abraham Lincoln," Quantrill said, as he raised his cup, "[I'm]_hoping his bones may serve in Hell as a gridiron to fry Yankees on."[25] When an inept farrier lamed Charley, Quantrill took it as a premonition. A few days later he was terribly wounded in a skirmish near Louisville and died a slow, painful death. Kate used money from his estate to open a fancy brothel in St. Louis.

Gradually, the guerrillas in Missouri degenerated into outlaw bands like the James and Youngers. A thousand-dollar reward was posted for the remaining pro-Southern partisans. Federal cavalry combed the woods, hunted them down, and shot them. The guerrillas had no options. To give up meant a noose or a bullet. Along the roads they waited to rob returning soldiers, as well as, civilians. Missouri became known as the "outlaw state." The Radicals controlled the State Government until 1872. Returning Southerners were disenfranchised. The courts and authorities, controlled by their enemies, sought revenge. Unionists could file lawsuits against their Southern neighbors and take what little they had. In most counties, including Douglas, Southerners were gunned down with impunity. Again in 1866 all men over eighteen were required to register with the local militia. Pro-Southern preachers were often the targets of the Radicals, who considered them heretics. They were shot, hung, whipped; their churches, torched. "Their [has] been a greate deal of murdering done in this state this summer," a farmer wrote to his brother in North Carolina. "…a greate many ministers of the gospil have been shot at their churches whilst ministering the gospil by the Radicals."[26] Joseph King wrote, "[After returning home] I found it impossible to preach in peace as my life was constantly being threatened and the people were afraid to come together."[27]

In the late 1860's a renewed wave of lawlessness swept the state. Banks and trains were robbed boldly in broad daylight. Federal troops joined local sheriffs to hunt down brigands. Many of Missouri's guerrillas and outlaws went west to form the bandit gangs celebrated in novels and movies.

Booger County's postwar years mirrored those of the rest of the state. The ballot box, county government, courts, and sheriff were controlled by the Alsups, their kinsmen, and allies. What they couldn't take legally, the Alsups took by force. The eastern townships seceded to Howell County; the county seat was forcibly moved. Though the Alsups were killed off, one by one, the Radicals would return. As masked riders in the night, they wielded the hangman's noose, the bullwhip, and the Bible. People called them the Baldknobbers.

Notes

1. Shea and Hess, 261, from a letter by General Curtis to General Halleck, April 6, 1862, Official Records.
2. Shea and Hess, 301, from a letter that appeared in the June 12, 1862, Aurora Beacon (Illinois).
3. Shea and Hess, 301, from a letter that appeared in the Little Rock, Arkansas, State Gazette, July 28, 1862.
4. Monaghan, 135. Mr. Monaghan does not give a source for this quote of General Lyon.
5. Monaghan, 197, Cincinnati Commercial, October 11 and 16, 1861.
6. Fellman, 154, Dan Holmes' letter to his family, December 21, 1861, Chicago Historical Society.
7. Fellman, 155, E.T. Lane letter to his cousin Sam, "Lucien Case Letters," Chicago Historical Society.
8. Fellman, 155, David Garver letter to his sister, April 15, 1862, "David Garver Letters," University of North Carolina.
9. Monaghan, 234, speech by Van Dorn to his army.
10. "The Battle of Hartville," Wright County Historical Society pamphlet. The Marmaduke quote is not given a source.
11. "The Battle of Hartville," Wright County Historical Society pamphlet.
12. "The Battle of Hartville," Wright County Historical Society pamphlet. The Marmaduke quote is not given a source.
13. Brownlee, 25, taken from War of the Rebellion: a Compilation of Official Records.
14. Fellman, 113, from William Strachan's December 10, 1862, letter to the New York Times, reprinted in the Official Records.
15. Brownlee, 35-36, from the Official Records.
16. Fellman, 35, from a letter by Dan Anthony to Aaron McLean, "The Letters of Dan Anthony," Kansas Historical Quarterly, XXIV, 1958.
17. "The Civil War Letters of Colonel Bazel Lazear," Missouri Historical Review, July 1950.
18. Fellman, 179, taken from the Sardius Smith Diary, May 28, 1862, Illinois Historical Society.
19. Fellman, 180, Keowuk Weekly Gate City, February 12, 1862, by a soldier in the Third Iowa Cavalry.
20. Fellman, 44, letter from G.O. Yeiser to General Schofield, July 19, 1862, Record Group 393, National Archives.

21. Brownlee, 162, letter from Surgeon George Rex, Official Records, Series 2, Vol. VIII, 367-377.
22. Monaghan, 343, from the diary of Private J.H.P. Baker, Missouri Historical Society.
23. Vineyard, from his manuscripts.
24. Bradbury, "Refugees in Rolla," Phelps County Genealogical Society, April 1993.
25. Monaghan, 346, from William Elsey Conelley's <u>Quantrill and the Border Wars</u>, 465,467.
26. Fellman, 239, letter from S.S. Steig to his brother James, August 26, 1866, "Samuel S. Steig Papers," Duke University.
27. Fellman, 239, "Joseph King Autobiography," Jackson County Historical Society, Independence, MO.

Baldknobbers

Drive south from Ava on Hwy 5 four miles and turn right on A Hwy. To the southwest a prominent timbered ridge dominates the horizon. Our route today, the Glade Top Trail, runs along this ridge. Built by the WPA and the CCC, construction of the trail provided work for many Ozarkers during the Great Depression. Follow the signs and stop at the parking area where the National Forest begins. No water is available.

Take 147 up Bristle Ridge to the summit. On the left is the first of many vistas. Caney Mtn. lookout tower is six miles from the start. Beyond it is a sheltered picnic area, and across the road is narrow, muddy Caney Cave. Four miles further at Wolf Junction the Glade Top Trail splits. With panoramas of Arkansas 147 descends to Longrun, an old Hippie settlement with a church and a few buildings. Road 149, also called Glade Top West or Skyline Drive, veers to the right at Wolf Junction; it is fairly level and an easy ride. For six miles it follows the forested ridge top to Hwy 125 near the Hercules Glade Wilderness. The numerous forest service and ATV trails that crisscross this area are a mountain biker's paradise.

Few people live here; however, in October when the forest colors, many drive up to see the spectacular neon pink and orange displays of the rare smoke tree, *Cotinus Obovatus*, endemic to these ridges. Water drains into the Little North Fork and Pond Fork to the east. Caney and Brushy Creeks flow into Beaver Creek to the west. These tributaries empty into Bull Shoals Lake, a colossal impoundment of the White River with 1000 miles of shoreline.

Today we'll pass several areas of extensive "cedar removal/glade restoration" where the forest service hopes to reestablish native plant and animal communities. Wildfires once swept across these hills, killing brush and rejuvenating meadows. The Ozarks was a patchwork of prairies interspersed with copses and treeless balds. It was on these desolate balds that the feared post-Civil War vigilante group, the Baldknobbers, held their rendezvous.

For generations Douglas County has been solidly Republican. Congressmen from the 7th District are unflinchingly conservative. Republican candidates in the general election receive two or three times

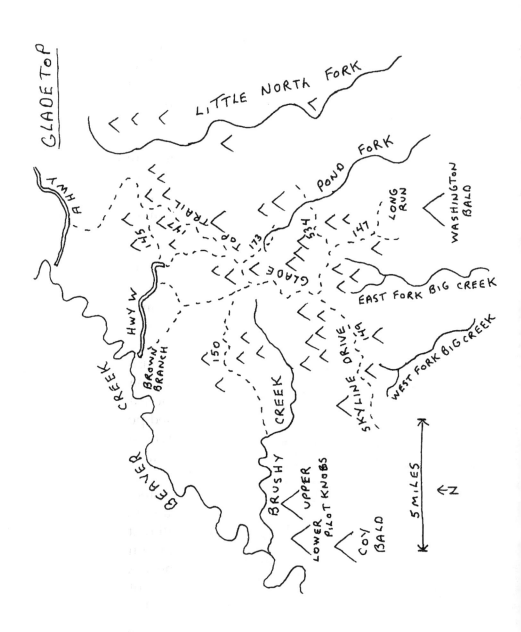

Gladetop

as many votes as Democrats. In the primary many Democrats and Independents take a Republican ballot to have a voice in choosing the next sheriff, clerk, or road judge.

Ironically, when the county was established in 1857, it was named for the most famous Democrat of the time, Stephen Douglas, the "Little Giant," the silver-tongued Senator from Illinois. Three years later, as the Democratic candidate for President, he carried Missouri. His opponent, Abe Lincoln, received few votes in rural Missouri; in Douglas County he garnered none. Lincoln's election brought a generation of war, instability, and crime.

During the war Douglas County was a battleground. Rebel units out of Arkansas raided Federal forts and wagon trains. Bands of bushwhackers, Jayhawkers, and deserters ambushed travelers and farmsteads; regular U.S. Army units pillaged as they marched. The local militia under Locke Alsup, headquartered at Vera Cruz, Co. H of the 46th Mo. Mounted Infantry, was the only law and order. How could Locke's thirty or forty part-time soldiers control 600 square miles of rugged terrain?

When the war ended, the surviving Booger County Rebels walked across the shattered South to worse devastation at home. The land they had so laboriously cleared and fenced had reverted to wilderness. Their livestock was gone; family members, missing. Most were penniless, their Confederate money just worthless paper.

Unionists blamed these former Rebels for the war. The new Republican Party, centered on the Alsups, controlled postwar Douglas County. Trouble started right away. Families whose men folk had joined the Rebels were brutalized. Vengeance was taken and answered by retribution.

The county was open range. Everyone's livestock, branded and earmarked, was scattered. It was easy to take a pig or calf in some lonely hollow. With high postwar prices, a small rustled herd could bring a family out of poverty. Allen Rankin's grandfather told him how a family from Illinois had homesteaded near Ann. One day a "bad bunch from Fox Creek" rode up. Ignoring the folks, they caught several chickens, built a fire, and ate a meal before they rode off with the family milk cow.

Sheriffs, judges, and prosecutors risked retaliation from relatives of someone they'd arrested. A few years after the Civil War, Pennsylvanian Dan Fogel, a tanner, farmer, Methodist preacher, and Union veteran, walked through south-central Missouri looking for land to homestead. In letters to his wife, Elizabeth, he described a ravished landscape nearly "entirely depopulated" where "everything that could be burned was destroyed." Every day he walked past charred chimneys overgrown with brush. There were "few men but many widows." "These lands," he wrote, "sell for near nothing—but it is considered very hazardous to buy and occupy them, as they mostly belonged to the men who went into the southern army and dare not return and there is a large band of them sworn together…who will and do kill every man who attempts to occupy their former homes."

In the summer of 1885 a holy man traveled out of Taney County into Booger County. He was six-foot-six and 300 pounds yet quick and athletic. He rode his blooded horse like a cavalryman and was a crack shot. A Bible was in his saddlebag and crossed pistols in his belt. His name was Nathaniel Kinney, chieftain and warrior priest of the Baldknobbers. God had sent him to purify Douglas County. Originally from Old Virginia, he had served as a private in the 6th West Virginia Infantry throughout the war. Afterwards he traveled west, making his living as a bare-knuckle prizefighter, gunman, and Pinkerton agent. He made a dubious fortune as a Springfield saloonkeeper.

He spent hours memorizing Scripture, which he quoted in conversations. He told people he had been a captain in the war and embellished his record. People called him "Captain" or "Cap." His sprained ankle became a war wound. He wooed and wedded Maggie Delong, a respectable widow, and bought a bottomland farm in Taney County. Their house was the showpiece of the neighborhood, with exquisite furniture and the county's first piano.

Like Douglas, Taney County had only one town, Forsyth, a port on the serpentine White River at the mouth of Swan Creek. During high water steamboats unloaded cargo into smaller boats or oxcarts. Throughout the Civil War Rebel forces periodically occupied the town, until the Federal Army burned it. Just after the war the newly rebuilt courthouse was set ablaze along with most of the documents.

Just down the road from Kinney's house stood the abandoned Oak Grove School. With his own hands Kinney renovated the building into his church. Before delivering a sermon he would dramatically pull the Colt revolvers from his belt, a snub-nosed piece he called "Short Tom," and a long-barreled piece he called "Long Tom," and ostentatiously place them on the pulpit. We are living in a time of moral laxity, he would say. Criminals, adulterers, and fornicators walk boldly among us, stealing our property and making a mockery of decency. Forty murders have been committed in the county with not one conviction. Gather by my side! We shall raise the cross and drive out the heathens! Afterwards, with his rich baritone he led the singing of hymns and invited the congregation to dinner.

Soon he was one of the most admired men in Taney County. Charismatically he gathered followers. Prosperous and influential families opened their doors and hearts to Maggie and the Captain. During these visits Kinney persuaded a group of prominent gentlemen to form a citizen's committee to institute law and order.

A clandestine meeting of thirteen was held in the back of a store. All were well-to-do and highly respected—lawyers, mill owners, businessmen, and large-scale farmers. Most had served with the Union Army. At least half of them were Freemasons. They agreed that the lawless rabble needed to be suppressed by whatever means necessary. Simultaneously, they wanted to elect county officials dedicated to strict law enforcement.

Their candidates, all Republicans and members of their committee, swept the next election. Soon one hundred carefully selected men secretly gathered atop Sharps Bald, a treeless knob near Kinney's home. Kinney showed up first and warmly greeted each arrival. He delivered a fiery speech. Crimes and moral transgressions have gone unpunished for too long! No longer can we sit back and let lawbreakers mock us! For the sake of our children's future, the time has come to act!

The cheering men joined hands and swore a solemn oath, under penalty of death, to never reveal the names and secrets of the organization. Like Jesus and the disciples, they were organized into "bands" of thirteen. Six bands under a captain became a "legion." Kinney, called "Chieftain," had overall command. They called themselves the Law and Order League of Concerned Citizens. All records were burned; henceforth, nothing was written down. Secret handshakes and passwords were created. Before they left the hilltop, Kinney exhorted them to recruit their neighbors to form a powerful voting block. The men imagined themselves as crusaders on a sacred quest for decency. The righteous sword of God was about to be unleashed across the Ozark hills and hollows.

A few nights later they rode en masse to the Taney county jail and broke down the door with sledgehammers. Kicking and screaming, the infamous Taylor brothers were dragged out of their cells, thrown on horses, and galloped off. Beneath an ancient black oak the posse stopped, threw two ropes over a limb, and lynched the brothers. A crude sign was pinned on one of the bodies:

> **BEWARE!**
> **THE WRATH OF OUTRAGED CITIZENS**
> **MORE WILL FOLLOW**
> *THE BALDKNOBBERS*

The lynchings were immensely popular; the Baldknobbers, heroes. At night bands would gather on bald knobs and then ride to the homes of their victims. Capitalizing on people's fears of Indian depredation, some of the Baldknobbers disguised themselves as Native American warriors. Others just used a flour sack for a mask.

Young men were prone to excesses. Life was dull and work monotonous on the Ozark frontier. As Baldknobbers the men found adventure. They galloped across the moonlit hills and imagined themselves as gallant knights protecting the innocent. Their courage was tested against other young men marked for expulsion.

Arriving in a clatter of hooves, they would fire a volley of shots and order their quarry out. He or she would be given a warning to either mend his ways or leave the county. Another volley of shots was fired as the Baldknobbers rode away, and a bundle of hickory switches was thrown at the person's feet. The number of switches was the number of nights until the Baldknobbers returned.

Fires burning on the knobs were a symbol of warning, though sometimes no warning was given. The victim was carried off and given a short military-style trial followed by flogging or lynching. Men simply disappeared, perhaps buried or weighted down and thrown into deep pools. Terrified families would hurriedly pack whatever belongings they could carry and move on. Often they abandoned crops and livestock.

Hog thieves, rustlers, squatters, and ex-Rebels were the usual targets. Kinney himself punished moral transgressors. Gamblers, debtors, philanderers, and the indolent he personally flogged. From the pulpit he repeatedly denounced common law marriages. At night by torchlight, surrounded by his men, he chastised those who married outside the church. He whipped men and women for flirtatiousness. Later, his lash was used increasingly on those who spoke out against the Baldknobbers. His whip fell especially hard on the flesh of

Baldknobbers who had lost their zeal.

With Taney County nearly cleansed Kinney rode into Douglas County to organize another legion. Joe Walker was elected Captain. (His kinsman, "Bull Creek" Dave Walker, originally from Douglas County, was Captain of the Christian County Baldknobbers. Dave eventually suffered a slow, agonizing death at a bungled public hanging in Ozark.) Soon bands of vigilantes operated in Booger County, often coercing newcomers off land they had settled under the Homestead Act. One night the Douglas County legion rode around the Ava Square, denouncing county officials for mishandling county funds.

A bizarre accident made former state representative, Achilles "Kel" Ellison, the best-known Booger County Baldknobber. Arriving early to a secret meeting atop Pilot Knob west of Ava, Ellison sat down to wait, setting the butt of his rifle on the ground with his fingers over the barrel and his chin on his fingers. Somehow he slipped, jarring the weapon. A bullet blew off three fingers, passed through his chin and tongue, and lodged above the roof of his mouth.

When the other members arrived, Kel was comatose. His only hope, they decided, was to carry him on a four-man litter to the doctor in Ozark. Kel was a big man. Ozark was forty miles away across rough terrain cut by numerous ridges and streams. The entire community was called out for the rescue. By horseback and wagon neighbors gathered for miles around. Teams of men traded off carrying the heavy litter while women served food to the tired men. Though near death Achilles slowly recovered and lived several more years.

Back in Taney County opposition to the Baldknobbers grew. Although the charismatic Kinney inspired devotion, many people instinctively hated him as a sanctimonious sham. Unscrupulous men had used the Baldknobbers' zealousness to drive out their neighbors. Farms and livestock could be bought for pennies on the dollar from terrified families. Others waited and bought land from the Baldknobber-controlled courts for back taxes.

With so many people leaving the county and so few willing to move into the violence-prone region, land values plummeted. Families saw their life's work dissolving. The community began to polarize. A group eventually known as the anti-Baldknobbers formed. Its nucleus was the old cabal that had controlled the courthouse before Kinney's candidates swept the election. Some families targeted by Baldknobbers turned their farmsteads into fortresses and grimly held on. They were joined by men who, though sworn members, had renounced the group and now lived in fear each night.

Douglas County's leading Democrat and anti-Baldknobber was Samson Haws. Originally from DeKalb County, Alabama, Haws moved with his parents to Dent County, Missouri, while still a boy. Inducted into the Union Army, he contracted typhoid fever, which caused him a lifetime of health problems. After the war he married a Dent County girl, Mary Wallis; they moved with his parents to a farm near Ava.

Born a gifted orator, Haws often presided at weddings and funerals in addition to preaching at the Antioch Church. Religious debates were then popular entertainment; Haws was Douglas County's favorite debater. Once he and the Reverend S.B. Davis of Vera Cruz debated "Christianity or Infidelity-Which?" at the Ava Baptist Church for three days. Folks referred to Samson as "Parson," "Pastor," or "Elder."

At that time Republicans had not yet become dominant; men from several parties held county offices. However, candidates were either "Alsup" or "anti-Alsup." In 1878 and again in 1882, Haws was elected county clerk. While in office, the power of the Alsups was broken as, one-by-one, they were gunned down.

Unfortunately, soon after his re-election, Mary died suddenly. Four months later, the thirty-nine-year-old widower with six children, ranging from eight months to fifteen years, married seventeen-year-old Allie Miller. The Millers were influential and well-to-do. Allie would bear him three children.

When the Baldknobbers organized in 1885, the outspoken Haws became their most vocal enemy. In October of that year, he was tried and found not guilty of "failure to make a report." Animosity between the political factions grew as federal agents intervened and arrested a handful of Baldknobbers. On the night of the arrest, someone entered the courthouse, splashed kerosene in Haws' office, and burned the building. Haws' enemies claimed he'd tried to destroy evidence of fraud. Others said the east-enders, still angry over moving the county seat, had done it. Many thought the Baldknobbers were responsible. Haws resigned.

One year after the fire Parson Haws' opponents indicted him for forging a $33.70 bill related to the grand jury investigation of Abraham McDaniel. Haws' assistant, Oliver Gentry, had prepared the bill. The signatures of Judge Woodside and Prosecuting Attorney John Payne were required before the bill could be sent to the state auditor and paid. Woodside claimed his signature was forged. Haws denied any knowledge of the forgery and said his enemies had made up the incident to discredit him. That night a posse of Baldknobbers rode into his yard, called him out, and told him to either confess or face the consequences.

On change of venue the trial moved to Ozark County. Haws was convicted and sentenced to two years imprisonment. After the Missouri Supreme Court denied his appeal, Haws was incarcerated at the state penitentiary at Jefferson City. While imprisoned Haws petitioned Governor Francis, presenting new evidence of his innocence. After a year Haws was pardoned.

Ironically, Elder Haws was elected to the Douglas County Democratic Central Committee one month after his conviction and remained a member during and after his incarceration. Later, he became an activist in the fledgling Union Labor Party.

Throughout his ordeal Elder Haws maligned the Baldknobbers as "dastardly cowards." They might lynch him or drive him out of the county but not without a fight! The Baldknobbers chose to ride at night because their deeds were evil, he proclaimed. "I am not going to quit short of death. Coercion is a poor law and proves nothing."

Elder Haws never let his problems interfere with his preaching. In 1897 he carried God's message into the Indian Territory, a hard fourteen-day journey by wagon. During an epidemic he spoke at twenty-five funerals in twenty-five days. Many times he returned to Booger County to preside at the funerals of prominent people.

When he died at seventy-one, Samuel Haws' assets were $31. He was interred in Wheeler County, Texas, near the home of his daughter Maude.

The Coggburns in Taney County were also anti-Baldknobbers and neighbors of the Kinneys. Robert Coggburn, a local wit, found Kinney's self-righteousness ripe for jokes and ridicule. He took a popular ditty and composed a mocking doggerel that he called the "Ballad of the Baldknobbers." Robert's teenage nephew, Andrew, had more courage than wisdom and publicly taunted the Baldknobbers, humorously parodying their secret handshakes and rituals. He and his friends referred to Kinney as "Old Blue Gobbler" and made gobbling noises at him. The flogging Andrew received only increased his hatred for Kinney.

Strangely, the Coggburns regularly attended services at the Oak Grove Church. Robert often made disparaging remarks during

Kinney's sermons. One night after prayer meeting, Kinney confronted Andrew and his friend Sam Sapp in the churchyard. Angry words were exchanged. A moment later Andrew lay dying with Kinney's bullet in his chest. At the inquest the Baldknobber-packed grand jury quickly exonerated Kinney on grounds of self-defense.

The murder brought public outrage. Churches split. Anti-Baldknobber congregations prayed that God would strike Kinney down with lightning. Kinney now traveled with bodyguards and delivered three-hour sermons. Barns were burnt, cattle killed, men shot as they plowed. The governor was petitioned to declare martial law.

Fearful that the Sapp boy would testify against him to state authorities, Kinney hired a fifty-year-old Union veteran/farmer/Baldknobber with eleven children, George Washington Middleton, to kill Sam Sapp. One Sunday afternoon on the front porch of the Kirbyville Store, in front of numerous witnesses, Middleton gunned Sam down and fled into Arkansas. The Sapp family raised $1000 and put it in escrow in a Springfield bank for the capture of Middleton, dead or alive.

Meanwhile, five young men, friends of the murdered boys, met secretly after dark. Over cups of moonshine they dealt out a grisly hand of poker. Billy Miles won the game and pledged to kill Kinney or die trying.

The Baldknobbers were now front-page news. Sensationalized and embellished tales of vigilantism sold newspapers coast to coast. Church groups in Europe considered sending missionaries to Missouri. Soon journalists would have much more to report.

Federal Judge Arnold Krekel, shocked by newspaper accounts of the Baldknobbers, quietly sent Federal agents into Douglas County to investigate infringements of the Homestead Act and other Federal law. Their report was laid on the desk of highborn Assistant U.S. Attorney General Maecenas Benton, nephew of former Senator Thomas Hart Benton. Briefly U.S. Marshals occupied Douglas County, arresting Baldknobbers suspected of intimidating homesteaders. Eight men were captured and taken to Jefferson City for trial.

Judge Krekel presided. "Colonel" Pony Boyd, the "loudest hollering lawyer in Missouri," represented the defense. Asking for mercy from the court, the defendants pled guilty with mitigating circumstances. Federal authorities, Boyd argued, were interfering in a local matter. The Homestead Act had no connection with criminal cases. Those accused, he claimed, were respectable citizens—preachers, businessmen, and prosperous farmers—trying to uphold the law. Benton presented the Federal case, describing the defendants as a scurrilous gang of outlaws who preyed on honest citizens. A traveling sewing machine salesman testified for the prosecution that after he refused to sell his property, the Baldknobbers dragged him, with a rope around his neck, and beat him with a bullwhip.

In his decision Judge Krekel said that the duty of the Federal government was to protect homesteaders. The Baldknobbers were an "evil disposed set of men" who undertook to determine who would and who would not be allowed to settle on public lands. They had interfered with Federal law in a criminal way. Krekel imposed maximum sentences, six months, to be served in various county jails where the government rented space.

Cleverly using the notoriety he received as the law-and-order prosecutor of Booger County vigilantes, Benton won four terms in Congress. In Washington his son Thomas began an education in art and eventually became a world-renowned painter and muralist.

Meanwhile in Taney County, a bizarre twist of fate would violently end the Baldknobber era. Jim Berry was a prominent Forsyth businessman. He owned the store, hotel, mail contract, and other enterprises. A leading anti-Baldknobber, he once had a Baldknobber hangman's noose around his neck. Business required Berry to travel out of town. Along the way he'd begun an amorous affair with a Kansas woman. Unfortunately, while he was in Kansas City on "business," Mrs. Berry discovered a love letter in his coat. Outraged, she took the letter to George Taylor, a Baldknobber lawyer and friend of Kinney's. They sued not only for divorce but also for most of Jim Berry's property. While working out the details of the lawsuit, Taylor and Mrs. Berry were smitten. He moved into the hotel with her.

A few days later when Berry returned, there was a wild scene on the public square as Taylor and Berry emptied their revolvers at one another. Both were arrested, Berry for felonious assault, Taylor for illegal cohabitation. After much legal maneuvering Berry, on very poor advice, declared bankruptcy. Quickly, the Baldknobber-controlled court put his property into receivership and named Kinney guardian.

The showdown came on a Saturday morning. Kinney was in the Berry store, inventorying merchandise for a public sale that afternoon. It was August, another hot, humid day. The doors and windows were wide open. Kinney's bodyguards, fearing for his life, wanted to stay, but he told them to take the day off. Witnesses remembered seeing him carefully clean, oil, and load Long Tom and set it on a shelf beside him.

Around nine A.M. Jim Berry walked across the square carrying a Winchester rifle and sat down on a bench. A few minutes later Billy Miles came into the store and confronted Kinney. Furious words were spoken. Both men reached for their pistols. Billy had a lucky shot. The heavy bullet from his Smith and Wesson .44 smashed into the forearm of Kinney's gun-hand, shattering the bone and sending Long Tom clattering across the floor. Screaming with pain and frustration, Kinney tried to duck behind the counter, but the next bullet tore through his ribcage. Billy stepped closer to the fallen chieftain and coolly pumped three more bullets into him. Meanwhile, Jim Berry leveled his Winchester at the few Baldknobbers who had gathered outside. Billy left the store, mounted his horse, and galloped out of town.

The funeral was the grandest held in Taney County. The slow, mournful procession stretched from the Forsyth Square to the Swan Creek Cemetery. Nat Kinney was laid to rest as a minister of the Gospel, war hero, upholder of the Union and Constitution, defender of justice, and backbone of the Republican Party. Children from the Oak Grove Church sang hymns as the grave was filled.

The trial of Billy Miles was national news. Venue was moved to Springfield. The anti-Baldknobbers raised $8,000 for Billy's bail. The Baldknobbers raised $1500 and hired gunslinger Ed Funk to kill Billy.

The day of reckoning came on the 4th of July. Billy and his girlfriend, Etta, drove into Kirbyville for the annual community picnic. They were dancing when Billy saw Funk ride up, accompanied by Baldknobber Sheriff Galba Branson. Billy slipped away to the spring where a group of men, including his brothers, were sampling Mason jars filled with moonshine. Boldly and foolishly Funk walked up to Billy and reached for his gun. Instantly bullets from the Miles brothers' pistols blasted into Funk and Branson. With a Baldknobber posse in hot pursuit, the Miles boys fled into Arkansas.

Back in Taney County the Baldknobber era ended. The Miles brothers turned themselves in. On grounds of self-defense Billy was declared innocent of killing Nat Kinney. George Taylor was State's Prosecutor in the Miles brothers' trial for the murders of Sheriff Branson and Ed Funk. A Greene County jury found them not guilty. Later, Jim

Miles would serve ten years for killing a clerk at Heflin's Grocery and Meat Market in an argument over money.

Jim Berry was tried in Springfield and acquitted for the felonious assault on George Taylor and as an accessory in the death of Nat Kinney. Mrs. Berry was severely beaten by her husband.

George Middleton, the killer of Sam Sapp, was tracked by Arkansas bounty hunter Jim Holt to a remote hollow near Jasper, Arkansas. At the Mount Parthenon 4th of July Picnic, before numerous witnesses, Holt boldly shot Middleton down. He escaped to Springfield to collect the reward that the Sapp family had posted.

Lawyer George Taylor led a Baldknobber posse that broke into the Taney County Jail. The men killed a deputy and hanged a wife-murderer, using the rope from the public well. Again the Baldknobbers were a national sensation, especially after the lynched body was partially eaten by open-ranging hogs. Taylor and thirteen others were indicted for murder, but after much legal wrangling, charges were dropped.

Legend says that the Douglas County Baldknobbers last met on Jess Bald south of Ava. They set a giant ring of wood ablaze and held their final meeting in a circle of flames. The Baldknobbers never rode again.

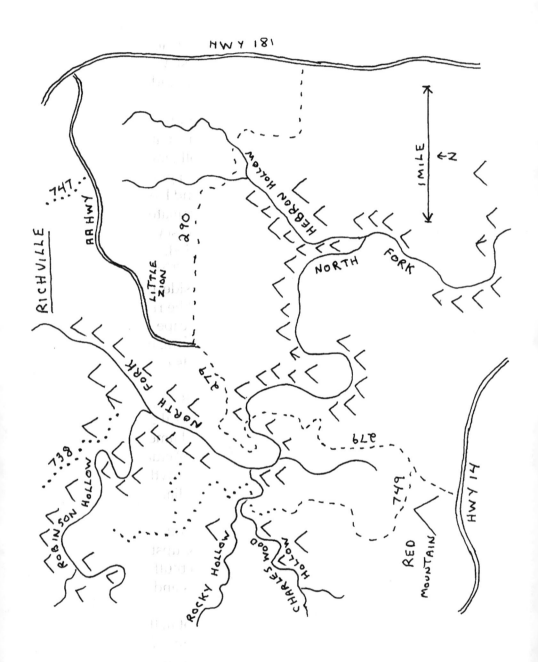

Richville

Old Richville

Exhausting uphills are ahead on today's ride into a secluded section of the Mark Twain National Forest. We'll cycle narrow trails, hop logs, duck limbs, and dodge boulders. Use caution and bring plenty of water.

Turn off Hwy 181 four-and-a-half miles north of Twin Bridges onto AA Hwy. AA passes through stunted forest and onto an open ridge top scattered with farmsteads. On a knoll among oaks are the Little Zion Church and Cemetery. Park facing a gravestone marked **OSBORN**. Beside it, next to the fence, lie Doc and Hester Osborn, the subjects of our next chapter. Nichols Knob dominates the horizon to the north. Bear Mountain is a low hump in the west while Saul's Knob rises in the southwest, the direction we're headed.

Bike down the pavement until it ends. CR 279 descends to the river and winds through steep, forested countryside. Look right across the canyon at the imposing slopes where we'll be riding. To the left several small, unnamed drainages cut the landscape. Nearby are dramatic bluffs and interesting caves. The oldest human artifacts found in Douglas County, which date back thousands of years, were discovered in seldom visited Huffman Cave.

A narrow metal bridge that we call "Steel Bridge" or "Old Steel Bridge" spans the North Fork above a wonderful swimming hole. When it was built in 1914 for $5900, skeptics claimed that it would never withstand heavy loads of railroad ties. Actually, foxtrotting horses were a greater threat to the span. The rhythm of their feet caused the bridge to modulate; the slap of the diagonal trusses produced an eerie sound.

The boat ramp, primitive campsites, and pit toilets are maintained by the Missouri Dept. of Conservation. Walk upstream along the fisherman's path to a deep pool at the base of a bluff. Further up, the North Fork surges over rapids where canoeists and kayakers laugh and shout over the waves.

Waterpower brought Miles Pease to this spot in the late winter of 1867. With his sons George and Myron and an African-American named Julius, he had walked the long, slow journey from Rolla beside the oxen and wagons. On St. Patrick's Day they made camp and staked out a claim. Miles had borrowed money to build a large-scale mill powered by the North Fork in the forest of virgin yellow pine.

A few days later, Julius and the boys began building a cabin while Miles trekked back to Rolla for supplies and to check on the rest of the family, a three-week roundtrip.

For twelve-year-old Myron this was high adventure. At dawn he would "hunt up" the steers, yoke them, and skid the logs that George and Julius had felled and limbed. Though their shack wasn't level, plumb, or square and the logs not tightly-fitted, they were proud of their work. They chinked mud into the cracks to keep out the wind and attached an awkward stack of sticks and clay for a chimney.

Miles was a wanderer from Vermont with a genius for machinery. After he married Susan Metcalf in New Hampshire, they moved to Rhode Island and later to Massachusetts; Miles worked as a mill supervisor. By train and steamboat the growing family then traveled to Minnesota, and Miles set up the state's first printing press at St. Paul. During the Civil War Miles owned a hotel in Rolla, where Myron shined the shoes of Federal officers. Occasionally, Myron visited his father's steam-powered wooden tub factory in Gasconade County.

After the years of roving, Miles was determined to stay in Douglas County. He brought a carpenter from Rolla, and work began on a large house. Myron was amazed at the tightly-fitted joints of the adzed logs and how perfectly the carpenter stacked rocks and clay for the five-foot-wide fireplace.

While Miles, George, and the carpenter worked on the house, Myron and Julius cleared a field for crops with a team of steers. Until they harvested corn, pumpkins, and potatoes in the autumn, everyone subsisted on rough corn grits made by rubbing hardened corn-on-the-cob across a grate and boiling it. Venison and turkey were a welcome addition to the monotonous diet. George hunted deer with his Colt revolver.

The following spring Miles brought Susan, his eldest son, Clarence, and the younger children—Clinton, Alando, Ida, Ella, and Minerva—to their new home. Work had begun on the mill, and everyone was expected to help out. Myron and Julius felled and skidded logs to the mill site where they were squared into timbers, mortised and tenoned, and pinned into bents. The bents were raised with ropes and poles, interlocked and knee-braced, to create an immensely strong timber frame. A dam was built across the North Fork to divert water down a race and over the water wheel, which drove a circular saw blade. Soon the mill cut three thousand board feet of lumber each day. The choicest boards were hauled to rebuild West Plains, the Howell County seat that was partially destroyed during the Civil War. Many times Myron walked the slow three-day roundtrip beside the straining oxen.

By the summer of 1869 Miles had the gristmill grinding corn and wheat. He installed a carding machine for wool, as well as, a gin for cotton. The mill ran day and night. Soon the Pease general store opened for business. Only then did Miles take time out to build a schoolhouse. He hired a young woman teacher for $23/month plus room and board. Most of the kids walked or rode to school for drilling in basic math and English. But the Pease's most numerous neighbors, the Collinses, wouldn't send their children. "I don't want children 'round me that knows more than I do," "Uncle" Pete Collins told Miles. Later, when Myron needed a tooth pulled, Miles sent him to Pete, who did dentistry on the side. The Collinses all wore store-bought "factories," long-tailed shirts or nightgowns. There was a "great parcel" of Collins children, Myron said, who at the sight of him ran into the woods and hid. Myron's formal education lasted only two years. George married the teacher, and Miles never hired another. Susan taught her children at home when there was time.

Pete's dad, old "Uncle" Saul Collins, was often a guest at the Pease home and entertained listeners with stories of the old days. He came by oxcart with the Collins clan from Carolina. There were no roads, and Native Americans still lived in Booger County. The Collinses traveled across the upland savannas and drove their oxcarts "right through" thickets. When the grain was gone, they lived on bear meat and honey. Pete went into the woods nearly every day to find and cut a bee tree and would bring back buckets of honeycomb. Each spring, Saul told Myron, the North Fork teemed with schools of migrating fish so thick "a man could not cross the shoals without stepping on them."

Since the Pease house was the largest, it became the neighborhood meeting place for religious services, dances, and *shivarees*, as well as, the polling station for this part of the county. After the Civil War everyone voted Republican, but in 1876 "old" Frank McCarty shockingly asked for a Democratic ballot. When Tommy Rice suggested thrashing Frank, Myron, then eighteen, angrily spoke up. Though he was too young to vote, he said, he'd read the Constitution and believed in democracy; anyone who wanted to whip Frank would have to whip him first!

Those were turbulent times. Bushwhackers and outlaws still lurked in the woods. Newcomers were suspect. The Yankee Peases had peculiar speech patterns and odd customs. An accident and a misunderstanding nearly caused their banishment. A local man disappeared while out hunting; search parties combed the forest. Simultaneously, two men from Mtn. Grove came to hire Miles to set up a carding machine. Miles' neighbors assumed the men were outlaws and appointed a committee to investigate. When Julius was asked if two "suspicious characters" had spent the night at the Pease house, he told them, "No." Since witnesses had seen the men, the committee concluded that Julius was lying. However, to Julius the two men were "gentlemens." The committee ordered the Peases to leave the county. Ed, a young Union veteran who worked for Miles, announced that the day the Peases were driven off was the day he died! Men readied their weapons. Luckily, just in time, the missing hunter was found dead from an accidental, self-inflicted gunshot.

The nearest post office, Vera Cruz, was twenty miles away. Miles wrote to the Post Office Dept. in Washington and established the Richville Post Office in a corner of the Pease house with George as postmaster. Once a week one of the boys made the long, rough ride to get the mail. Later, Miles initiated mail service from West Plains to Ava; twice a week his sons carried the mail on horseback.

Let's continue south on CR 279 toward Red Mountain. The bottomland fields on the left are private, but soon we'll enter Federal land on a long uphill. To the left the river makes an abrupt bend circled by a dramatic bluff above "Shavey Hole," a popular fishing spot. On the right is a clear-cut; watch for trails to explore.

Turn right onto FS 749 and wind over level terrain through mature oak-pine forest. Be careful when the road drops into Charles Wood Hollow! Weeds hide a furrowed surface gullied by 4x4s; pockets of deep gravel will skew your wheels. Visualize "spinning out" and crashing. Abrasions, lacerations, contusions, hematoma, road rash, and avulsions will become personal experiences. After you start uphill, look for brown boulders on the right. Stop and listen. Below, the North Fork churns through a series of boiling rapids. Though we've ridden miles, we're just a quarter-mile upstream from Pease's Mill.

Waterpower had drawn Miles Pease here, and his new mill attracted settlers. The village of Richville developed into "the greatest business place in southern Missouri." Big crops of tobacco, cane molasses, corn, and sweet potatoes grew in the newly cleared bottoms. Grain was hauled in from Wright, Texas, Howell, and Ozark counties, as well as, parts of Arkansas. Hundreds of thousands of board feet of lumber were cut and sold. During harvest fifteen or twenty wagons waited along the riverbank to be loaded.

People admired Miles. But just when he was established and successful, bad luck intervened. Like others he didn't realize Booger County's potential for flooding; the mill, dam, and crops were damaged several times by high water. Worse yet, Federal monetary policy kept money scarce. Customers were willing to barter but couldn't give Miles the cash he needed to pay his creditors. Prices for grain, cattle, and lumber, high in the post-Civil War period, fell. When Miles couldn't meet the interest on his debt, he frantically worked harder. He succumbed to a sudden illness and died; the mill shut down, and Richville shrunk into a ghost town.

Years later, near the turn of the century, Myron brought his family to old Richville for a picnic. Dense brush had overgrown the site. While the children waded in the river, Myron and his second wife, Eva, looked for the old home place. The house and barn had vanished. The mill was gone, as well as, the millpond. Only a small section of the dam, held by sycamores, remained. Two dilapidated buildings, now home to snakes and flying squirrels, were the last traces of Richville.

Myron's mother, Susan Metcalf, was born in New Hampshire in 1823. A devout Methodist, she insisted that Brother John, the circuit preacher, hold services once a month in the Pease home. To future generations she passed on Christian principles of faith, charity, compassion, industriousness, and Bible study. George became a fulltime Methodist minister. Myron, too, studied to spread God's word. To everyone's surprise he converted to Spiritualism, an ancient and complex set of beliefs with a worldwide following, and combined his Christian upbringing with the study of spirits, necromancy, dream interpretation, phases of the moon, and astrology. He believed that human will had the power to move inanimate objects, such as tables, and that people could communicate with the dead.

The Pease family stayed in Douglas and Howell counties and intermarried with other pioneer families. Clarence, Miles' and Susan's first born, married Liz Upshaw in 1868 and became a prosperous stockman on a farm near Blanche. Liz's father, Leroy, had been murdered from ambush near Rockbridge when she was a little girl. Her mother, Lydia Parsons, then married Bill Alsup, Locke's brother.

All the Pease boys became mill owners, sometimes in partnership with one another. Alando speculated unwisely in business and lived beyond his means. Myron had a mill in Pease Hollow south of Blue Buck and another near Dora. When the pines were gone, he moved his mill to Izard County, Arkansas, but kept his farm south of Saul's Knob near the Bethany Church. The fine, pervasive dust in his father's gristmill had caused Myron to develop white lung, a debilitating condition that weakened him for life. Nothing has been passed down about Clint or the girls.

In 1877 Myron married Winnie Johnson, a seventeen-year-old Cherokee. They had five children in nine years, but Claude and Clide died as boys. Cold Christmas floods of 1888 swept through the creek bottoms as Winnie went into labor for the sixth time. The twins born to her, Norma and Nora, came a day apart in a difficult delivery; Norma died on Christmas day and Nola the next. Winnie herself died not long after. At the time Eva Lina White worked as a hired girl for Myron and Winnie. She married Myron, and they had ten children. When their daughter Tula was ten, she contracted typhoid and seemed to recover, only to relapse while visiting her grandmother, and passed away. Morton, the eldest of Myron and Eva Lina, was a prosperous farmer and Eastern District Judge. Six of the nine other children became schoolteachers.

Miles' tragic bankruptcy and death profoundly influenced Myron; he criticized big government, over-regulation, and special interests. Outspoken and well read, he publicly debated important issues of his time, such as women suffrage, temperance, and the gold standard. Often he recounted how a government survey team had stayed at his father's home for several weeks. The best timber was set aside for agricultural college grants but later was bought below market value by well-connected lumber companies. Myron joined the Greenback/Populist party to champion common people, farmers, and small businesses. Twice he campaigned for state representative. During the election of 1892 he met Democrat Walter Jones of Willow Springs and Republican Ashbury Burkhead of Ava on the podium and denounced both major parties for voting against the best interests of their constituents. Later, Myron became a Socialist and spoke out, until his death in 1940, about the unequal distribution of wealth and power.

You'll need power to pedal up to the end of FS 749, which then winds as a faint, brush-choked trail into serpentine Robinson Hollow. Look for seldom-used FS 749A on the right and a well-worn ATV trail on the left. Be careful; respect private property.

On the way back to Little Zion you can take CR 290 east at the end of AA Hwy down into Hebron Hollow. There are several excellent springs; one is dammed up as a small lake.

After you load up the bikes, walk around the cemetery. Look closely at the graves of the Osborn family. Tomorrow we'll cycle to secluded Prairie Hollow and the ruins of Omba (pronounced locally like *zombie*).

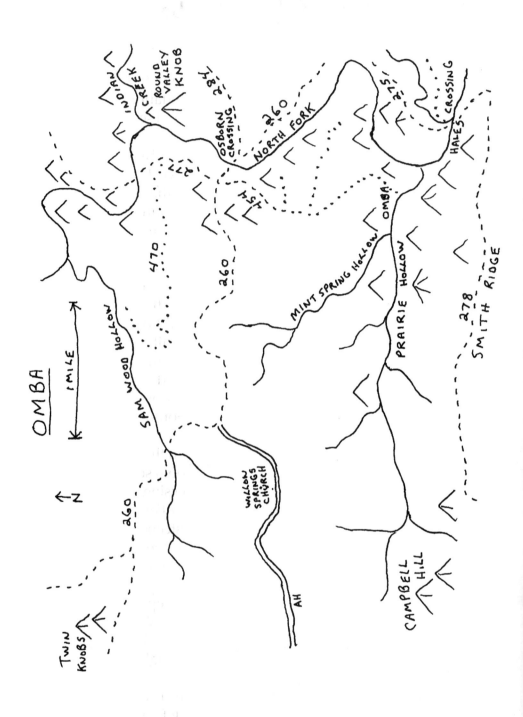

Omba

The Ruins of Omba

Deep in the forest, overgrown and virtually forgotten, are the ruins of Omba. All that remain are foundations. Today we'll take county roads, Forest Service roads, and seldom used trails to the once thriving site.

From Vanzant drive five miles south on W Hwy to CR 260. A small store stands at the junction. Looming above, topped by a lookout tower, is Twin Knobs. Park anywhere along the road. If the sky is clear, climb the tower. All of Eastern Booger County is spread out before you. Look for Blue Buck Mtn. topped with another lookout tower. Further south is Cedar Knob, the Yeomans, and Nichols Knob. Try to follow the looping course of the North Fork.

Ride past Twin Knobs on CR 260 through pasturelands. Pass several dairies; cross Sam Wood Hollow and turn left at the end of AH Hwy. The road drops steeply into an unnamed hollow that comes out at Round Valley. The Osage camped in the valley for months at a time and lived in conical thatched huts. Marmaduke's Confederate cavalry rested here after the raid on Springfield and the Battle of Hartville. They reported that Douglas County was "stripped bare" of provisions by Curtis' Federal Army of the Southwest, which had come through in the spring of 1862.

Forest road 454 is easy to miss. Look for it on the right just before CR 260 meets CR 277. The Round Valley one-room schoolhouse once stood at this junction. Before the Great Depression and Dust Bowl Drought many families resided on what is now Forest Service land. A quarter-mile down 454 is one of the roughest, steepest hills in Booger County. Only the strongest riders can pedal to the top. Stay on the main trail; pass two side paths, one to the left and one to the right. Watch out for rose thorns and deep, slippery mud puddles. Ride through dark stands of pine. Beyond the trees steep bluffs rise above the North Fork. After a mile 454 goes by a hunters' camp and starts downhill into Prairie Hollow. What is left of the road is badly eroded. Be careful. When the trail bends sharply to the right, stop and look around.

This is Omba. The ruins of a house and store are on the right, with a set of stone stairs leading up to them. On the left are the remains of the springhouse. Further on are the foundations of barns and other buildings. The trail forks. To the left is the North Fork. Straight ahead the trail goes up Prairie Hollow, enters private property, and eventually comes out on Smith Ridge. Geological features like Turnbull Cave, the Fiddle Spring Cave complex, and the knife-ridge above Punchout Hollow are nearby.

What was Omba? The story begins in Kansas in the years following the Civil War. A boy named Thomas Osborn, called Allen, his middle name, by friends and family, grew up on a farm. His family was friendly with Doctor Swank, the local physician. As a boy Thomas accompanied Doc Swank as he made his rounds and learned about illnesses and treatments. Thomas helped care for the sick. It was only natural that he took over Doc Swank's practice. How much, if any, formal medical education Doctor Osborn had is still debated.

A young schoolteacher from Ohio caught Thomas' attention. Vivacious and strong-willed, Hester Elliott shared Thomas' desire for adventure and his dissatisfaction with the windswept flat lands. They married.

Thomas had read about the vast forests of the Ozarks where streams flowed swift and clear among the hills. One night he told Hester about his dream of settling there. It wasn't hard for him to convince Hester that they should homestead in the Missouri hills.

Though they had four children and Hester was pregnant again, they sold Thomas' practice and many of their possessions. Hester and the younger children stayed with her parents while Doc, Will, and Bart, ten and seven respectively, packed up a covered wagon and began the long trek to the Ozarks. It was the spring of 1896; the roads were no more than trails. In Booger County Doc and the boys had to clear away brush for the team and heavily-loaded wagon.

Back in Kansas Doc had lived through droughts. He looked for land with plentiful water and found this six-hundred-acre farm where Prairie Hollow meets the North Fork. Hester, the two girls, Cora and Mabel, and the baby took the train to Missouri.

Reunited, the family moved into an old two-room shack. A few weeks later they awakened to find that the creek had risen and flooded the floor of the cabin. They bought lumber and further up the slope built a larger cabin with a small room in the front, which Hester made into a grocery and dry goods store.

The family began the arduous cultivation of a farm. They cleared trees with crosscut saws and by girdling them with axes. Some of the timber they used for a barn and for fence posts. They planted a garden for themselves and crops for the livestock, as well as, fruit trees. Doc bought a dependable sorrel saddle horse named Scotty and a collection of cattle, horses, pigs, mules, and some chickens for Hester. The mules were cantankerous. Doc joked that his neighbors could work his mules anytime they could catch them.

Their hill-folk neighbors tended to be clannish and suspicious of newcomers. The older folks remembered the long war with Kansas in the 1850's and 60's and the terrible depredations of the hated Jayhawkers. At first few people used Thomas as a physician, so he worked at a sawmill. Whenever someone needed him as a doctor, the boys would saddle up Scotty and fetch Doc at the mill.

Doc, Hester, and the children were warm, friendly people and gradually became accepted as part of the community. Hester's store business grew, and Doc became a full-time physician. There was little money in the area, so Doc took sacks of potatoes, honey, molasses, and eggs as payment; Hester then sold the goods at the store.

After the birth of their eighth child, Hester and Doc decided to build a larger home further up the hillside. The family gathered wagonloads of rocks and erected this five-foot retaining wall. With the team the boys plowed and drug dirt from further up the slope. They filled in behind the rocks to create a level building site. The two-story house was 16'x45' with three rooms and two porches downstairs and three bedrooms upstairs, plus a sun porch for drying fruit. They dug into the hillside behind the house and constructed a root cellar where Hester stored canned food, potatoes, apples, and vegetables. On the left, as you look up the stairs, they built a 14'x30' store building that allowed Hester to greatly expand the items for sale.

One corner of the store became the local post office with Hester as postmistress. Three times a week the mail carrier, John Freeman, journeyed from Vanzant on horseback to deliver the mail to Hester. The new post office needed a name. After much thought Hester chose *Omba*, from the first names of her children, Oakley, Mabel, Bart and Annis. She painted a big white sign with black letters, **Omba Post Office,** which Bart hung above the store.

People who came to Omba would come up the stone stairs and either turn left, into the store and post office, or right, down a boardwalk to the Osborn's front door where Thomas saw patients in the parlor. The house wasn't fancy, but Hester was a tireless decorator. She brightened the rooms with hand-crocheted furniture covers, hand-loomed carpets, lace doilies, and ruffled curtains that matched the wallpaper she'd installed. Prominently displayed high on the wall was the wreath of hand-woven flowers and tendrils she'd made from hair clippings of her family and faraway relatives. The organ was adorned with lace, and Hester played hymns to entertain family and friends. Outside there were beds of flowers. Visitors remember the fragrance of the big honeysuckle that grew over the porch and the clucking of hens from Hester's chicken coop. Further to the right was the springhouse that Bart built. Hester kept milk and butter in a box cooled by the cold water.

By 1906 the Osborns were established. Livestock dotted the pastures; the fruit trees and crops were bountiful, and the store thrived. The post office became so busy the boys put up mailboxes along the road.

However, that spring was unusually warm and dry. By late May everyone worried about the crops. Young corn plants wilted in the afternoon sun. Garden vegetables withered, and many springs slowed to a trickle.

Late on a muggy night there was a frantic pounding on the door. A young farmer had been sent by the midwives to fetch Doc. His wife was having a difficult labor: twins in a tangled breech birth. The boys saddled up Scotty while Doc hurriedly gathered his gear. When he arrived, the woman's condition was worse. Doc worked by dim lamplight. His shirt was soaked with sweat when he finally delivered the babies at dawn. Because the family was poor, Doc told the father to forget about the fee and use the money to feed his children.

By the time he got home, the thermometer neared 100°F. Cattle clustered under the trees along the hollow. Hardly a breeze stirred as Doc unsaddled Scotty in the shade near the house and then lay down for a well-deserved nap.

As usual the household was bustling. Hester moved back and forth from the store to the post office. The two youngest boys were plowing a new garden patch uphill from the kitchen while the older children were clearing out stalls in the big barn. Mr. Simpson, a livestock dealer, had promised to bid on some extra horses and mules Doc wanted to sell. The girls were doing the wash in the stifling house.

About 9:30 that morning the mail carrier drove up in his new car, one of the first in the county. (The rough roads kept him busy fixing flats.) He told Hester that one of the cows might be having trouble calving up the hollow. Hester yelled to Will to check the cow. Will returned an hour later. The cow and calf were fine, and all the cattle were bedded down contentedly along the branch.

By four o'clock that afternoon the heat was intense; the sky, cloudless. Hester was locking up the store when she heard a rumble. Glancing up, she saw dark clouds suddenly rolling in from the northwest. The next crash was deafening. She grabbed the big dinner bell and rang it furiously. The younger boys galloped in on the plow horses; the harnesses flapped and clanged against the horses' sides. The rest of the children came running. Doc woke up to an ominous black sky. Lightning struck a tree near the cattle. They stampeded up the hollow, their eyes wild; the wobbly-legged new calf vainly tried to keep up with its mother.

For a moment everything was still. Then a series of lightning strikes volleyed from the brooding clouds. Rain came with a roar. They say it was the worst flash flood Booger County had ever seen. In minutes Prairie Hollow was a foot deep in water. The deluge swept down the hillsides, rolling large stones. A six-foot wall of muddy water surged through the hollow. Logs twisted in the flood. The crest was alive with struggling cattle, pigs, horses, and mules. The barn was obliterated. Everything was swept downhill and into the North Fork. The screams of the drowning animals could be heard between booms of thunder.

Within an hour the worst of the flood had passed. Doc calmed the terrified Scotty. The new mother cow, minus her calf, had somehow survived along with two other cows. Tenaciously, a mule had held onto a rafter with her teeth and wasn't swept away. Afterward, many people came to see the deep teeth marks in the wood. All of the families had lost cattle and crops. Some lost everything they owned. The boys took the team and joined others in the grim task of dragging the dead animals back into the woods. Miraculously, no one was killed.

The Osborns surveyed their farm. The corn was gone, washed out by the roots. The cane (molasses) was destroyed. A foot of sand and gravel had buried the vegetable patch. Luckily, the sweet corn, tomatoes, green beans, and other vegetables planted above the kitchen were flattened but still alive. Later, Hester and the girls would fill dozens of Mason jars from the harvest. The older children roped the new mother cow and broke her to milk. Despite kicking and overturned buckets, she eventually turned into a good family milk cow.

A few months later an even greater tragedy befell the Osborns. Their eldest daughter, Ethel Marie, a young mother of two, died suddenly. Mabel became the temporary mother of the toddlers, and later their paternal grandparents, the Cobles, raised them.

Fortunately for everyone, the winter of '06/'07 was mild. Spring came early, and the summer yielded a bumper crop. But Thomas struggled. A flu epidemic struck that winter; for many the flu turned into pneumonia. There were more people sick than Thomas had time to treat. He and Scotty traveled the roads, checking the gravely ill and trying to save as many as possible. He slept little. Back on the farm, the barns needed to be rebuilt and new fences erected to keep livestock out of the crops. There was harvesting to be done and firewood to cut. Doc became pale and thin; his hair receded and grayed. Though still his cheerful self, he now wore a tired expression.

The Osborns were part of the Willow Springs community and attended services and Sunday school there. The church was also the local schoolhouse. They were a fun-loving family, always off to singings, pie suppers, "play parties," and picnics. In season there were pea-hullings and apple-peelings where the young men and women would throw hulls and peels at one another. The biggest event of the year was the two-day Osborn Picnic in early August alongside the North Fork below the house. The day before the picnic the sound of hammers and saws would ring through the hillsides as the men folk put up family stands and hauled in ice packed in sawdust. One stand sold lunches, another homemade ice cream; others sold soda pop, pies, and balloon whirlers. There was a swimming hole with a big rope swing and all kinds of races and contests. Politicians gave speeches.

When they became big enough, the boys took jobs at local sawmills, saving their money for saddle horses. Later, they went out on the high plains and worked the wheat harvest. Eventually, all the boys married local girls and built cabins on the home place. Doc jokingly referred to the three tiny cabins as "weaning houses."

Hester was stricter with the girls, especially after Ethel's death; they had to stay at home until they married. Occasionally, they were allowed to "hire out" at a home where there was illness or a new baby. The work was long and hard and the wages meager. The money would be spent on shoes or special clothes.

Will is remembered as a workaholic, always busy at something, often far into the night. He became a storeowner and merchant.

Bart was proud, good-looking, and gifted at business and organization. He became a master carpenter and owned the adjoining farm.

Mabel was called a "tomboy" because she liked to work outdoors with her brothers. She was a skilled equestrian and handy with livestock. She married into the well-to-do Pierce family.

Annis was Hester's "homebody," content to stay indoors, cleaning and cooking.

Oakley played the fiddle in the local bluegrass style and ran a sawmill.

Dale was gregarious, always joking and laughing, the "life of the party."

Richie, the baby of the family, was a hunter, fisherman, and trapper. He prowled the deep holes of the North Fork with a cane pole and a can of worms and seldom returned without a string of "good ones" for supper.

Doc delivered most of his grandchildren. On Sunday afternoons the house was overrun with youngsters playing on the front steps, investigating the hen house, wading in the river. Doc sat in his old wicker rocker, joking and teasing them. Occasionally he opened the store and passed out stick candy and chewing gum.

In the newspapers there were rumblings of war in Europe. In 1917 the U.S. became involved, and the young men of Eastern Booger County left for faraway battlefields. Sad letters arrived at the Omba post office of sons killed, wounded, or missing.

Conditions at the front were appalling. Soldiers lived in muddy trenches. Constant shelling made sanitation impossible. Stark terror and unwholesome food weakened the men. In the final weeks of the war disease spread among the armies. Virulent and extremely contagious, the 1918 flu brought high fever, congested lungs, and death. A sick soldier got off the train at the nearby small town of Norwood. Within days the epidemic spread across Booger County.

Doctor Osborn rode through the hills trying to save lives. He was seldom home. Entire families died near Omba. Often everyone became sick at once, and there was no one to milk, feed livestock, or keep the fire going. Fear gripped the community; families refused to help neighbors. They kept themselves isolated. Later, many of those raised to believe that charity was a Christian imperative were wracked with guilt and depression. There was little Thomas could do other than make his patients' last few hours comfortable. When a patient succumbed, Doc had a low, plaintive song he hummed as he rode. Hearing the tune, people would know that someone had died. The epidemic wore him down. His hands became unsteady; his eyes, lusterless. At times he drank heavily. He increasingly depended on midwives Harriet Brisco, Kate Altermatt, and Ella Hopkins.

But there were troubles with the neighbors, too. Often, Doc took Mason jars filled with moonshine as payment. When he was "in his cups," Doc could be contrary and disputatious. After the war he convinced himself that the army was going to need to replace all the horses and mules sent to Europe. He bought livestock, sure that prices would rise dramatically. The Army, of course, like the rest of the nation, was mechanizing. Draft animals were no longer in demand. Doc found himself with a small herd of nearly worthless stock and turned them loose.

Booger County was open range until the late 1920's. The mules became a nuisance in the neighborhood. Virtually starving, they knocked over or jumped fences into crops and gardens. Many times Doc was at the center of a storm of indignation over his "damned mules." Eventually, they were rounded up and sold at a loss.

Drought came. Cisterns and springs families depended upon grew sluggish, brown, and full of bugs. Contaminated water caused an outbreak of typhoid fever. There was no way to combat the fever, delirium, and uncontrollable sweats. When a patient went into a "cold sweat," Doc knew that the blood pressure was dangerously low. Typhoid took a heavy toll on the young. Eva Wood, a neighbor of mine, recalls that her parents called in Doc Osborn when she and her brother caught typhoid. He gave her mother little paper sacks with doses of goldenseal and quinine. The taste was revolting.

In 1926 Hester's health failed. She needed help with her chores. Arthritis set in, causing painful sleepless nights. The veins in her legs distended, and slow-healing sores broke out. Bart laid an underground pipe from the spring and installed a hand pump in the kitchen so that Hester wouldn't have to haul water. Eventually, she forgot the names of her children. She cried for hours and hallucinated that lizards and snakes were crawling across the bed. Annis and her husband, Clyde, moved back home and cared for Hester until her death at age sixty-eight. She was laid to rest at the Little Zion Cemetery near Hebron.

Afterward, someone gave Doc a jet-black pup with bright eyes. Doc named him Coalie. They were constant companions. Old Scotty had been put out to pasture; Doc now rode a gray mule named Jack. Coalie trotted alongside. Doc bought a used Cadillac that he took great pride in, but he never learned to drive. Occasionally, a neighbor or grandchild would chauffeur him in it.

Thomas was nearly deaf. He didn't have much stamina these days and took the front stairs one deliberate step at a time. The neighbors, remembering his kindnesses, brought him food and had him over for supper. They saw that there was firewood at the house. Hester's friend Epsie Ball, a divorcee, would sometimes spend an afternoon at Doc's to clean and cook a warm meal for him. One day, to her surprise, Doc proposed marriage. Epsie blushed like a schoolgirl. Yes, she said, though she had reservations about his drinking.

Another era began in Doc's life. Epsie kept the house immaculate and always had home-cooked meals on the stove. The children and grandchildren loved her.

At Christmas 1938 nearly all of the family came back home. Obviously, Thomas was too feeble to live at Omba anymore. They moved him and Epsie into a house in Willow Springs. Just before his death in the spring of 1947, there was one last big family reunion. Doc was eighty-four. He was buried at Little Zion alongside Hester.

The children couldn't agree among themselves about the land and sold it to the Federal government. Now it's part of the Mark Twain National Forest and has grown back much as it looked when the Osborns arrived in 1896.

From Omba you can ride back to Twin Knobs, call it a day, or continue. Forest road 470 into Sam Wood Hollow, seldom used by anyone, is a possibility. Or ride across Osborn Crossing up CR 284 and take one of the trails to the left into the Hell Hole region. There are many trails to explore, and several lead past deserted homesteads.

In the next chapter we'll traverse lower Fox Creek, the ruins of Tetrick, and beautiful New Hope Cemetery. I'll tell you about the Great Depression/Dust Bowl Drought, a family named Giles, and another named Cooley. Ever heard of a "pulling guard?" What's the difference between a KO and a TKO?

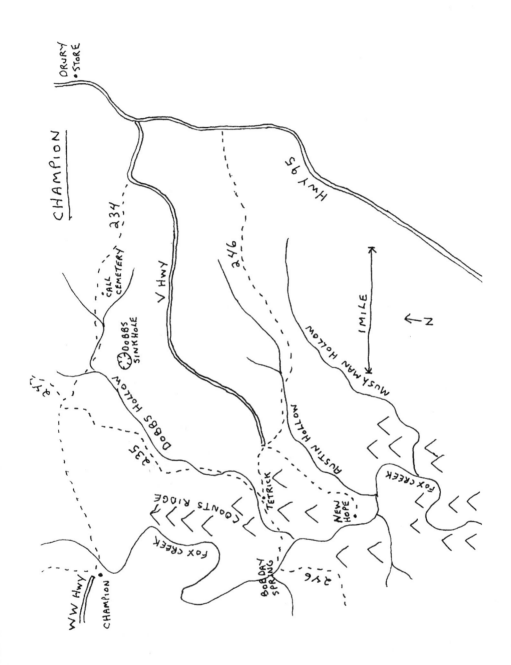

Champion

Champion

Dobbs and Austin Hollows are our destination today. Numerous hills will test your fitness. Wear bright colors; motorists don't expect to see cyclists. Do you have a spare tube and a reliable pump?

Drive south on C Hwy three miles from Hwy 76 and turn east on WW Hwy. Cross a rolling upland of scattered farms and woods and gradually descend to Fox Creek. The pavement ends at Champion. Find an out-of-the-way place to park.

On the right is tiny, anachronistic Henson's Store. Built in 1928, the store was purchased by Ed and Anna Henson in 1940 when their son Duane was two years old. The Hensons bought live chickens and rabbits, cream, and eggs from local farmers and used a gasoline-powered mill to grind grain. Ed always made room for passengers on his Monday, Wednesday, and Friday trips to Mountain Grove for supplies. Take a look at the Champion one-room schoolhouse beyond the store. Years ago dozens of children played in this yard.

Much of old Champion was washed away by the June 1942 flood. Imagine floodwaters up to the porch of the store! Duane saw his home unearthed from its foundation and dragged away with many of his family's possessions. By Christmas Jay Austin finished building the new Henson house you see on the hillside above the store.

Pedal east across the slab over Fox Creek. Try to visualize the force of the September 1993 flood that created the "dunes" of gravel in the streambed. Back at the store Duane has photos of the torrent. CR 234 winds up a narrow canyon and emerges onto the Coonts Ridge fields. Turn right on narrow CR 235 and descend through stunted blackjack, hickory, and post oak into pastoral Dobbs Hollow.

In the decades following the Civil War people homesteaded wherever there was water and decent soil. They felled trees for cabins and barns and rocked up springs. Split-rail fences kept livestock out of the crops. There was hay to cut, firewood to saw, split, and haul, plowing, hoeing, brush cutting, harvesting, and storing. Large families lived in cramped houses with little privacy. Money was scarce; wages, low. Surprisingly, most people who grew up in the hardscrabble times look back fondly on those years. We laughed a lot, they say. Neighbors gladly helped one another.

Through the 1880's, '90's, and the early years of the 1900's settlers moved into Booger County. Some filed for land under the Homestead Act. Others bought existing farms. They built mills, stores, churches, and schools. As you ride look for abandoned home sites. Sometimes there are foundation stones and a scattering of broken Mason jars, medicine bottles, and rusty metal. In a few places weathered little houses remain. Look for introduced plants such as honeysuckle, daylily, daffodil, iris, vinca, raspberry, and agave that live on long after the houses collapsed.

Where Dobbs Hollow narrows at the intersection of CR 246 and CR 235, there is a crumbling but well-built, two-story house on the right and a sagging barn on the left. Look at the dramatic rock ledges behind the house. This is Tetrick.

Mary "Liz" Riley, the mistress of Tetrick, was born in 1868 near Buckhart. People remember her for her striking Native American features, inherited from her Cherokee grandmother. Liz and her husband, Bill Dobbs, were drawn to Tetrick by the beautiful spring at the base of the cliff. They homesteaded here after their marriage in 1886 and began building to "prove" on their land claim.

Bill died suddenly in 1889 and left Liz with two infants, Josiah, or Joe, and Sylvia. Meanwhile, Billy Giles (b. 1862 Bristol, England) immigrated to Boston, where he found work in a hospital. Someone from Douglas County convinced him to move to the Ozarks and take up land, so Billy filed for 160 acres near Yates Cemetery along the ridge road. When he married Liz, he gave up his ridge top claim and moved here.

Theirs was an unusual marriage. Billy was short and bandy-legged; neighbors jokingly referred to him as "Hames Legs" (from the curved portion of a harness collar). Billy wasn't interested in farming and the out-of-doors. He'd had an excellent education and had studied Missouri law. In this house he worked as a paralegal, justice of the peace, and postmaster. He performed marriages, wrote wills, and handled land transactions. People remember "Uncle Billy" as kind and scrupulously honest. He served on the grand jury and set up his own library where neighbors could borrow books. Billy also oversaw his children's early education. He sent them to the Champion and Bakersfield grade schools and later to board with families in Ava to attend high school. All six of his children became teachers.

Liz ("Aunt Lizzie"), on the other hand, was a farmer and stockman. She raised wheat, corn, cattle, horses, sheep, and goats and worked the land with a team of horses and a hired hand. Below the barn Liz raised a big vegetable garden. When Joe and Sylvia and six of her seven children by Billy—Ralph, Florence, Bill, Harry, Ada, and Frank—were big enough, they joined Liz in the fields. Later, Ralph and Frank went into partnership with their mother. They used profits to buy adjoining parcels of land and divided everything into thirds.

Tragedy visited the Giles' home. The summer he turned sixteen, Joe went to Oklahoma to work the wheat harvest. He contracted pneumonia and died. Harry, also, died of pneumonia, at thirteen. At twenty Sylvia was the mother of four daughters. While brushing her little girl's hair one day beside the wood cook stove, Sylvia's dress caught fire. She could neither smother the flames nor tear off her dress. In her panic she raced through the house, slapping at the blaze, and caught part of the house on fire. She ran outside. Wind fed the flames; all her clothing, her skin, her hair, burned. Sylvia lived twelve more hours and died in the company of her family. Fannie, Frank's twin, lived six months.

Billy died in 1931 just as the drought years began. By 1934 springs had long been dry; fields, fallow. Liz, Ralph, Frank, their wives and children, plus another family drove west in the Giles' International farm truck to join Bill and Florence, who were living in Bakersfield, California. The journey was cramped and interminable. They rigged a canvas canopy "covered wagon" style over the bed and camped beside the road. Fortunately, Frank and Ralph found good jobs at sawmills in the Sierras. The Giles clan survived the worst depression years with few hardships.

In 1938 they returned to Tetrick and began to farm again. They concentrated on dairy and hog farming. Cream, they sold in ten-gallon cans; milk, they fed to the pigs.

When Liz died in 1945, the place was divided between Ralph and Frank. Frank was badly injured when he fell while attaching a hay rake and was run over by his tractor; he recovered, and in '48 and again in '52 he was elected Eastern District Judge.

The wet winter of '49 made Fox Creek impassable. Frank's boy Billy needed to cross the creek to catch the bus to Ava High. Ralph and Frank decided to drop a sycamore as a temporary bridge. With a two-man crosscut saw, they notched and back cut the big tree. Suddenly, though, the log kicked back from the stump, struck Ralph in the chest, and shattered his ribs. He died instantly.

Let's ride further down Dobbs Hollow. Notice the beautiful rock outcrops on the right. The Frank Giles place is on the left. The annual community 4th of July Picnic was held here. On Sunday mornings neighbors would gather to ride in the Giles' farm truck to Sunday school and services at the Bakersfield School. As the road bends to the right, look downstream for sunlight glittering off water. For miles Fox Creek has been a dry losing stream, but now it has abundant water.

Cross Fox Creek on a slab. This is a popular swimming hole. At the second slab stop and look to the right. Notice the beautiful arched barn built into the bottom of the hillside. In front of it is the Bob Day Spring complex, the source of this water. Other water flows down Coonts Hollow from the Seven Springs. Watch for beaver, otter, herons, and kingfishers.

Turn around. At Tetrick turn right, up the hill. The Ralph Giles place is on the right across from his mother's house. They used the same spring for household water. At the end of V Hwy follow the signs to New Hope Cemetery and the Saddle Rock Ranch. We're riding into lovely Austin Hollow. The road passes through majestic trees and imposing limestone formations and opens up into a lush, little valley. You can see the buildings of the Saddle Rock Ranch on the left; this was originally the Bill and Effie Giles Place. A carpenter, Bill built the barn at Tetrick when he was only seventeen. He was eighteen when he bought eighty acres here.

In 1925 Bill and Effie moved to Bakersfield, California, where Bill became a contractor and Effie, an ordained Assemblies of God minister with a church in Pismo Beach. The house you can see through the trees is the one they built when they returned in 1945; though, it now has an addition on each end. Water for the house was raised from a shallow well, by hand, with a tubular bucket attached to a rope and wheel. Bill worked the farm and built custom homes. He and Effie milked Jersey cows by hand, cut hay, and bred Hereford cattle.

Further on, around the end of the ridge, is New Hope Cemetery, established before the Civil War. The lush riparian woods and timbered slopes are soothing and serene; I think New Hope is the most beautiful place in Douglas County. Walk through the gate past the chapel. The Gileses are buried here. Beyond Billy and Liz's graves, near the back fence, is the flat marble monument of Lydia Hicks "Granny" Sweeton of Drury, the beloved midwife who delivered many of the people interred here. Try to find Ed and Anna Henson. Look for the Cooley family's markers, especially those of Fred, Elsie,

Lee, and Maggie. Notice the woven-wire fence around the cemetery. During the Depression years the cemetery was neglected; afterwards, wethers were used to browse off the broad-leafed plants.

Ride back to the end of V Hwy and take CR 246 into upper Austin Hollow. At one time this area was dotted with small farms. The population peaked around 1920. Few realized it, but people and livestock had degraded the land. Much of the wildlife disappeared, first the bison, cougar, elk, bears, wolves, and prairie chickens; later, deer and turkey became extinct. The marketable timber was cut and hauled away. The stands of virgin pine vanished. Houses, barns, sheds, smokehouses, and fences were built with wood. Meals were prepared on wood cook stoves that every day needed a stack of finely split faggots. All winter fires blazed in parlor stoves to warm the drafty houses.

The early settlers wrote of native grass as high as a horse's belly. For generations Douglas County was open range. Livestock, branded and ear marked, roamed freely, and bands of semi-wild "razorback" hogs eked out a precarious existence foraging for roots, acorns, and small creatures. As the native sod began to disappear, people set fire to the cutover woods to encourage more grass. Invasive plants rooted down in the overgrazed fields: sassafras, persimmon, blackberry, poison ivy, and rose. People chopped at them with axes and hoes, but they sprouted back and threatened to turn pastures into thickets. Cedar was the worst. Unpalatable to livestock, the seed was scattered by the millions in bird droppings. In a few years productive land, so laboriously cleared, became choked with cedar copses.

Though the soil in Booger County is thin, stony, and acidic, the settlers grew corn, a demanding crop best suited for deep rich soil. Runoff from pounding rains, held back for centuries by forest litter and native sod, now poured off the barren slopes and filled the creek beds with gravel. The land absorbed less water and caused formerly dependable springs and streams to slowly dry up.

Weather is volatile in the Ozarks. Warm moist air from the Gulf of Mexico collides with cool dry air from Canada and produces violent storms. Sometimes the dark cloud masses spawn tornadoes that leave swaths of devastation. Temperatures can approach -30°F in winter and 110°F or higher in summer. November 11, 1911, began balmy. By early afternoon a record high of 80°F was reached just before a powerful cold front pushed in. The thermometer dropped thirty degrees in two hours. Gusting winds broke windows and tore shingles off roofs. Before midnight a record low of 13°F was recorded amid hail, sleet, and snow. On the 18th of March 1925, a colossal storm was born in the sky above Booger County. Three-hundred-mph winds obliterated farms and towns. Foundations were sucked up and blown away. A half-mile wide, the monster storm raged across Missouri, jumped the Mississippi, and cut a path of destruction across Illinois before it lifted back into the clouds over Indiana. Seven hundred people died; fifteen thousand homes were destroyed.

There are unseasonable frosts and freezes. Though heavy snowfall is unusual, ice storms are not. Tree limbs break; the ground glazes over and is impossible to walk upon without crampons. Cattle fall and can't get up or slide into ponds and freeze.

Summers are sultry. The Ozarks hosts chiggers, ticks, biting flies, scorpions, wasps, hornets, and mosquitoes. Yet insect pests were few when the early settlers arrived. The newly broken ground had natural fertility built up over millennia. Crops and orchards thrived. Potatoes were an important subsistence crop; most old home sites have some sort of root cellar for storing them. Native to the South American highlands, they were brought to Europe by the Spanish and then taken on ships to Colonial America. Frontier families carried them west in their oxcarts.

When potatoes were planted in Colorado in the 1850's, a strange thing happened. A local beetle, *Leptinotarsa Decemlineta*, adapted to feed on potato foliage. By 1865 the pest, later known as the Colorado Potato Beetle, was ravaging potato crops in Missouri and by 1874 had moved as far east as New Jersey. The bright orange adults overwinter in the soil. In the spring as the potato plants emerge, the females lay masses of yellow eggs on the undersides of the leaves. The larvae, soft and bulbous, grow astonishingly fast. They suck the life from the plants and soon pupate into egg laying adults. Pioneer families hand picked them by the bucketsful and drowned them. Eventually, *Lydella Doryporae*, the Tachid Fly, adapted to parasitize them. The female fly lays a single egg on a potato beetle larva; it hatches into a maggot, burrows into the larva, and devours it.

But the potato beetle wasn't the only pest to spread into Booger County from the west. An ordinary grasshopper, *Melanopus Spretus*, the Rocky Mountain Locust, is native to the high grasslands of Colorado and Wyoming. Birds, animals, predatory insects, fungal disease, and its own cannibalistic appetite check the population. However, when conditions are right, the locusts reproduce prodigiously, and millions of them can take flight in dense clouds. Swarms were blown into Douglas County and all over Missouri in the 1870's. Ravenous, they stripped the land bare. Trees stood like skeletons; the earth lay naked without even a vestige of green. Governor Charles Hardin proclaimed June 3, 1875, a day of prayer, worship, and fasting to seek Divine intervention against the grasshoppers. State Entomologist Professor C.V. Riley suggested eating them. A bounty of $1/bushel for adults and $5/bushel for eggs was established by the state legislature.

Strangely, the most pernicious pest in Booger County, *Epicauto Vitlata*, the Striped Blister Beetle or old-fashioned potato bug, is a major predator of grasshoppers. The females lay eggs near the burrows that grasshoppers have laid their eggs in. Beetle nymphs emerge with long legs, large heads, and strong jaws and feed on grasshopper eggs. After eating the beetles pupate and metamorphose several more times. The benevolent traits of the nymphs, however, are overshadowed by the devastations of the adults. Blister beetles defoliate tomatoes, potatoes, beans, and beets. Their highly toxic body fluids blister the skin, and a few of them baled in hay will kill a horse. In Booger County families would "drive" them with branches into windrows of straw and burn them.

In 1860 *Pontia Rapae*, the Imported Cabbage Worm, was first noticed in Quebec. By 1880 it had spread throughout Missouri. In adult form it is a familiar while butterfly. The Plum Curculio and the Coddling Moth ruined thriving orchards. Mexican Bean Beetles, Asparagus Beetles, aphids of many species, Onion Maggots, Squash Bugs, Flea Beetles, Corn Borers, Horn Worms, and many others laid waste to crops. *Heliothis Obsoleta* adapted to feed on several plants. Though it is one species, it is known variously as the Corn Earworm, the Tomato Fruit Worm, the Tobacco Bud Worm, and the Cotton Bollworm.

Honeybees were brought to America aboard ships in straw skeps. Swarms escaped, spread across the continent, and established "wild" colonies in hollow trees. Settlers harvested the honey and sold wax in rendered blocks. But there were problems. *Galleria Mellonella*, the Wax Moth, laid eggs in crevices near beehives. The emergent larvae crawled into the hive and fed on beeswax. Later, a deadly bee disease, foulbrood, was imported from Europe. Finally, in the late 1970's *Varroa Jacobsoni*, the Throat Mite, completely eradicated honeybees in Booger County, including mine.

Hypoderma Lineatum, the Heel, Bot, or Warble Fly, attacks cattle in

April. Sometimes, insane from incessant torment, the animals stampede through the pastures; tails held high, they futilely try to escape. Docile cattle become dangerous and unpredictable. Yet the Warble Fly neither bites nor stings. The females lay eggs on the hair above the hooves. The maggots burrow through the skin. For eight months the growing maggots migrate through the tissues to the upper back, where they cut breathing holes. Eventually, they fall to the ground and pupate into winged adults. Other parasites include Roundworms, Tapeworms, Lungworms, Bladder Worms, Liver Flukes, and Lice.

In Austin Hollow the road turns abruptly to the right at a farmstead between buildings, crosses the branch, and turns left. Up the hill on the right is the imposing rock and wrought-iron main entrance to Saddle Rock Ranch. Further on look for a stone house on the right. In front of it is the crumbled foundation of the Bakersfield School. Imagine times long past when children walked here from every direction, carrying their textbooks and lunches. CR 246 dead ends at Hwy 95. Turn around and go back to the end of V Hwy. As we cycle up the pavement, notice how few old home sites are still occupied. Most of the families moved away as the soil was depleted and pests became intolerable. Old timers say that after the 1918-19 influenza epidemic, many discouraged people migrated west to California, Oregon, Idaho, or wherever there were jobs.

Fred Cooley was twenty-seven when he took his sixteen-year-old bride, Elsie Doane, to Dewey, Oklahoma. Kinfolk helped Fred get a job at the cement factory. Conscientious and hard working, he eventually became a head burner and earned six dollars a day, a high wage. Few men could take the work because heat from the kilns was intense, and the caustic, pervasive dust provoked fits of coughing and lung disease. Cement poisoning caused skin ulcerations akin to poison ivy; one of Fred's kinsmen would die from it.

Fred and Elsie were cousins within the Dobbs family; their grandfathers were brothers. It was a troubled marriage. Fred had been married before. He'd just turned eighteen when he married Oma Rhodes. They had four children in four years. Ida (b. 1912) was handicapped; self-centered, Orville was spoiled by Fred. Hazel, though, was a helpful, pleasant child. The baby born in 1915 lived only a few months and was soon followed to the grave by Oma, a victim of TB.

For Elsie those first years in Dewey were miserable. She was a country girl far from home, and she had to watch helpless Ida constantly. Orville would not obey Elsie; insultingly, he mocked her and refused to do his chores. Though Elsie pleaded with Fred to help her, Fred couldn't. He ignored the chaos in his home and the suffering of his wife. Eventually, Ida went to live with Fred's mother, Granny "Wumps." Orville left home at sixteen and was seldom heard from again.

Lee was born in 1919. Fifteen months later, Elsie gave birth to Janie. Frederick was born in '25 and Joanne in '27. The Cooleys lived in a comfortable rent house and had plenty of money. Fred worked the night shift, and the children were expected to be quiet and let him sleep. One day Fred came home in a brand new '26 Model T Ford that he'd purchased for $500.

Prosperity ended for the Cooleys when the stock market crashed in 1929. Demand for products diminished; massive unemployment, bank failures, and widespread bankruptcy ensued. When Fred was laid off, he couldn't find another job. Desperate, he decided to move his family back to Douglas County, where he owned a forty-acre ridge top farm adjacent to his mother's place near Drury.

It wasn't much: a tiny three-room house with an outhouse out back. Water was a quarter-mile down Austin Hollow at Chaney Spring, a seep that filled a concrete tub where buckets could be dipped. Fred bought six head of dual-purpose (beef and dairy) Shorthorn/Jersey cows, a sow, and a flock of chickens. He and Elsie planned to raise their own food to survive the hard times. When Elsie's brother, Herbert Doane, decided to move to Washington State to pick apples, Fred traded the Model T for Herbert's team of black draught mares, Dopsey and Ribbon, as well as, harness, a wagon, a plow, and a double shovel. Though the Cooleys never could afford a saddle horse, Lee and Janie rode Dopsey to the Drury Store bareback with a bucketful of eggs to trade. When the garden needed cultivation, Dopsey was careful with her hooves and never stepped on a plant.

Watch for traffic as we ride up V Hwy. The Cooley Place is on the left, two miles up the pavement on the ridge top. Every trace of the homestead has disappeared. Look for rocks piled between two big trees in the fence line. The ruins of a barn are in the woods to the right. The house used to sit where a lone cedar now stands. Notice how steep the slope drops off into Austin Hollow, and imagine carrying water up a path through the woods.

Concern for water dominated the Cooley's lives because the crops, garden, and pasture depended on rain. Far away in the Eastern Pacific changes in ocean currents affected weather worldwide. The Dust

Bowl Drought began in Douglas County. Summers were miserably hot and arid; unseasonable frosts damaged tender plants, and sudden cold snaps plagued the winters. Crops failed; pastures withered; gardens dried up. Dust particles suspended in the atmosphere created eerily vivid sunrises and sunsets.

The Cooleys struggled. Fred occasionally worked for Bid Reynolds, fixing fence or cutting brush for long, sweaty hours in exchange for a gallon of molasses. Often, the Cooleys subsisted on cornbread and "water gravy" made from tins of lard purchased at the Drury Store. Poor hygiene and an unhealthy diet caused bouts of sickness. New shoes had to last two years. In the warm months they went barefoot; during winter they wrapped their feet in burlap tied with binder twine. Their clothing became ragged. Nevertheless, there were soon more mouths to feed. Elsie gave birth to Francis in '32, Janice in '34, and Landon in '36, the worst drought year.

Lee was a chubby eleven-year-old when he moved to the farm. Realizing the hardships his family faced, he did his best to help out. Numerous times each day he carried water from the spring. He cut and split firewood with a saw and axe and stacked it beside the cook stove. He learned to harness the horses, drive the wagon, use the plow, and handle a hoe. On Saturdays he carried two big cast iron kettles to the spring and started a fire. While Janie watched the babies, Elsie and Lee would boil the soiled clothes, scrub them on a rub board, and hang them to dry on wires strung tree to tree. If the weather was inclement, the Cooleys went dirty. Years of work went by. Lee chopped brush and hauled innumerable wagonloads of rocks out of the fields. He milked twice a day and tended the garden. With a two-man crosscut saw, he and Fred cut cords of firewood. Whenever the sow or one of the cows needed to be bred, Lee would drive her to Bill Call's to breed her to his boar or bull.

In their tattered clothing the Cooleys joined their neighbors and relatives at church, Sunday school, square dances, hymn singings, and picnics. When a family needed a new home, the community gathered for a house raising: the house was built and roofed in one day. At midday there was a picnic amid jokes and pranks.

When squirrels were plentiful, Lee borrowed his Uncle Henry's .22 rifle and his squirrel dog, Sam. Henry taught Lee how to trap rabbits. The Drury Store paid five cents for small ones and ten cents for big ones. In cold weather gutted rabbits were stacked like cordwood on the store's porch.

Uncle Joe Lambert was a beekeeper and wild bee hunter. He and Lee captured a jarful of bees, shook flour on them to make them more visible, and released them one at a time; they followed the bees until they found the bee tree, which they cut down with a crosscut saw. Just before it fell, Joe had Lee stand back. Angry bees swarmed the air when the tree crashed down. Stripped to the waist, seemingly immune to stings, Joe chopped out the colony, found the queen, and moved her to a hive box. The other bees soon joined her. Finally, Lee and Joe carried bucketsful of honeycomb and the newly boxed colony home.

Lee and his siblings attended the Bakersfield School. Grades one through eight were taught in one room. At first the noisy confusion of the tiny schoolhouse bewildered Lee. Frank Giles was his teacher; Frank stressed spelling and math and demanded that his students study seriously. Lee was dyslexic; he confused his b's and d's and jumbled his numbers. Often during recess, with the laughter of his frolicking classmates filtering in, Frank had Lee stand at the blackboard and corrected his mistakes. In time Lee became a good speller and mastered the multiplication tables. He loved to read. Bill and Ethel Call let him borrow freely from their home library.

Later, Florence Roper Reese, just graduated from high school, taught at Bakersfield. She believed that education should be fun and organized spelling bees, ciphering matches, and geography hunts and arranged academic competitions with Champion and other nearby schools.

Until the late '30's Douglas County kids who attended high school boarded with families in town. Roads were primitive; vehicles, few. Hwy T [present day 95] was a rough, potholed dirt track. When money was finally allocated for buses to transport rural students, Lee and Janie rode the first school bus into Mountain Grove. What a long day! They left in the dark, walked the two miles to Hwy T, and returned home in the dark. Evening chores had to be finished before doing homework by the light of the kerosene lamp.

As we cycle up V Hwy, imagine Lee, Janie, and the neighbor kids walking toward Hwy 95 under the predawn stars. Turn left on CR 234. To the left is a branch of Dobbs Hollow. Beyond, on the opposite ridge, is the Cooley Place. West of it, on the slope facing us, is Grandma "Wumps" Cooley's old place beside a year-round spring. On this long, gradual downhill you can coast and enjoy the pastoral scenery.

The Cooley's financial situation grew progressively more desperate. They sold the farm in order to have food to eat. The cattle brought $12/head. Afterward, they moved from one rent house to another.

It took years, but Federal relief money reached Booger County. In 1929 Republican Herbert Hoover became President; Republican St. Louis lawyer Henry Caulfield, Governor. By 1930 182 Missouri banks had failed, and 115,000 Missourians had lost their jobs. While shivering families stood in soup lines, farmers destroyed their crops rather than sell at prices below the cost of production. Hoover and Caulfield kept saying that prosperity was just around the corner and stuck with policies of small government, low taxes, and resistance to expenditures for public works (roads, bridges, public buildings, etc.). Though the Great Depression was a worldwide phenomenon, both men would be blamed for the widespread misery.

Meanwhile up in Kansas City, "Big Jim" Pendergast, an Irish American saloon keeper, had been elected alderman from the First Ward, an area of packinghouses, slums, brothels, and bars. He founded a faction of the Democratic Party called the Jackson Democratic Club. Jim helped his younger brother Tom move up the political ladder from deputy constable to superintendent of streets to a seat on the city council. Tom was a large man with a gravelly voice and a quick temper; ruthless and violent, he intimidated those who disagreed with him. By allying the Pendergast "goat" faction of the Democratic Party with the Republicans, he squashed the "rabbit" faction and seized control of the city. The heart of his power was a padded election roll of "ghost" voters. At the polls Pendergast thugs decided who could vote; they threw ballots in the wastebasket and beat up complainers. Tom could deliver majorities of 100,000 votes.

He ruled from a plainly furnished office in a modest downtown building. Hundreds of people, from janitors to would-be governors, came up the stairs, hats in hand, to ask Tom for jobs or favors. Thousands, including everyone on the municipal payroll, worked for Pendergast. He provided services for the poor: food, clothing, and shelter. For businesses large or small, Tom could cut through red tape.

His private wealth grew. The P.T. Pendergast Wholesale Liquor Company was a virtual monopoly in the Kansas City area. His Ready-Mixed Concrete Company, one of the first in the nation to deliver on site, did a lucrative business with local government. Money from bribes, payoffs, and kickbacks poured in; businesses paid for "protection," usually ten percent of gross, to the Pendergast machine, and gambling houses and brothels bought police protection from Tom.

At the 1932 Democratic Convention, when Franklin Roosevelt's nomination seemed impossible, Tom Pendergast swung the Missouri delegation to Roosevelt. In return Roosevelt rewarded Tom with control of Federal relief programs in Missouri. Soon a billion Federal dollars would create tens of thousands of jobs that were administered by Pendergast appointees.

Tom's nephew Jim introduced his war buddy Harry Truman to the boss, who made Harry an aide, then a judge, and later manager of the Federal Re-Employment Agency. Truman eventually became the "Senator from Pendergast," a compromise nominee for Vice President and President for seven years when Roosevelt died.

Tom's luck finally ran out. His ally in the Italian North End, Johnny Lazia, owner of the Cuban Gardens, a lavish nightclub and casino, was ambushed outside his fashionable townhouse and shot eight times. On Election Day 1934 Pendergast thugs killed four people and injured dozens at the polls. Tom's health failed. He had a heart attack, stomach surgery, and a colostomy operation. Following a sensational trial, Tom was convicted under the new Income Tax Act and served a year in Leavenworth.

When Federal money came to Booger County, Fred got a WPA job building roads near Denlow. Lee dropped out of high school to work for the CCC. The Federal Government had bought up large tracts of land, much of it derelict or tax delinquent, to create the Mark Twain National Forest. For the next year Lee lived at the Pond Fork Camp near Thornfield with a large group of young men. They built roads (including the scenic Glade Top Trail), campgrounds, picnic areas, trails, bathrooms, benches and tables, and planted trees. Clothing and medical care were provided. Lee used $5/month for spending money and sent twenty-five dollars to Elsie.

With the Cooley's finances improved, Lee went back to high school. During his year with the CCC, Lee realized that he was athletically gifted. Pound for pound he could run faster, lift more, and work longer than the other boys. Though he'd never handled a football or seen a football game, he decided to join the team. That first day at practice he proved himself. He outran everyone. He could hit hard and make difficult open field tackles. Filled with confidence he told Coach Lowell Wade that he wanted to be quarterback. Later, after practice, Coach Wade took Lee aside and explained that small town football wasn't fair. The sons of prominent families held the most desirable positions; country boys played the line. Lee took his advice and became a starter on offense, defense, and kickoffs.

These were the "Wade years" at Mountain Grove High. Lowell's younger brother Morris was quarterback; another brother, Clell, center. Morris dominated the gridiron. It took several boys to tackle him. He went on to be a star at MU and then had a long career as a winning college coach. Mountain Grove won by vast margins. At the end of the season, Mountain Grove played in the "Ozark Bowl" against the best Springfield team. A Frisco Railroad special passenger train carried Mountain Grove fans to the game.

Lee loved the violent clash of helmets and shoulder pads, the bone-jarring hits. Coach Wade didn't believe in razzle-dazzle. He seldom passed the ball or used pitch outs, reverses, or trick plays. Mountain Grove played "smash mouth" football, running the ball at, over, and through their opponents. They exhausted teams with their swarming defense that forced fumbles and interceptions. On offense Lee "pulled" from his guard position. The instant he heard Morris give the snap call, he stepped back and to the side and plunged into the gap created by tackle Junior Prock and end Joe Finley. With Morris right behind, Lee would hit the linebacker and then race ahead to block the safety.

Games were on Friday nights under electric lights. After the game the country boys would drag out tumbling mats and sleep on the gym floor; in the morning Lee hunted through the town square for a neighbor to drive him home.

Sadly, Fred and Elsie separated. Renewed war in Europe had stimulated the economy. Fred got his job back at the Oklahoma cement plant. Janie married Elmer Hicks of Gentryville and had four children in quick succession. They never had much money but always had something to eat. Elmer was a crack shot and a wizard at gigging fish. Janie and the kids survived on squirrels and rough fish (suckers and red horse) and tins of lard to fry them in. Following Pearl Harbor Elmer enlisted and lived through weeks of desperate combat with the 82nd Airborne.

Ironically, Lee's draft notice came to the Drury post office the day he graduated from high school in May 1941. He reported to Fort Riley, Kansas. To his delight he became a horse soldier with the 2nd Cavalry Regiment. For several months Lee's company was detached for border patrol duty in southern Arizona. They returned to Fort Riley the day before Pearl Harbor. Fort Riley was isolated; the men had few diversions. To relieve the boredom the post commander ordered every company to furnish men for a boxing tournament. Though Lee had never been in a fight or worn boxing gloves, he was willing to try. "All they can do is whip me," he thought. When he was a boy in Booger County, his family and the neighbors had gathered around Frank Giles' radio as Gene Tunney, Max Baer, and Joe Louis defended their titles. To his surprise Lee became battalion, regiment, and division Middleweight Champion in a series of wildly awkward slugfests. Later, the colonel called Lee into his office and introduced him to Young Stooley, the division boxing team's manager/trainer, a formidable looking former middleweight contender.

Lee was assigned to the boxing team, which trained on Mondays, Tuesdays, and Wednesdays. In the morning they worked the light and heavy bags, skipped rope, and ran around the base shadow boxing. In the afternoon they sparred. For Lee that meant getting into the ring with Coach Stooley. If Lee lost concentration or didn't follow instructions, a flurry of sharp punches would get his attention. Boxing is complex, Coach Stooley told Lee. It takes years to develop skills to compete at the highest level. If Lee boxed conventionally, he would lose to more experienced men. But if he was aggressive, Lee could compensate for his lack of finesse. Lee became a "brawler" and used his speed and upper body strength to pin his opponent against the ropes. When Lee felt his opponent weaken, he intensified the attack and hoped for a knockout or a TKO, a referee's decision to stop the fight.

On Thursdays the team rested or traveled to other military bases. Since he was only a private, Lee "hid out" at the base library and read dozens of books to avoid being "volunteered" for work details.

Weigh-ins were at 9 A.M. on Friday. Lee was naturally a 175-pound man. Making 160 pounds was difficult. Starting Thursday he wouldn't eat or drink. Anyone who didn't make weight got a second weigh-in at 1 P.M. Often Lee would have to skip rope heavily dressed in a furnace room. Coach Stooley would stick a wad of tobacco in Lee's mouth and have him chew and spit. Lee never failed to make 160 pounds.

Fights were on Friday nights. Lee's aggressive style made him popular with the soldiers. He always fought last in the feature fight or main event. Amid smoke and noise Lee fought scores of men in sweat and blood-splattered rings.

As part of the war effort, Heavyweight Champion Joe Louis toured military bases with the Negro Champions chosen from African American units of the segregated army. Lee had seldom seen black folk. In the main event, though, he faced a muscular, ebony-skinned man with reddish hair. Midway through the first round Lee took a devastating punch; he felt himself black out and fall. Dimly he remembered being half carried through a screaming crowd; later, when he woke up in the dressing room, he was being congratulated for winning the fight. Lee had gotten up off the canvas and had instinctively fought on.

On Saturdays and Sundays the boxers nursed their bruises and rested for another round of training and fighting. After a year-and-a-half, Lee was tired of beating young men to unconsciousness, and he was sick of black eyes, headaches, and swollen knuckles. He'd only lost two fights, both to a tough artillery sergeant with years of ring experience. In the first round of their first fight, Lee stunned him but uncharacteristically—to Coach Stooley's wrath—failed to "bore in" for a knockout. During the next two rounds the sergeant nimbly sidestepped Lee's bull-like charges and landed enough punches for a close decision. In their much ballyhooed rematch, Lee was knocked out. His request to rejoin his unit was granted.

The horses were gone. The 2nd Cavalry was the nucleus of the new 9th Armored Division, designed, rumor said, to spearhead the final offensive against Germany. Lee was nervous because he didn't know how to drive. For months they trained in the barren Mojave Desert and learned to operate and maintain armored vehicles. Then they moved to Louisiana for extended maneuvers in mud. They practiced crossing rivers under fire and establishing bridgeheads. Their metal barracks were ovens in the intense Mississippi Delta heat.

Lee went home on furlough. One evening his sister Joanne took him to a square dance at a neighbor's home. Lee got into a conversation with another soldier, Dick Burge, who, like himself, was dressed in uniform. Dick asked Lee to introduce him to Joanne; in return Dick introduced Lee to his sister Maggie, who would become Lee's wife and lifelong friend.

We're on our way home now, too. Continue down CR 234 into Dobbs Hollow past the Call Cemetery. On the right, just past the cemetery, was the farmhouse Elsie rented while Lee was in the Army. Cross the usually dry streambed and start up a steep hill. Farm dogs sometimes harass us here. At the top CR 244 is on the right and CR 235 on the left. Champion is a mile-and-a-half straight ahead. If you're still energetic, turn right for a seven-mile addition to your ride and snake along the ridge top on CR 244. Turn left on CR 245 downhill across Greasy Creek. Atop the opposite ridge turn left on CR 240 until you intersect the Fox Creek Road. Champion is downstream.

When Lee returned from furlough, orders had come to ship out. The men were told to pack one small bag and leave everything else behind. Trains took them to New York City where they boarded the behemoth luxury liner, Queen Mary, stripped down to hold 26,000 men. Tightly packed, the men operated in three shifts. One shift slept deep inside the ship on mats or in hammocks. Another shift crowded the passageways and stairwells while the third shift, regardless of weather, jammed the decks. Though the kitchen ran twenty-four hours a day, it could only feed the men twice: porridge in the morning and cold cuts in the evening. The Queen Mary sped unescorted on a zig-zag course with anti-submarine aircraft prowling overhead. She arrived at the Firth of Clyde, Scotland, lucky to have avoided U-boat "wolf packs."

In England they were issued new equipment: uniforms, rifles, toothbrushes, tanks, and trucks. Combat ready, the 9th Armored Division sailed for France. Lee, now a corporal, commanded an 81mm mortar halftrack armored fighting vehicle. The mortar fired projectiles in a high arcing trajectory over trees and buildings. Explosive rounds burst red-hot metal shards called shrapnel. Incendiary rounds threw fiery white phosphorous in every direction.

The Normandy beach was still littered with wreckage when Lee came ashore. Day and night the wind roared; sand filled his clothing and food. Further inland it rained for days. Viscous "gumbo" mud stuck inches thick to his boots. In Paris and all across France, people greeted them warmly, enthusiastically waving French and American flags.

Ahead, beyond the front lines, Germany was beginning to collapse. Her armies, decimated by attrition, were relentlessly pushed back. Firebombs set German cities ablaze and created "firestorms" that incinerated tens of thousands of noncombatants, many of them slave laborers from occupied lands. Fuel for German vehicles was in critically short supply.

Though their situation was hopeless, German leaders refused to capitulate. Sophisticated propaganda created a "religion" of patriotic nationalism that stirred the hearts of the German people. Germany, they were told, was an innocent nation being attacked by barbarians; defending her was a sacred duty. Boys, middle-aged men, and the handicapped were drafted to replace the lost armies. They received limited training and rebuilt equipment and were rushed to the front.

As Lee neared the front he saw burned out tanks and trucks, and ghostly, shattered villages littered with the rotting bodies of enemy soldiers. His platoon took over a quiet sector in Luxemburg, a farmstead with a house, barn, and outbuildings. Forward observers decided to have some fun. They waited until a group of Germans were busy at the straddle trench latrine and brought a tank forward. They lobbed shells at the Germans who had to scurry for cover with their trousers around their ankles. It was so funny they tried it again the next day. With everyone watching the tank came up to fire, but a waiting German anti-tank gunner sent an armor-piercing shell into the tank's turret, killing the crew.

Everyone hoped the war would be over by Christmas, but in early December Lee was fighting in the snow along the Belgian/German border. Secretly, the German High Command had been waiting for cold, cloudy weather to launch a massive counterattack. Veteran units had been pulled from the line, rested, reequipped, and clandestinely moved into the Ardennes Forest. Joining them were dozens of regiments just out of recruit training. To succeed the assault would have to capture American supply dumps before they could be moved or destroyed.

Before dawn on a foggy, snow-covered December day, the Germans attacked. Artillery pounded American positions. German tanks churned through the mud, captured crossroads, and spread panic. Behind them regiment after regiment of German infantry marched into the breach in the American lines, later known as the "Bulge."

Lee became part of a hastily assembled armored relief force commanded by Colonel Creighton Abrams (later Supreme U.S. Commander in Vietnam). They were sent to stop the German spearhead. German planes bombed and strafed them as they neared the front. During an intense artillery barrage, they took shelter in trenches alongside frozen corpses of German soldiers.

On a bitterly cold Christmas night, they reached the front. The sky was alight with flashes and explosions. Ahead the 101st Airborne Division was encircled and cut off in the crossroads town of Bastogne. Lee's six-man mortar squad set up in the slush and frozen mud. Truckloads of mortar shells were stacked like cordwood. At dawn they attacked. Tanks and infantry moved forward as Lee's squad worked like demons, loading and firing hundreds of shells into the German positions. They had no food, and their boots were soaked through. Late that night, exhausted and shivering, Lee could hear German officers shouting orders and blowing whistles to line their men up for an assault. It was a massacre. As the screaming Germans rushed toward them, tracer rounds lighted the night. Flares and explosions surrealistically illuminated the Germans as they were decimated. When daylight came, the snow was a crimson slush studded with bodies. The wounded cried, "Comrade, Comrade." Orders were issued to take no prisoners.

The German offensive halted; their vehicles, out of fuel, were abandoned. The sky cleared, and the temperature plummeted to record lows. American planes circled over the Bulge and turned intersections into killing fields. Day after day the Americans counterattacked with appalling losses. Lee could barely walk on his partially frozen feet. Everyone in the squad was ill or slightly wounded: lips, noses, ears, fingers, and toes were blackened and scarred by frost. Yet none of them would report to the hospital because they were afraid of being released as infantry replacements.

In mid January Lee's battered unit was sent to France to rest and reequip. A French woman knitted a pair of thick, soft slippers for Lee's injured feet.

The 9th Armored forced its way across the Rhine in early spring. They routed the demoralized Germans and raced into the heart of Germany. Resistance was crushed with machine gun and cannon fire. Refugees jammed the roads: the homeless from bombed cities, slave laborers trying to return home, deserters. Lee's company liberated a large farm worked by Russian, French, Polish, and Jewish prisoners who were guarded by German women with rifles. The workers showed the Americans where the Germans had hidden their valuables. That night the Americans partied on German wine and cognac.

The "no prisoner" rule still stood. Lee, like most soldiers, couldn't kill in cold blood. His unit had a Kansan who led dozens of unlucky Germans into the woods.

In the heart of Germany Lee's armored column rounded a bend in the road and halted suddenly. They were face to face with the Russian Army. After an awkward pause, everyone began to laugh. Hugging and pounding each other's backs, they realized the war was over.

Lee returned to Booger County. Maggie hadn't heard from him for over a year when they met by chance at a softball game. The old flame was still there. They married. Lee took out a veteran's loan and bought the farm now owned by Marilyn and Charley Byerley a mile north of Ray's Store. Lee and Maggie purchased three draught horses, Pete, Nig, and Doll, as well as, a small herd of Jersey milk cows they gave names like Flashlight, Knothead, and Goldie. They milked by hand twice a day in a tiny three-stall shed. With second-hand horse-drawn equipment, they plowed, planted, and put up hay. There was no electricity; roads were unpaved. Despite the long hours and little money, Lee and Maggie were happy.

Though neither of them was from a strongly churchgoing family, they attended a revival at the Fieldstone Church of Christ. The words of eighteen-year-old evangelist Billy Horton opened their hearts and filled them with God's joy. They were baptized in the North Fork at Topaz. To this day they remain deeply committed Christians with warm compassion for everyone. Eventually, they broke with the Church of Christ over three issues: the shared communal cup and the tenets against instrumental music in church and against Sunday school.

The local FHA loan officer, Allen Rankin, insisted that the Cooleys modernize and buy a tractor and up-to-date farm equipment and build a milking parlor. Lee and Maggie were just making ends meet. How could they take on more debt? Rankin persisted, and Lee became discouraged. The Cooleys sold everything and paid off their debts. They were lucky! In the early 1950's drought returned, cruelly hot and dry. Many families went bankrupt and were forced to move. Between 1950 and 1960 the population of Douglas County declined by 24%!

Lee and Maggie bought a new Chevy sedan and drove to southern California where high paying jobs were plentiful. They purchased a new "tract" home. Years passed, but no children were born to them. They tried to adopt, a slow and frustrating process. One evening a friend called to say that he knew a couple in San Diego with a large family who were expecting another child that they wanted to have adopted. Lee and Maggie met with them and agreed to pay all the medical bills. The couple, however, wanted to "sell" the baby. No compromise could be reached. Unexpectedly, a few months later, the couple called. The Cooleys could have the newborn, a boy.

They named him Billy. He was a joy. Billy made friends easily, excelled in school, and always tried to "do the right thing." He seldom needed discipline and had a close relationship with his parents. After Billy worked his way through college, he became an army officer. While serving in Germany, he was killed in an automobile accident. His death rent Lee and Maggie's hearts; their lives were never the same.

The Cooleys adopted two other children, Shirley and Patrick. By then the "rat race" of California was increasingly dissatisfying, with its congestion, traffic, and constant growth. When automation took Lee's job, they sold out and bought an Arkansas chicken farm. For eighteen years Lee and Maggie worked long hours, gathering and sorting eggs, hauling manure, feeding, watering, and maintaining buildings. Just as they were prospering, disaster struck. A fire broke out at 3 A.M. on a sweltering August night. Thousands of chickens and years of hard work went up in smoke. Lee and Maggie sold what was left and moved back to Douglas County.

Today—the summer of 2000—the Cooleys live in Mountain Grove's senior housing. Mild mannered and dressed in bib overalls, Lee is a fit eighty-one-year-old.

Are you feeling fit after today's ride? Let's buy a soda and a snack from Duane and load up the bikes. Get a good night's sleep. Tomorrow we'll take a long, arduous excursion through the Topaz area. What do you know about "flower children?"

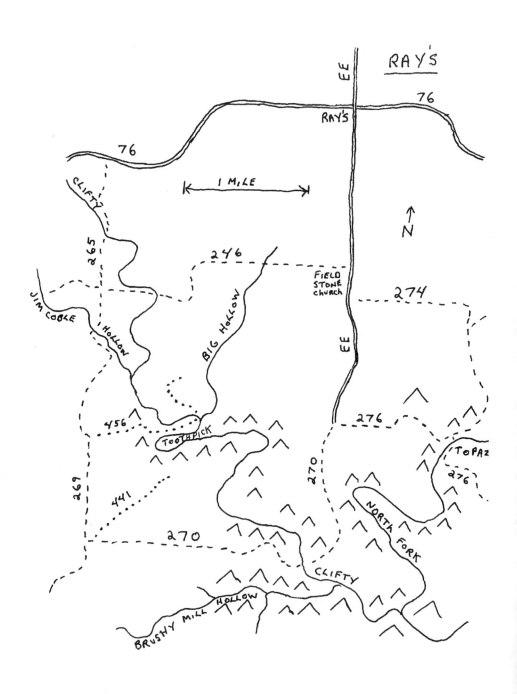

Ray's Store

Topaz

Today's excursion begins at Ray's Country Store at the junction of 76 and EE. Built in 1932, the store was successively Holt's, Gregor's, Coble's, and Finley's. It sold feed, farm supplies, groceries, and gas. In 1980 Ray McCall bought the store from Herb and Carol Finley. Today Grateful Dead and hippie-era memorabilia and tie-dye shirts are for sale. Why is the store so different now? Perhaps it's Ray. The son of a Santa Fe Railroad man, Ray grew up in Wichita. As a young man, he worked as an independent trucker. His partner, John Hamby of Dora, talked about the Ozarks as a place that would suit Ray's personality, which was profoundly influenced by Herman Hesse, Martin Luther King, Rudolf Steiner, and the Eastern religions. Ray is a "Rainbow Person" who believes in the ideals of the 1960's counterculture: love, peace, compassion, and social justice.

Owning the store is not an easy life. The front door opens at dawn and closes after dark seven days a week. Forget weekends and vacations. After several years Ray was "burned out;" he leased the store, moved to Springfield, and bought a house near Southwest Missouri State University.

Maria Ramos, Ray's wife, was born in Rio Bravo, Mexico, on the south bank of the Rio Grande, fifty miles inland from the Gulf. The youngest of eight children, Maria grew up in four houses side-by-side with her extended family. The houses had concrete walls, tin roofs, and dirt floors. Jobs were scarce; wages, low; sanitation, primitive; social services, non-existent. Through her teens, twenties, and thirties, Maria neither married nor had boyfriends. She and her sister Sophia converted to the Assemblies of God, and Maria embraced her new religion with fervor. Jesus, she said, was her husband. To help her family financially, Maria crossed the border illegally to find work. A church in McAllen, Texas, provided her with a truck bed that had been converted to a small bedroom; she held dry-cleaning and dishwashing jobs. When amnesty was offered to undocumented workers, Maria was granted a green card.

Meanwhile in Springfield, Ray joined the Unity Church. At an Advanced Adult Metaphysical Theology study group, he befriended a man who planned to start a business as a "coyote" under the pseudonym "Señor Bob." Bob intended to transport Mexicans to work in chicken processing plants; in exchange, his clients would pay him a portion of their wages. In McAllen Señor Bob recruited Maria and another woman and man. On a bitterly cold January night, they arrived in Springfield. Maria had never seen snow; she was forty-one and only spoke a few English words. Señor Bob awakened Ray late that night. Could he help Maria and the others? Disastrously, the coyote's schemes had unraveled; there were no jobs or places to live for his group. For the next several weeks, Ray slept in his '48 Chevy school bus, so the three Mexicans could stay in his house.

When the others left, Maria was alone, confused, and surrounded by strangers she couldn't understand. Ray's study group urged him to marry Maria who saw Ray as a man of means, the owner of a house and business. Together they would make Ray's Store a thriving enterprise; she would send part of the profits to her family. In 1994 they married and moved into the back of the store. Maria serves delicious tamale dinners in the tiny restaurant section. The ambiance is unique. Occasionally, Ray will serenade his guests with a song. Sit awhile and chat with other customers; before we leave, remember to tell Maria how many of us will dine later.

Park across the road on the highway right-of-way near the sawmill. This will be our longest, hardest ride—thirty hilly miles over a variety of surfaces, through large tracts of Forest Service land, as well as, private property. Ride south on EE to the Fieldstone Church and turn right on CR 246. We're on a ridge top between Clifty Creek and the North Fork. Nearby are many sinkholes. Clifty is a losing stream. As you cross the gravel-choked creek bed, notice the large, flat-sided boulders on the left. This sandstone can be "split out" with wedges for building material.

Turn left at the crossroads onto CR 269 and descend into scenic, forested Jim Coble Hollow. [Look for a faint track to the right across the streambed. A challenging ride through dense forest over a deeply eroded old logging road will eventually take you to W Hwy.] Further south on CR 269, at the top of a long hill, turn left onto FS 456. This track leads to the geologically anomalous Toothpick area. The Toothpick is a knife-like ridge just wide enough to walk on, and where it meets the ridge, Clifty Creek makes an abrupt turn. Imagine the force of a flash flood as it collides against the precipitous slope! Leave the bikes at the campsite near the creek and explore on foot. Climb the rock formations; look for Clifty Cave and the sinkhole.

Go back to CR 269 and continue south. You'll see the Twin Knobs fire tower ahead. Turn left onto CR 270 and pass FS 441 on the left. Forest Service land, much of it clear-cut, is on the left, and private pastureland with scattered trees is on the right. A long, rough downhill descends back into the Clifty Creek bottoms and passes between an arch-roofed barn and a house. Master Gardener Faye Coble lives here. Stop for a few minutes and look at Faye's wonderful garden and yard. Local plant enthusiasts eagerly anticipate her spring plant sale. Armadillos have destroyed some of her prized plants, however. Notice the steep "backbone" ridge behind the house. Faye's springhouse is built into the entrance of Coble Cave, which is associated with a sinkhole over the ridge in Brushy Mill Hollow. Years ago a sawmill operated near the sinkhole. After heavy rain particles of sawdust flowed out with the spring water.

Faye's late husband, Buster, son of the tragic Cora Osborn, was a gifted stockman and horticulturalist. In order to purchase this portion of his grandfather's farm, Buster worked for seven years in the hazardous logging industry in Oregon. During the 1930's Faye and Buster survived low crop prices and extreme drought with perseverance. In the '40's and '50's they farmed large acreages with a 9N Ford tractor they'd bought new for $865 in 1941, the last one available until after the war.

From Faye's the county road goes uphill to the end of EE. Turn right on CR 276 and ride past Wrinkle's dairy. This road, seldom used or maintained, is sheer, rocky, and dangerous with deep gravel at the bottom, a sure trap for a speeding mountain biker. Cross the North Fork on the concrete bridge. This is Topaz, the jewel of Eastern Booger County.

An enormous spring pushes ten million gallons of water a day into the beautiful mill pond, down the race, and into the mill. The old-style water wheel is just a novelty, put up recently by Joe O'Neal, owner and restorer of Topaz Mill. The mill is actually powered by a water turbine. Though rustic and weathered-looking, the fully operational mill is a sophisticated timber frame structure built with massive beams that were painstakingly mortised and tenoned together. Inside is a complex system of drive-belts, conveyors, elevators, and valves. One is for corn, and one, for wheat; the equipment not only grinds the grain but also separates the bran, germ, and chaff from the flour. During harvest wagons lined up, sometimes for days, and waited their turn at the mill. Bart Hutchinson, the original owner, took a percentage of the grain in exchange for the grinding.

Take a good look at the two-story store building next door. In its day it was a fabulous, bustling place that employed five clerks. A gallery ran around the upper story inside. Glass-fronted cases displayed goods for sale. There was a post office, a barbershop, and a blacksmith business that later became a garage. Much of the exchange was barter: farm goods such as eggs, chickens, cream, vegetables, grain, and honey were traded for tools, barbed wire, cloth, bullets, and lamp oil.

Topaz was the commercial hub of the area. Heavily laden wagons and later, trucks, hauled goods back and forth from the railroad depot in Mountain Grove. The Hutchinsons bought livestock, weighed them on a heavy scale, and "drove" herds of cattle and hogs into town. When WWI began, the army came here and offered top prices for mules. With stalls for thirty-two mules and horses, the red barn behind the white milking parlor was originally much larger, with a tall hip roof. At the onset of the Civil War, Jesse B. James operated the Topaz Mill. Jesse and a Mr. Brown were tried, convicted, and hung by Southern sympathizers because they furnished flour to Federal troops.

When prospector Henry Schoolcraft passed through in 1818, he found a massive set of elk antlers and hung them in a tree. He named this Elkhorn Spring. That name was forgotten. In 1839 Aaron "Posey" Freeman (b. 1783 Rowan County, NC) and his sons-in-law, Henry Wood and Bill Clinton, laid claim to the spring. They had come from the Meramec River settlements west of St. Louis to hunt and look for land suitable to homestead. They struck a large creek at its headwaters and followed it downstream. Because there were many Indian huts scattered along the bottoms, Freeman named it Indian Creek.

The Delaware had recently moved further west; a few friendly Shawnee still lived along the North Fork; they told Freeman that they had lived many good years in Eastern Booger County because game was plentiful. The Seminoles had settled on the Jacks Fork thirty-five miles to the east. The tribes visited and traded so often that a well-worn trail, knee deep in some places, led around the north side of Blue Buck Mountain to the Seminole villages. Somehow, however, war began with raids across Blue Buck. Most of the Shawnee, Delaware, and Seminoles moved away. Talking about it made them sad.

As winter ended the next year, the Freemans, Woods, and Clintons cut their own trail for the heavily laden oxcarts across ridges and streams to Topaz. They camped here on March 10, 1840. Aaron's wife,

Alabeth, was a Choctaw; friends and family called her Dolly. She and Aaron had lived among her people in Crawford County, Mississippi; they had thirteen children over a twenty-two-year period. The Freemans built a gristmill and a distillery beside Topaz spring. Their peach brandy became widely popular. People later spoke of enormous piles of peach pits beside the distillery. Bill Clinton homesteaded further south, near a spring at the mouth of Indian Creek. Henry Wood, his wife, Sarah, and his fifty-year-old father, Hiram, settled two miles north of Topaz where the North Fork loops. Henry was a blacksmith and farmer who lived to be 103. Hiram had been a corporal in the Tennessee militia during the War of 1812, and in the 1830's he campaigned with Witt's Alabama Mounted Volunteers against the Seminoles in Florida. When their son James died, Henry and Sarah hollowed out a large pine log for a coffin with boards from a wagon bed for a lid. James was the first person buried at Mt. Ararat. The Woods nearly lost their property when another man left for Springfield to file a claim on it. Henry mounted his best horse, Barber, and rode hard for Springfield. As Henry was leaving the land office, the other man came through the door. The Henry Wood place is still owned by the Wood family; Russell and Joanne Wood raise prime beef cattle there.

The Johnsons settled in the area soon after and intermarried with the Woods. John and Lovy owned a gristmill in northern Alabama; they moved west with the Cherokee along the Trail of Tears. John died young of "dropsy." During the Civil War the Johnsons had nearly all their possessions stolen by soldiers and bushwhackers. They went to Rolla as war refugees and found work on the Federal trains. Eventually, they were able to move back to Booger County.

James "Bushy" Wood served with Henry Coble and his son Peter in the militia. Henry was from Lincoln County, Tennessee; he and his wife, Catherine, were early pioneers in the Topaz area and had three sons. Catherine died of complications soon after she gave birth to Alf. After the war Henry married Mary Russell Owens, a war widow whose husband, William, was hanged by Rebels at Rockbridge. Peter and James were lifetime friends; Peter's three sons married James' three daughters (John/Mary, Alf/Xeriviah, and Peter/Caroline).

After a flood destroyed the original mill that was built on the other side of the millpond, Bart Hutchinson hired master carpenter Lawrence Smith of Vanzant to construct this mill. Smith later built the fabulous Basin Park Hotel into a steep hillside in Eureka Springs,

Arkansas; nine stories tall, each floor of the hotel extended to ground level. He superintended the construction of portions of Drury College in Springfield, as well, and erected many of the buildings still in use on the square in Mountain Grove. Unfortunately, he broke his back when he was thrown from a horse and lived only a few more years as an invalid.

It's time to ride on. If you have the energy, continue up the hill on CR 276. Straight ahead the Mt. Ararat Church and Cemetery are among the oldest in the county; stop awhile and wander among the monuments. The church was a convenient meeting place for families who settled along the North Fork and Indian Creek. Beyond the cemetery turn right onto FS 483, a rugged trail along a gentle slope patched with fields, forests, and dense copses of large pine. Except during hunting season, this trail is seldom used. It ends at the gate of Helen Freeman's Hell Hole Estate, a cattle ranch that spans both sides of Indian Creek. At one time the trail crossed Cedar Knob and the Yeomans to Hwy 181. I know from personal experience that Helen does not appreciate mountain bikers on her property.

Turn around; go past Topaz and over the concrete bridge. This is the Blue Hole, popular for swimming and wading. Occasionally, a thick rope is fixed on a tree limb for the adventurous to swing out and drop into the middle of the pool. Just beyond is a park-like picnic area. Turn right (north) on CR 273 and climb a steep, rocky hill. Ironically, the pasture on the right is National Forest land leased for grazing. During the Depression/Dust Bowl era a man from Oregon named St. Claire bought up farms and cheaply amassed a large tract of land that he later sold to the Forest Service. Beyond the pastures the North Fork makes a series of bends. High white limestone bluffs form a razorback ridge between the North Fork and Reese Hollow. Just past a farmstead the road forks; stay to the right on CR 273 and ride down Reese Hollow. For two miles CR 273 twists and turns and ends at Hwy 76. Turn right onto the pavement, ride past the Mark Twain National Forest sign, and take CR 162 up Freeman Hollow. The road T's at the Donald Stillwell place.

Donald grew up nearby and was related to many people in the neighborhood. Clever and hardworking, with a natural aptitude for tools and machinery, he joined the Navy and became a machinist who served aboard various warships, including the battleship New Jersey. After he retired in the 1960's, he and his wife, Ada, built this homestead, as well as, the barn and springhouse further up the road,

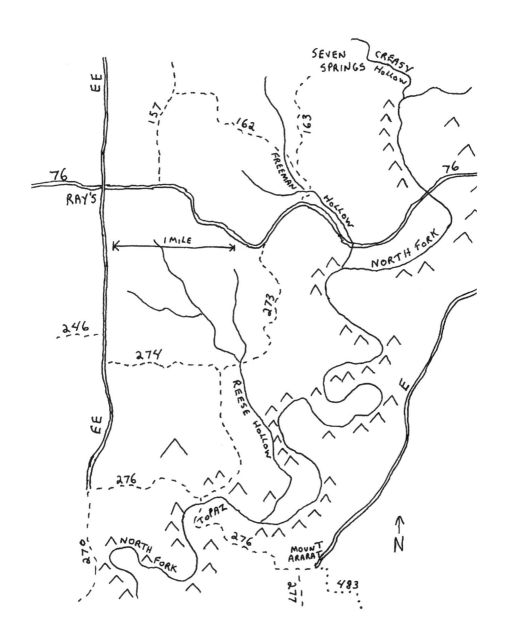

Seven Springs

where dependable Freeman Spring gurgles out of a rock ledge. Cheerful and generous, Donald graciously helped fix his neighbors' machinery. In the early 1990's he had a heart attack and passed away.

Go up CR 163 between the house and the shop. When Donald built the shop in the streambed, floodwater was inadvertently diverted into the road. After "gully washers," people who use this road have to fill it in with rocks and gravel. Rough, steep rock-strewn roads like this are normal in Booger County. Before the Civil War folks complained about the roads just as they do today. In the 1950's many of the gravel roads, such as EE and 76, were paved.

At the same time the way of life that the people of Booger County had known for generations—planting, harvesting, milking, and haymaking—began to change rapidly. Bulldozers pushed acres of forest into piles to burn, and farmers built hundreds of miles of barbed-wire fences. With milking machines families could have larger dairy herds; they borrowed money and constructed Grade A milking parlors. New breeds of large, fast-growing cattle—Charolais, Simmental, and Holstein—replaced Shorthorn, Angus, and Jersey. Larger cattle meant more hay and necessitated bigger tractors and equipment.

Deer and wild turkey, extinct for a generation or more, were reintroduced by the Missouri Department of Conservation and began to multiply. Out in the fields the MDC encouraged progressive farmers to plant "living fences" with the wickedly thorny, non-native multiflora rose. The invasive new species spread quickly. The berries, called hips, were devoured by birds that scattered the seeds far and wide. The exquisite clusters of fragrant white flowers soon had no charm. Farmers rode over the bushes with tractors and shredded them with bush hogs, only to shake their heads in disbelief when the roses sprouted back vigorously. Entire farms became giant briar patches. To reclaim fields men crawled painfully into the thickets, wrapped log chains around clumps of rose, and yanked them out by the roots with a tractor.

The REA strung power lines to every home and provided electricity for modern appliances. Industry saw a hardworking labor pool that would accept low wages and moved factories into the small towns: Emerson in Ava, Brown Shoe in Mountain Grove and Cabool, Rawlings in Willow Springs. People had less time; they bought their food at the supermarket rather than grow it themselves. Television antennas were erected, and families sat in front of the glowing screens and visited their neighbors less often. They didn't always like what they saw—the Civil Rights movement, protestors, Hippies, riots, tear gas, graphic footage of combat in faraway, exotic Vietnam. The flickering images made them uneasy and challenged their core beliefs in God, family, and country.

However, in the autumn of 1972, the rapidly changing outside world moved into the community. Aboard old school buses converted into nomadic homes, the "flower children" arrived from every corner of America. Most of them were likeable young folks with polite, well-behaved children. That first winter the neighbors remember meeting Manny and Sandra Brandt and their three children, Balin (called Kevy), Heather, and Erin. From Iowa, Manny was a minister's son; Sandra grew up on a prosperous "black dirt" farm. Both were keenly intelligent. They met as students at the University of Iowa where their exposure to the Civil Rights and anti-war movements left them deeply disillusioned with both politics and academia. Simultaneously, they were influenced by American philosopher Henry David Thoreau, who proposed the rejection of material things and the cultivation of a delight in the natural world—the songs of birds, the star-filled sky, the changing seasons. Thoreau also wrote of the duty of citizens in a democracy to oppose unjust government policy with acts of civil disobedience; he was subsequently imprisoned for his refusal to pay taxes in support of the U.S. war with Mexico in the 1840's.

Before they moved to the Ozarks, Manny and Sandra rented an old farmhouse outside Iowa City. They planted a big garden and kept a milk goat and some chickens. Juggling school, work, and farm chores wasn't easy; after Balin's birth, it became even harder. Just down the road the Brandts met Patty and Leon Van Weelden, kindred spirits who also rented a small homestead. The Van Weeldens were high school sweethearts from Oskaloosa with an infant daughter, Anna. A carpenter's son, Leon, plainspoken and forthright, had dedicated his life to artistic expression. Tall and strong, Leon was a formidable basketball and volleyball player. Patty was the daughter of a podiatrist who bitterly opposed her alternative lifestyle. The "generation gap" between them created a long, heartrending estrangement.

When school ended at U of I in the spring of '71, Leon and Patty drove their '54 Chevy sedan to northern California. They rented a house in the tiny town of Elk, perched on a cliff above the rocky, fogbound coast. Patty worked part-time at the Greenwood Cove Cafe;

Leon found odd jobs. Just north of town a small river, the Navarro, rises in the redwood-clad Coast Range. (Back then during the summers, hundreds of flower children would "hang out" along the river to make music, camp, and frolic in the sun.) When the Brandts and Patty's brother, Jeff, visited that summer, everyone was enthusiastic. On the riverbank among the towering redwoods, anything seemed possible.

Manny had a friend named Paul Clark. The son of an upright Des Moines newspaperman, Paul was a student activist in the Civil Rights and anti-war movements. Deeply idealistic, he believed that young people like himself could organize students to bring about social change and an end to the war. Robert Skolnick was a Jewish New Yorker recently graduated in art from Carnegie Mellon; he was on his way to San Francisco to take up a graduate scholarship/teaching assistant position. When he met Leon, their shared passion for art launched a warm friendship; Robert never made it to San Francisco.

Robert, Paul, the Brandts, and the Van Weeldens were caught up in the "counterculture." At evening get-togethers they spoke of forming a community. Manny, Sandra, and Robert, the group decided, would go ahead as "scouts" and locate a good parcel of land. Robert and the Brandts bought old school buses and converted them into nomadic homes. They had to depart suddenly in the middle of the night when a young woman acquaintance of the Brandt's, her personal life a mess, gave Manny and Sandra her newborn twins. A few days later in another state, Sandra told officials that she had given birth to the babies at home and received birth certificates. She and Manny named the girls Heather and Erin.

The old buses labored ponderously in low gear up the Rockies. They camped along the roadsides on the way to Spokane, Washington, where they'd heard there was cheap land. Spokane at the time was a mecca for "back-to-the-landers" looking to set down roots. On the street in his amiable way, Robert met a freckled, pregnant young woman named Valerie Ring. The daughter of a Filipino war bride and a journalist/professor, Valerie was complex and outspokenly radical. From the Chicago suburbs, she and her husband, David, lived and worked on a ranch near Newport, Washington, close to the Idaho border. David was an intense, highly focused Irish Catholic known for quick-witted repartee. Like his schoolmate John Belushi, David had a talent for song and dance. The Rings wanted their own place in the country, but without money or job skills, that seemed impossible.

However, they would throw in with the group if the right tract could be found.

The buses drove on. Day after day Manny, Sandra, and Robert visited real estate offices and chased down leads on pieces of property. They crossed the border into Canada, where they met many young American expatriates—deserters, draft-evaders, and disillusioned peace activists who now called themselves Canadians. They considered immigration, but British Columbia, like Washington State, had no land they could afford. The places they'd seen in their price range were marginal at best, with no water, a short growing season, and bitterly cold winters. At the real estate offices they picked up catalogues that listed property all over the U.S. One evening around the campfire, they read about the Missouri Ozarks, where land sold for $100/acre. The long growing season, timber, and plentiful springs attracted them. One morning in September of 1972, the group decided to give up on the Northwest and "check out" the Ozarks. They stopped at the Ring's. Valerie had a newborn, Joe, at the breast. Yes, the Rings would go with them! Robert made room for their belongings in the back of his bus while David loaded their Arab/Morgan filly, Gala Crescent, into the stock-racked bed of his Datsun pickup.

The convoy crossed Idaho into Montana. They camped along streams, where David staked Gala to graze through the night. As they crossed the Black Hills and the Badlands, they observed the devastation of Rapid City from a reservoir-bursting flood. One night as they camped along the Missouri River in Iowa, tragedy struck. Somehow, Gala fell hard on her stake; it pierced her ribcage and penetrated her heart. They buried her in the deep river bottom soil and continued on.

The travelers had only a vision of their community when they made camp at Noblett Lake on their first night in Missouri. They stopped at the cafe in Willow Springs the next morning. When Robert accidentally knocked a woman's purse onto the floor, he congenially began a conversation. Her name was Banner, and her husband, Neal, was a realtor. A few hours later, Neal showed them a piece of property near Topaz. It was perfect: 120 acres, mostly wooded, with a thirty-acre ridge top field speckled in wild flowers; rugged Creasy Hollow cut through it with a year-round stream. Two waterfalls and a small swimming hole added to the land's appeal. Though quiet and secluded, there was a county-maintained gravel road to the boundary, and the land adjoined the Mark Twain National Forest.

The price: $15,000. Manny called Iowa. The Van Weeldens had no money but were very interested; Paul Clark sent $2000. The Brandts had $2000 and the Rings $1000. Luckily, Robert had received an inheritance; he put up $10,000, an unselfish act that deeply angered his parents. Though it took many years, Robert was eventually paid back.

They had a farm, and it needed a name, something catchy like the nearby Hippie settlements of Stars End, Garden of Joy Blues, Edge City, and Dragonwagon. For days they tried futilely to think up a name. When their newfound friend and neighbor, Elmer Brown, rode his horse over for a visit, he said, "There are seven springs here, God willing." Seven Springs became the name, not only because of the seven springs of water, but also because there would be seven shareholders. The households would be "springs" of life, energy, and creativity.

Only the Brandts overwintered that first year. They picked a lovely building site on a south-facing slope above the juncture of two streams. Atop a sandstone ledge, with salvaged materials and hand tools, they built a sturdy three-room cabin that is still lived in today. Below the ledge was a two-acre bench of sandy loam, a prime gardening spot. The clear, gurgling waters of Creasy Hollow flowed among towering, white-barked sycamores below the garden. Sandra built a cold frame and planted seed; she bought two beehives. Elmer plowed the garden with his 8N Ford tractor and afterwards bounced the kids on his knee.

In the spring the Rings built a cabin on the edge of the big field. Paul Clark started a house, also. Robert never did spend much time at the farm; he was a magnet for ticks, chiggers, and poison ivy, which made his life in the Ozarks a misery. He soon left, never to return. Valerie left, too. She told David that she'd married and become a mother too young. The solitude of country life wasn't for her; she wanted to go back to school and "make something" of her life. David raised Joe as a single parent.

Leon and Patty moved to the farm aboard their own converted school bus. Their son, Jason, was an infant. Patty's brother, Jeff Dunshee, and his new bride, Jan, bought in and moved onto a secluded corner of the property. Jan was from Chicago and had an ardor for living things; crushing ticks, pulling weeds, or felling trees was traumatic for her. Jeff was wiry, soft-spoken, and capable. He'd let his tightly curled hair grow out into an Afro. He loved music and played whenever he could, strumming guitars with Paul Clark or singing duets with Patty.

Two other couples, the Spaeders and the Rosses, had traveled to the Ozarks to join a community. They showed up one day after a night spent near Birch Tree at Garden of Joy Blues. Everyone got along, and soon there were two more households on Seven Springs. Nancy and Nick Spaeder came from California, but both had been raised in Pennsylvania. They had two little boys, Josh and Noah. Nancy was a flamboyant extrovert who loved theatre; she was most at home on stage. Nick was a smooth-talking woodworker described by his peers as a "wordsmith" and a "woodsmith" and a "ladies' man." An attentive "hands on" father, Nick worked hard to make a living for his family.

Viki and Arrow Ross arrived from New Orleans with their children, Michael and Natasha, whom everyone called Rainbow. Viki was a southern belle from a well-to-do North Carolina family. Vivacious, with elfin looks and an infectious laugh, she made friends easily. She organized birthday parties, potlucks, games, and evening get-togethers. The kids said she was a "fiend" at slapjack. Arrow was a Dane with a dark tan, luminescent, pale blue eyes, an earring, and a thick accent; he looked like a sailor or pirate. His mother, Ems, was a diplomat and the former Danish Ambassador to the U.N. Arrow, a graduate of the Royal School of Photography, had toured the world with his camera. He loved adventure; while at the farm he bought and sailed a sea-going yacht, explored Booger County in an ultralight airplane, and journeyed to Nepal.

Both couples practiced "open marriage." Although they believed in shared finances, mutual responsibility for childrearing, and an orderly home, they were open to romantic liaisons outside their marriages. Viki was a romantic, self-proclaimed "love junkie" who had several affairs. Other, more conservative, Seven Springers resented the guilt by association Viki's behavior gave them in the neighborhood and the way it destabilized the community they were striving to solidify.

Nevertheless, a community was born. Slowly, a Constitution was written and the farm incorporated. Each household owned five acres, with the bulk of the property held in common. There would be regularly scheduled farm meetings, annual dues, and farm workdays where households would provide labor for road maintenance, construction, farm beautification, and haymaking. Procedures were worked out to buy and sell shares; new members would have to be acceptable to every household. The farm bought an 8N Ford tractor, a Dearborn sickle-bar mower, and an old dump-style rake. A well was dug; Bob Squirrel brought his ditch witch and ran waterlines to everybody's place. The REA strung power lines to all of the houses.

When Jan began her labor, she chose to have the baby at home with the aid of a midwife and insisted that the entire farm share in the birth of the first child born at Seven Springs. Everyone remembers the day vividly; they felt a "oneness," strong fellowship, and spiritual warmth. Jan and Jeff named the healthy baby girl Maya.

The Seven Springers were young, optimistic, and full of exuberance. They tended gardens, raised children, constructed homes and outbuildings, and found jobs. So what if copperheads were in the kitchen, blacksnakes in the bedroom, and black widows in the outhouse? In the summer they scratched their tick bites and poison ivy; in the winter they huddled by the fire and learned to put tire chains on their vehicles. They started their own school, a one-room, green asphalt-shingled geodesic dome, in a copse of pines. Kids from off the farm came to attend. Every adult taught at the school.

They knew how to have fun, too. In the deep pool below the bluff on the North Fork, they swam in the nude. On Sunday afternoons they played volleyball in the field with their own "Booger County rules." Saturday nights they jammed and danced to their own band, Hot Mulch. Jeff played rhythm or bass electric guitar and did the vocal for "Cripple Creek" and the Everly Brothers' "Bye Bye Love." Nancy worked the drums with verve and showmanship and provided backup vocal. Patty was the lead singer; she delivered a sultry version of "Fever" and Hank Williams' "Mind Your Own Business." The crowd loved Patty and Jeff's duet version of Louis Jordan's "Choo Choo Chooboogie."

"Freaky" friends filled out the band: New Yorker Jan Madras hit the hot licks as lead guitarist; Ron Hughes from Brixey switched back and forth with Jeff from rhythm to bass. Ron wrote "Ozark Mountain Mother Earth News Freak" and "Hot Mulch Blues":

> *So come on baby,*
> *Put your dancing shoes on.*
> *Hot Mulch gonna boogie-woogie*
> *All night long.*

> *Lock the chickens in the house,*
> *The cows in the barn.*
> *'Cause it darn near will be daylight*
> *When we get back to the farm.*

When the band took a break, other Seven Springers would take the stage. David played the flute and could sing "Heard it Through the Grapevine" and "Kansas City" like a Motown man. The musically gifted Paul Clark would sit on the edge of the stage with his acoustic guitar and somehow slip from his precise upper Midwest accent to a thick, Deep Delta version of "Trouble In Mind" or to the easy, liquid tones of the mid-South in "Brand New Tennessee Waltz." Hot Mulch always finished with "Goodnight Irene."

Money was scarce and wages low in Booger County. The Seven Springers occasionally traveled for high wage jobs. Viki worked on the river barges. David became a recording studio carpenter and thrived on the complexities of the projects. One winter Manny took a job in Boston. In the spring the Brandt's marriage ended when Manny realized that he wasn't a rural person. He needed a fulfilling career and the intellectual and cultural stimulation of the city. The family separated; Sandra, embittered, her dream of a peaceful rural life shattered, left and never returned. Viki and Arrow divorced, too, but amiably, and became neighbors.

In the meantime Paul married Jane Devries. Thoughtful, introspective, and conscientious, Jane grew up in the Detroit suburbs, the daughter of a GM engineer and his Alabama bride. When Jane met Vinnie Wittenberg, owner of Elixir Farm near Brixey, in Mexico, Vinnie persuaded her to move to Ozark County. Naturally strong and hardworking, Jane worked on hay crews; she could pour concrete, do carpentry, or clear brush. Artistically gifted, she became a skilled spinner, weaver, and stained glass craftsman. Her garden was the delight of the neighborhood. Paul and Jane built a house with a Frank Lloyd Wright inspired design.

Viki married a tall, deliberate, dry-witted minister's son from California, Paul Goodwin. The Seven Springers called him Paulo. Occasionally for laughs, Paulo and Paul entertained the farm with a hilarious rendition of the teenybopper hit, "Paul and Paula." Paulo was the single parent of a young daughter, Asha; earlier they lived at the Dragonwagon community near Ava but left when it became exclusively female. Cramped in a school bus with three rapidly growing children, the Goodwins started an imposing two-and-a-half-story house with telephone poles set in concrete for the vertical structure. They moved into the uninsulated, partially built house and endured the severe winter of '78-'79; their water froze solid in milk jugs set by the fire. Everyone, though, slept comfortably under electric blankets.

David married a "radiant" blonde Californian, Beth Spangler. Her father worked at Universal Studios; her mother was Blaize Malone, the acupuncturist. Beth was exuberantly outgoing and a graceful volleyball player. At their wedding the pianist, who had been playing traditional wedding tunes, broke into rock 'n roll; David danced down the aisle in a tux, singing "Chapel of Love." Soon David and Beth had a son, Jesse.

Nancy loved puppets and puppetry. People called her "Puppet Lady." She would work on a half-made puppet as she chatted. With the help of the Seven Springs kids, she staged many enjoyable performances. Leon began to work with Nancy and to fabricate a wide variety of puppets. Their collaboration became a romance; the Van Weelden's marriage ended. Nancy and Leon's partnership continued. They created the Chameleon Puppet Theatre and for years staged elaborate shows filled with drama, pathos, humor, and music; Leon became a harlequin.

In the spring of '81 the Seven Springers, with help from their friends, began a production of Shakespeare's "A Midsummer Night's Dream." It was a huge undertaking with many scenes, characters, and costumes. Week after week they studied their lines, worked on their costumes, and rehearsed; all the while they held down jobs, raised children, and tended gardens. They performed the play in high summer, outdoors, in a meadow on a full-moon night. Fireflies swarmed; songs of katydids, cicadas, and frogs filled the night.

Act One began as the moon rose; tendrils of mist from the sun-heated grass encircled the actors. David was the mischievous forest spirit, Puck. Viki was Titania, queen of the faeries, and Paulo was Oberon, king of the faeries. Jeff played the "rude mechanic," Bottom, who was given the head of an ass and the love of Titania by Puck. Paul had a hilarious role as Thisby, man-turned-woman in the play-within-a-play. Jane and Beth, fancily costumed and gossamer-winged, were Titania's faerie consorts.

In Act Two, as Oberon waved his arms and called on the forces of nature, lightning lit the horizon as if on cue. Intense flashes backlit the actors and added to the drama. In the finale the sky opened; a torrent of rain soaked everyone. Costumes and clothing plastered to their bodies, the troupe and audience hiked the slippery half-mile back through the woods to their vehicles. Here in Booger County a soaking summer rain is considered a blessing.

Years went by. After Seven Springs School closed, the kids caught Junior Haywood's Bus #11 at Donald and Ada Stillwell's for the long, noisy ride to Cabool. Paul and Jane divorced; Viki and Paulo divorced. When Beth left, David was emotionally crushed. His beautifully crafted home now held only empty, haunting memories. He moved to Springfield. Arrow repeatedly but futilely sought a long-lasting relationship.

A few of the original Seven Springers still live at the farm, but the dynamic energy is gone. The Seven Springs kids, grown up, stop in occasionally and tramp around the old homesteads nostalgically. Most of the Seven Springers became professionals whom no one would suspect were once flower children.

CR 163 ends at the Seven Springs gate. Ahead are the meadow and side roads that branch out to separate homesteads. Turn around; take CR 162 up Freeman Hollow to CR 157. Turn left and pass two dairies, Rogers' and Sloan's, built across from one another. Ray's Store is a half-mile right on Hwy 76.

Remember the tamale dinners we ordered? Forget them! Maria has passed away. She seemed so strong and energetic, up very early and busy until well after dark. Just as she was beginning to hold conversations in English, she became ill, with nausea at first and then bouts of vomiting. One doctor said she had indigestion and prescribed antacids. Another treated her for an ulcer. A third speculated about a "twisted bowel." In the meantime Maria became weaker. Her nephew Raul took the long bus ride from Mexico to help Ray at the store and to care for Maria. By the time she was diagnosed with a malignant tumor, Maria was too feeble for chemotherapy or surgery. Ray drove her back to Rio Bravo to live her last days among her family. ¡Vaya Con Diós, Maria!

The next chapter will be our last ride together. We'll explore the wildest portion of Booger County. Serious cyclists can hop logs and jump rock ledges; the rest of us will get off our bikes and walk. Who were the Leni-lenápe? What happened at Satsang that fateful August morning in 1979? Ever had your hand around a Little Yeoman?

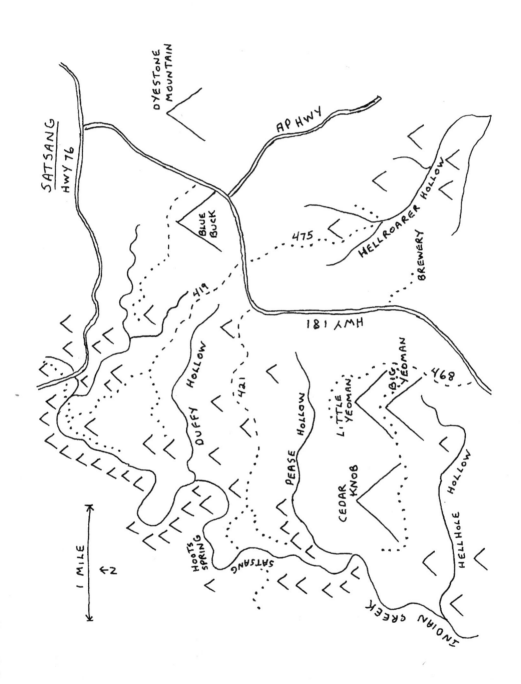

Satsang

Little Yeoman

Indian Creek, the focus of our final ride, cuts a deep canyon through the most mountainous, densely forested part of Booger County. As you drive south on 181 from 76, look for Blue Buck Mountain topped by a fire tower. Pull in at the gate and climb the tower for a view of the landscape we'll bicycle through today. Pause for a moment to appreciate the venerable white pines planted years ago on the north slope of the mountain.

Further south 181 passes AP Hwy on the left and then FS 419 and FS 421 on the right. As 181 bends to the left and enters private property, notice three prominent hills on the right: Big Yeoman, Little Yeoman, and Cedar Knob. On the left is the entrance to the Little Yeoman Brewery, open for retail sales 9-5 everyday except Wednesday and Sunday.

Two miles beyond the brewery, where 181 bends to the left, turn right onto FS 468 and park. Pedal north toward the Yeomans. The land is deceptively level; to our left is rugged Hell Hole Hollow, Indian Creek's final tributary. At the foot of the Yeomans turn up the steep slope. Most of us will have to walk our bikes to the hunters' camp that lies in the saddle between the peaks. Stop a moment and admire the wonderful views to the north, and notice how the cedars have overgrown the glades on the south slope of Cedar Knob. Be careful not to get lost as you ride down the west slope of the Yeomans toward Cedar Knob; the road deteriorates into a seldom-used trail choked with brush and broken with rock ledges. In warm weather look for scorpions and the brilliant yellow-green Western Collared Lizard, known locally as the "mountain boomer." Further on the trail passes through mature oaks, prime habitat for the raucous, brilliantly colored Pileated Woodpecker, and ends at the back gate to Hell Hole Estate. Stop awhile to savor the panorama north up the Indian Creek drainage.

People think that pioneer families like the Collinses and Upshaws were the first to settle in Booger County. However, when Aaron Freeman rode alongside Indian Creek in 1839, he passed ruins left by the Lenápe, the "People," also known as the Leni-lenápe, the "Real People," and as the Loupes by the French, the "Wolves." Other woodland tribes referred to the Lenápe as "Grandfather" because they were the oldest people; archaeologists believe that for thousands of years they lived along the streams that flowed into Delaware Bay. Artifacts carved with images of mammoths have been found in Lenápe rock shelters in present-day New Jersey, Delaware, lower New York, and eastern Pennsylvania. The English dubbed them the Delaware after Lord de la Warr.

Early European visitors remember the Lenápe as a tall, agile, and handsome people who could run great distances and endure hardship without complaint. Industrious, sensible, and astute, they took great pride in feeding and entertaining guests.

Lenápe children were cherished and indulged by their kin. However, as soon as Lenápe youths could walk, they were given tasks. Boys were encouraged to make their own bows and arrows; girls, to till the soil and plant seeds. Like everyone else children were addressed by nicknames. At a solemn ceremony a shaman, called a "name giver," christened each child, but the name would remain a secret within the family.

Premarital chastity was not important. Children born out of wedlock were treated the same as "legitimate" offspring. Boys married outside their clan and lived among their in-laws. When a girl became marriageable, she wore a special headdress, and suitors wooed her with gifts and worked for her parents. Eventually, a one-year betrothal was arranged. There would be no marriage ceremony or exchange of vows; the couple simply began living together. If, after a time, one of them desired divorce, all property and children belonged to the woman. Adultery, however, was considered a disgrace, and public displays of affection, even between husband and wife, unseemly. Showing emotion in the presence of strangers, too, was inappropriate. Though profanity was alien to the People, both sexes enjoyed bawdy banter.

The Lenápe dressed flamboyantly. Women wore rouge and eye shadow, and they dyed their hair. Earrings, anklets, and brooches accented their colorfully beaded clothing. Men shaved their heads and let thin braids of hair grow down their backs. Cockscombs, crests of greased and painted hair, bristled atop their bald heads. Some men pierced their noses and inserted porcupine quills. Both sexes carried cosmetic kits and wore animal-symbol tattoos and body paint. The term "Red Man" comes from the Lenápe's fondness for vermilion paint. The People bathed regularly in streams and cleansed themselves in sweat lodges. In the warm months the Lenápe wore nothing and lived out-of-doors on raised platforms among the crops to keep deer, groundhogs, raccoons, and crows away. During winter they wrapped themselves in fur shawls, bearskin cloaks, leggings, and waterproof capes of turkey feathers.

Lenápe women farmed corn, beans, and squash; they gathered fruits, nuts, roots, berries, and shellfish. From corn meal women made Johnny cakes, a blend of meal, nuts, berries, and maple syrup; persimmon bread; and dumplings, which they ate with grape juice. Talented weavers and ceramists, they wove baskets, sewed clothing and footwear, made pottery, and tanned hides. The men hunted. Deer, elk, bear, muskrat, beaver, raccoon, fox, and fish fell prey to their arrows, snares, traps, and nets. Dog, beaver tails, clams, animal entrails, wild rice, grubs, and cicadas they considered delicacies.

In the early spring Lenápe men set fire to huge tracts of land, probably to improve the hunting and gathering. In troubled times they erected a defensive stockade around the village. Every twelve years or so they moved the village. New fields grew more vigorous crops with few weeds or pests. The men cleared fresh fields with stone axes and fire; they built oval-shaped wigwams and the "Big House," or church, with its symbolically carved wooden beams. This large, circular structure formed the center of Lenápe social and ceremonial life.

The Leni-lenápe weren't a nation. They had no central government or oligarch. Rather, a group of forty-to-fifty autonomous villages, each of several hundred people, composed the loosely-knit tribe. Each village had a Council of Elders and a hereditary chief who together made important decisions. Since the Lenápe didn't believe they were related to their fathers, a new chief was chosen from among the sons of the deceased chief's sisters. His authority was based on his ability to persuade and to organize; a negligent chief was ignored by the Elders and eventually replaced.

The Lenápe did not amass personal wealth; chiefs had no more assets than had anyone else. Individuals gained respect and status through acts of kindness and generosity, especially toward the elderly. People who committed outrages like robbery, rape, or murder were publicly scolded by the chief and then shown disrespect by fellow villagers. Habitual offenders were shunned.

The Leni-lenápe were a peace-loving people surrounded by warrior cultures like the Mohawk and Cayuga. When raids and provocations by another tribe became intolerable, the Council of Elders appointed a war chief and sent messengers to other Lenápe villages to invite men to join a war party. In battle the People wore wooden helmets and body armor; they carried war clubs and symbolically decorated moose-hide shields. Stealthy night attacks and surprise were the People's way of war. They avoided pitched battles. After a hit-and-run raid, the Lenápe would vanish into the forest and lure vengeance seekers into ambush. The Lenápe tortured their fierce warrior captives and respectfully listened to their defiant death songs. Often they assimilated captives into the tribe. In later years many white women preferred to stay with the Lenápe rather than return to their families.

"Manitou" was the Lenápe's word for God. God was everything, and everything was God. The soul, they believed, lingered near the body for twelve days before it passed into the afterlife. All living things—birds, animals, trees, fish—were kindred spirits with souls. The sunrise and sunset, the stars, and the growing corn answered prayers. Each Lenápe sought a personal vision through a dream or trance that was brought on by fasting or a cathartic experience. Through this vision the individual gained a private guardian spirit, usually an animal or bird, and he carried a charm in a leather pouch—a rock, feather, or carved piece of bone—that was his spirit's essence. During a twelve-day religious ceremony called the "Gamwing," amid drumming and chanting, individuals sang and danced a testimony to their vision.

In the beginning the world was covered by water. Land rose. Out of the depths of the sea, a turtle emerged and climbed onto the earth. From the water shed by its shell a cedar tree grew; from the cedar sprouted all living things, including the first Lenápe man and woman. Cedars and turtles were sacred, as was the number twelve, because there are twelve plates to a turtle's carapace.

The Lenápe played a game called "paw-sah-hum-man" that was based on the number twelve. Everyone participated. Women competed against the men. Two saplings, six-feet apart, were set like soccer goalposts at each end of a field. A respected Elder kept score with twelve cedar sticks. At the start, as well as between goals, he threw up a deerskin ball high between two players for a jump off. Men and boys could not touch the ball or the women with their hands. However, the females could run with the ball, throw it, and tackle the men. The males scored by kicking the ball through the women's goal; women, by throwing the ball through the men's goal. The game ended when twelve goals had been scored.

Around 1600 small Dutch sailing vessels appeared off the Atlantic Coast. Presumptuously, the Dutch laid claim to the land the Lenápe had occupied for centuries. They named the territory New Amsterdam and referred to the Lenápe as their "subjects." For years there were only a few Dutch traders, and the Lenápe eagerly exchanged furs for metal tools, cooking utensils, trinkets, and bright cloth. As more Dutch arrived, trouble began. Free-grazing livestock destroyed Lenápe crops, and the Lenápe couldn't comprehend taxation. Worse yet, private property was contrary to Lenápe culture. Though families and clans had rights to gather and farm certain areas, land, air, sunlight, and the sea belonged to everyone. The People's philosophy of being part of nature was incompatible with the Europeans' need to conquer the environment.

War broke out intermittently in the 1640's and '50's. The Dutch burned villages and placed a bounty on Lenápe scalps. Captured children were sold into slavery in the Caribbean. The stockade the Dutch built to keep the People off Manhattan Island later became Wall Street. After the English seized New Amsterdam, more and more Lenápe land was taken through various legal pretexts.

Reluctantly and with great sadness, the Lenápe abandoned the land of their ancestors. For the next two hundred years they migrated west, away from the advancing white frontier. Historians believe there were perhaps 20,000 Lenápe when the Europeans arrived; 10,000 moved west. Smallpox, mumps, chicken pox, and measles further decimated them. Implacable enemies of the Americans, the Lenápe fought beside the French in the Seven Years War, and later, the English, in the War of Independence and the War of 1812. After each defeat settlers seized Lenápe land and distributed it as veterans' bonuses. In 1778 the Lenápe were the first native people to sign a treaty with the United States. They were promised legal title to their own land, protection from white squatters, and their own representative in Congress. The Americans breached this agreement and forty-four subsequent treaties.

In the Ohio Valley the Lenápe, numbering only 5000, joined their Algonquin cousins, the Shawnee, who had similar customs and language. In the late 1700's a woman remembered as the Munsee Prophet had a vision and began to preach among the Lenápe bands: Manitou, she said, had deserted them because the People had given up the traditions of their ancestors. Refute the white man's trade goods, like cloth and alcohol; use traditional tools and the bow and arrow; make fire by rubbing sticks together rather than with flint and steel. Only Manitou and the ancient religion would make the Leni-lenápe strong again. The Gamwing revived. The People celebrated old chants and prayers.

Other prophets appeared. Neolin, a reformed alcoholic called Delaware Prophet, had a revelation. He saw an alliance of tribes powerful enough to halt American encroachment and to negotiate a just and lasting peace. Cannon fire and bayonets dashed Native American hopes at the Battle of Falling Timbers. U.S. troops sacked villages and burned crops; destitute native families starved over the winter.

An important text emerged out of the religious foment and violence at the end of the eighteenth century. Over the millennia the Lenápe had developed a written language of painted and carved hieroglyphics. Traditionalists Talking Wood and Naked Bear recorded the folklore of their people in a document called the "Walam Olum". Part heroic epic, like <u>Beowulf</u> or the <u>Odyssey</u>, and part history, the Walum Olum describes how the Leni-lenápe long ago lived far to the north and west. Food was plentiful; war and sickness, unknown. Evil beings, however, drove them from their home, and for generations the Lenápe wandered. They crossed a frozen sea and many mountains until they reached the Mississippi, where they turned east toward the rising sun and settled along the Atlantic Coast.

Constantin Rafinesque, a French botanist/linguist, deciphered the Walam Olum. His translations took him seven years, but his work was ridiculed as a fictitious sham. Only after he died in poverty at fifty-seven from stomach cancer, did historians and anthropologists begin to appreciate his contribution.

In the late 1700's bands of Lenápe crossed the Mississippi into Spanish Missouri and established villages along Ozark streams like Indian Creek. Only a few thousand Lenápe remained. Like the "white" settlers who would follow them, many Lenápe were of mixed blood. They built log cabins instead of wigwams and wore cloth rather than skin garments. The villagers kept cattle, hogs, horses, and chickens. They carried rifles and a wide variety of metal tools, weapons, and cooking vessels. The women raised melons, potatoes, and cabbages alongside corn, beans, and squash; some of them had taken white husbands. Because beaver pelts were in high demand and the People master trappers, a few became well-to-do. Some Lenápe men hired out with the big St. Louis fur companies and traveled across the plains to trap the beaver-rich streams of the Rockies. There, the Lenápe encountered another Algonquin tribe, the formidable Blackfoot, the bane of the mountain men.

The Osage terrorized the Lenápe, and I believe that the legend of the Booger Man of Booger County began among the Lenápe here along Indian Creek. This was Osage territory, and the Osage were a bellicose warrior culture. The men shaved their body hair save a bristling, dyed "mohawk" that they festooned with feathers. Osage boys were raised to believe that robbing and killing trespassers were virtues and that death in battle earned an exalted place in the afterlife. Picture an Osage raid! Suddenly, sinisterly war-painted, tattooed, and muscular Osage, brandishing axes, swords, clubs, and muskets, attack!

When the U.S. Government banished Native Americans from Missouri, the Leni-lenápe were forced onto a reservation in Kansas. Unfortunately, white settlers soon squatted on tribal land. Worse yet, Lenápe territory would be fought over during the Kansas/Missouri Border War and the Civil War. Today, only a few Lenápe survive without a language or culture.

Turn around at the Hell Hole gate and ride back over the Yeomans. Look for paths that crisscross the main trail; I've only explored a few. Take FS 470 around the north side of Little Yeoman, through tangled, brushy forest, until the trail becomes impassable above Pease Hollow.

Isolated areas like this were used to hide illegal distillation equipment, or stills. Because they often worked at night, distillers were called "moonshiners" and their clear, potent liquid dubbed moonshine. A newspaper photo taken outside the Ava courthouse in the early 1930's shows Sheriff W.F. Givens and his deputies with the twenty-two "wildcat" stills they had confiscated. Imagine a time not so long ago when revenue agents prowled these paths in search of stills. From hilltops they looked for wafts of smoke rising from slow fires. Many people were arrested, fined, and imprisoned; nonetheless, moonshine is still made in Booger County.

The roots of Booger County moonshine go back to the beginning of civilization thousands of years ago. Beer was sacred to the Mesopotamians; Noah took it aboard the Ark, and Egyptian pyramid workers received a ration of three loaves of bread, a bunch of onions, and two jars of beer. The secret processes of making beer and bread are intertwined, and the ingredients—grain, water, and yeast—are the same. Bakers were often brewers.

The mystery of distillation—that alcohol becomes vapor at 176°F—was discovered in Persia around 800 A.D.; though, some scholars believe that ceramic vessels from a much earlier time were used to extract alcohol. Returning Crusaders brought distillation technology to Europe, and over generations the Irish and Scotch, in particular, perfected the art of whiskey making. Gaelic folk called liquor *visque breatha*, the water of life. Willy Rau became the patron leprechaun of distillers.

When English overlords began to tax stills in the 1600's, the resourceful and self-sufficient Scotch and Irish felt that their liberty and way of life were under attack. Militant societies similar to the present IRA formed. Tax collectors, derogatorily referred to as "gougers," were waylaid, beaten, and murdered. Simultaneously, traditional life underwent radical change. Common people were forced off the land, and tens of thousands of the so-called Scotch-Irish emigrated to British America. Often they had no choice but to accept seven years of indentured servitude to pay their passage. Many eventually took up land along the frontier away from government, taxes, and aristocrats where they could live independent, family-centered lives. Over generations the Scotch-Irish migrated from Virginia and the Carolinas, through Tennessee and Kentucky, into the Ozarks.

Early settlers like the Freemans brought distillation equipment into Booger County in their oxcarts. Liquor was their cash crop. Equipment and ingredients were simple: a large kettle, grain, water, and firewood. The first step to distilling whiskey is to make beer. Grain is soaked for several days until it sprouts into little plants high in sugar. The sprouts are boiled into a tea called "sour mash" and left to slowly ferment much like when bread is left to rise. As yeast feeds on the sour mash it exudes alcohol, and when this fermentation is complete, a lid is put over the kettle and sealed, usually with a cement made from flour and water. A slow fire is then kindled under the kettle. As gases build up they are forced into a tube or pipe where they cool and condense into liquid that drips into a crock. The more times this liquid is distilled, the higher the percentage or "proof" of alcohol. Most moonshiners took pride as craftsmen who produced a high quality product.

At Topaz the Freemans made peach brandy. Instead of using beer they fermented wine from fruit juice and then distilled the brandy with the same process of slow heat, vapor, and condensation.

Like the English the American government sought to tax and control liquor. When George Washington's Treasury Secretary, Alexander Hamilton, pushed an excise tax on spirits through Congress in 1791, there was angry opposition along the frontier. Eventually, Federal troops were used to crush the "Whiskey Rebellion." After a ball from Aaron Burr's dueling pistol ended Hamilton's life, thousands of cups were raised in celebration; Hamilton's tax lapsed.

At the onset of the Civil War, Abraham Lincoln used the Act of July 1, 1862, a 20¢/gallon tax on spirits, to help finance the Federal Army. By 1864 the tax had risen to $2/gallon. In 1868 a stamp tax was imposed on all liquors. Three years later the U.S. Cavalry under Custer scoured the Kentucky hills for stills.

Many Americans liked to drink. Ironically, the more liquor was taxed or prohibited and the higher its price became, the greater were the incentives for moonshiners. Before Prohibition was repealed, tens of thousands of gallons of illegal alcoholic beverages were produced annually that cost the government millions in uncollected revenue.

Let's ride back to the vehicles and load our bikes. Drive north on 181. Slow down as the road bends to the right, so you can pull into FS 421. Park, and unload the bikes. FS 421 is a narrow, 4x4 dirt track that runs along the knobbed ridge between Pease and Duffy Hollows. As we cycle through regenerating clearcuts and pine, oak, and hickory forest, we can admire the views of Cedar Knob and the Yeomans.

Two miles from 181 the road ends at two ATV trails. The left twists between trees and ends at a gate atop a bluff overlooking a small bottomland field on Indian Creek. To the left of the gate, across a precipitous ravine, Cedar Knob looms high. To the right, the trail runs along a ridge and then descends abruptly to the creek. Erosion has cut deep ditches in the hillside, so walk your bike down. The trail meets the water at a wide, shallow ford where we can take off our shoes and wade across. Upstream, Hoots Spring pours clear, shockingly cold water into the creek, so be prepared. The creek bottom is rocky, too.

The land across the creek is private property; in the 1970's it was a Hippie settlement called Satsang. Peter and Frieda Young built the log house facing us. Look at the pyramidal roofline. Peter believed that the symmetry and mathematical precision of pyramids had transcendental powers. Pete placed his son's bed under the roof's apex at the focal point of the pyramid's energy. Just past Pete and Frieda's house is another house built by Pete's brother, Joe, and Joe's wife, Janet; further on is the former home of Oman and Winona Divine and their children.

The words *sat* and *sang* are taken from ancient Sanskrit verses; *Satsang* is the spiritual bond that links a congregation. *Satsang* also means the attainment of self-realization through mental connection with a guru who need not be present in the flesh. This master teaches that silence and meditation induce mental energy and purify the soul. Speech interrupts this process of self-realization and breaks the flow of power from the guru.

The Hippies at Satsang believed that the material world was a web of delusion; they renounced the greed and selfishness that characterizes the scramble to acquire possessions. So, they settled here on Indian Creek to live off the land and attain Satsang.

Bill and Augusta Coffin raised dairy heifers on the 120-acre farm that would become Satsang. Bill had been exposed to asbestos as a young construction worker in St. Louis, and as his health failed, the Coffins sold off parcels of their farm: forty acres to the Youngs; seventeen to blue grass fiddler John Tickner and his wife, Marilyn; ten to composting toilet manufacturers Mike and Von Druin; two couples from New Mexico, John and Cindy Knoll and Bill and Lezlie Hemmert, bought forty acres together.

Try to visualize the Hippie days in this little valley: houses were being constructed, usually with salvaged materials, and gardens were planted. Children played along the creek bank. There were morning meditations and music in the evenings. Every 4th of July there was a big party. Imagine a hundred naked Hippies swimming in the creek! The "Firecracker 500" was held to see who could swim the furthest underwater in one breath. They played volleyball, shared a potluck meal, and "jammed" late into the night.

However, the peaceful life at Satsang ended suddenly at dawn on August 9, 1979. For months State Highway Patrol investigators had been gathering evidence about marijuana cultivation along Indian Creek. Frank Martin, a reporter for the <u>West Plains Quill</u>, was awakened that morning at 1:35 A.M. by a fellow reporter who invited him to join a massive police raid into Eastern Booger County. Before first light Troop G Highway Patrol headquarters in Willow Springs was thronged with reporters and law officers from the sheriffs' departments of Douglas, Texas, Howell, Wright, and Ozark counties and by municipal police from Mtn. Grove, Ava, West Plains, and Mansfield. Everyone crowded into a large room with a map of the Satsang valley drawn on a chalkboard. Sergeant Doug Loring and

Trooper Carl Watson, who had been conducting the investigation, began the meeting by dividing the officers into nine teams. Each team was assigned a "target" of the nine households (seven houses, a camping trailer, and a tent). At dawn the teams would converge on the households, seize evidence, and then systematically search the property for marijuana plants. Be careful, they were told. A dangerous fugitive might be in one of the households. Watch out for vicious dogs and crossbowmen. Maintain radio silence and avoid unauthorized searches. Before the meeting adjourned, Douglas County Sheriff Leonard Sanders stepped forward and swore them in as temporary Douglas County Deputies.

At 5 A.M. a long column of police vehicles headed west on Hwy 76 into Booger County. Over their CB radio the reporters heard someone say, "Look at that, a whole convoy of Smokies." As the sky began to lighten, the posse turned onto E Hwy and then down the Satsang driveway a mile north of Mt. Ararat Church. Quickly the separate teams pulled up to their targets.

Sweat stuck the officers' shirts to their bodies. Reporter Frank Martin was with the group that "busted" the Youngs. As he stepped into the house, Pete was getting dressed while Frieda and the kids huddled in the corner. Reporter Jerry Womack joined a band of officers who converged on John and Cindy Knoll's tent. Marijuana plants were growing beside the tent and in the garden. Just down the road Womack could see Bill and Lezlie Hemmert taken into custody when deputies found illicit plants along fence rows near the Hemmert's small camping trailer.

The Hippies didn't resist arrest or attempt to flee. Everyone was polite. After the households were searched, officers fanned out along both sides of the creek. In a few minutes a patch of seven-feet-tall marijuana plants was found. Around it was a monofilament fishing line trip wire connected to a battery and an automobile horn meant to surprise plunderers. As the sultry morning became hotter, other plants were discovered, uprooted, labeled as evidence, and loaded onto Sheriff Sanders' pickup truck.

Marijuana is known by the scientific name, *cannabis sativa*, and by the common name, Indian Hemp. Other cultures call *cannabis* "charas," "bhang," "ganga," or "hashish." The Hippies called it "pot," "grass," or "weed." Farmers across the Upper Midwest call the persistent nuisance "ditch weed" because it invades fields, roadsides, irrigation ditches, or anywhere rich, moist soil has been disturbed. It is a fast-growing annual native to Asia and the Middle East with a branching taproot and a coarse, hairy stalk; there are male and female plants.

Long ago, when people first began to save seeds and till the soil, *cannabis* appeared and crowded out food crops. While some experimented with the plant's narcotic effects, often in religious ceremonies, others gathered the frost-softened stalks for the strong, durable fibers in the inner bark. They wove mats and plaited baskets and eventually made twine, rope, fish nets, cloth, and paper and harvested the seed for food, beer, or oil.

Hemp was introduced to Europe at the time of Jesus and Julius Caesar. The Latin word *canvas*, hempen cloth, comes from *cannabis*. Over centuries people discovered that hemp fibers stand up to salt spray and intense UV, and it became a major crop. Ships needed miles of rope and acres of sailcloth. The English, French, Dutch, and Spanish fleets used tons of hemp on their wooden men-of-war and merchant ships.

Though the plant outgrows other weeds and has few pests, extraction of the fibers from the stalks is labor intensive. In Colonial America hemp became part of the slave system. After the growing season was over and the cotton and tobacco sent to market, slaves would gather hemp stalks into bundles and soak them in ponds. Called "water-retting" or "water-rotting," bacteria and fungi would soften the plant tissues enough to separate the stringy fibers from the pith and bark. After water-retting the fibers could be braided into rope. Central Missouri's rich soil and mild, humid climate was ideal for *cannabis*. Before the Civil War hemp was the state's major slave crop.

After 1900 mechanization revolutionized hemp production. With fiber-stripping machines hemp producers threatened to undersell other fibers, particularly wood pulp paper and the new oil-based synthetic fibers. Simultaneously, plant breeders were creating pliable varieties of hemp more suitable for clothing. However, President Warren Harding's Treasury Secretary, bank, timber, and oil tycoon Andrew Mellon, had a plan to eliminate hemp as a competitor with the wood-pulp paper industry. Mellon appointed his in-law, Harry Anslinger, Commissioner of the newly created Federal Bureau of Narcotics. With the help of the Hearst newspaper chain, Anslinger began a campaign to criminalize hemp. They used the pejorative Mexican word, "marijuana," and claimed that hemp turned men into homicidal maniacs. Jazz, they said, was a satanic, voodoo-inspired evil brought on by *cannabis* and aimed at the destruction of the White race. Under the influence of hemp, Negroes turned into carnal animals devoid of inhibitions.

Out of this hoopla Congress passed the Marijuana Tax Act of 1937, which outlawed hemp. Ironically, the Twenty-First Amendment had repealed Prohibition just a couple of years earlier. When the U.S. entered World War II, the ban was lifted. The War Hemp Industries Corporation planted hundreds of thousands of acres of *cannabis* and built dozens of mills. The USDA produced the promotional film, "Hemp for Victory." After the war Anslinger and the newspapers renewed their attacks on *cannabis* and claimed the drug made users so docile and entranced that they were easily converted to Communism.

In the Ozarks the Satsang bust created banner headlines. "Fourteen Charged Following Marijuana Raids Here," announced the Douglas County Herald. On the front page were pictures of Douglas County Deputy Alva Thurman reading Pete Young his rights and Sheriff Sanders beside a display of confiscated evidence. "Arrest Fourteen in Marijuana Cases South of Cabool," proclaimed the Cabool Enterprise below a photo of Sheriff Sanders and Texas County Sheriff Andy Johnson. The West Plains Quill declared, "Twelve Arrested, Marijuana Seized in Douglas County Raids," above pages of text and pictures. One shows Peter Young putting on his socks after being awakened by officers that morning. Another shows Frieda dressed in a bathrobe, the kids clinging to her, talking to Sergeant Harold Crafton. A third photo shows an officer pulling up hemp plants.

Later that morning, after the residences and grounds had been thoroughly searched and the arrestees handcuffed and read their rights, Sheriff Sanders had a school bus sent from Ava to transport the nineteen people (twelve adults and seven children) to Ava. Sheriff Sanders told the dispatcher that most of the internees were vegetarians. At the Ava jail the adults were searched and fingerprinted and the children released to family and friends. The next morning the prisoners were arraigned before Taney County Associate Circuit Judge Joe Chowning and released after they posted property bonds.

The cases went on for two years. There were hearings, court days, and meetings with lawyers. Some sold their property to pay legal fees; the Youngs hired a clever St. Louis lawyer to ease them through the legal entanglements. One person served six weeks in the Ava jail.

Today Satsang belongs to Vic Becker. Vic and his wife, Susan, bought the place after Pete and Frieda moved back to Michigan. I was hired by the Beckers to renovate the house. Susan later lost her life to breast cancer.

Let's head back to 181. Anyone who's still feeling energetic and adventurous can explore FS 419 just a half-mile north. FS 419 follows a nearly level, forested ridge top and has several side trails. Watch out when the trail descends into Indian Creek! The original logging road is now a deep, boulder-strewn gully. Look for small caves in the bluffs across the creek. If you ride across the ford, you'll come out on Hwy 76 just west of the Indian Creek Bridge. Other trails run north up the creek. Across from FS 419 a rough trail winds through scrubby forest and clearcuts and ends at a spring near an old homestead and cemetery.

Meanwhile, the rest of us will drive over to the brewery. Turn in at the Little Yeoman sign and follow the dirt road over the hill and into a copse of stunted oak and hickory. The brewery is on the left; the warehouse, straight ahead. Little Yeoman is the smallest commercial brewery in Missouri. Steve and Jane Markley sold their first case in the fall of '94. Earlier, they were in the feeder pig business for many years. At their farm just down the lane, in a row of homemade farrowing houses, they kept 10-15 sows and a boar and sold pickup loads of weanlings at the local livestock auction. Most of the piglets were trucked north into the grain belt to be fattened and slaughtered.

The Markleys didn't make a lot of money; the hog market fluctuated dramatically, as did the cost of feed. To be profitable Steve and Jane needed large litters of healthy piglets that grew rapidly and that had the same color and physical characteristics. Cold snaps, heat waves, storms, parasites, and disease thwarted them. Young sows sometimes foolishly crushed their piglets by lying on them. Other sows were aggressively protective, even dangerous, when the piglets were caught for vaccinations, castration, or tail and eye tooth clipping. Seven days a week Steve and Jane fed, watered, and shoveled manure.

In the '80's enormous corporate farms began to dominate the market; pig prices fell and stayed low. As other pig farms and the auction barns went out of business, Steve and Jane decided to risk their life savings to open a microbrewery. For two frustrating years they worked through the red tape of licenses, permits, and regulations. Sometimes different government agencies had seemingly contradictory ordinances. Patiently, the Markleys fulfilled each requirement and built the brewery.

When they started bottling, Steve and Jane cleaned recycled bottles and filled them by hand. They delivered "milkman" style to customers' homes, and steadily their business grew. In '97 Little Yeoman beer was distributed to local liquor stores. In '99 Steve hired artist Bruce Roberts as assistant brewer and began to sell beer in the Springfield area. Greg Braun, Fred Klug, and I built the warehouse in the spring of 2000. Nowadays, Jane concentrates on the paperwork and lends a hand only on especially busy days. "On tap" kegs for pubs and restaurants take up more and more of production.

Growing up in Wichita, Steve never dreamed he'd own a brewery in the Ozarks. His dad, Dwight, was an electrician at the Mobile Oil Refinery. On the side Steve's parents bought run-down houses to renovate and then rent out.

When Steve became involved in Boy Scouts, Dwight helped the boys arrange outing and camping trips. At Scout camp one summer Steve met a boy with a banjo. The look and feel of the instrument and the sounds it made intrigued Steve. He mowed neighbors' lawns and saved money until he was able to order a "Silver Tone" banjo from the Montgomery Ward catalogue. Throughout Steve's high school years, while his classmates listened to the Beatles and bought electric guitars to play in garage rock 'n roll bands, Steve's parents were subjected to countless hours of awful banjo picking as Steve tried to recreate the style of Flatt and Scruggs.

Steve began to master the banjo when he was a student at Emporia State College. In the late afternoons he played bluegrass music at the maintenance building with the janitors. At the same time Steve took a part-time job at the Iowa Beef Producers slaughter and packinghouse. The wages and benefits were good; Steve liked the work. After graduation, rather than become a teacher as he'd planned, Steve took a fulltime job at the slaughterhouse. He married and had two children.

As the years went by, Steve began to dream about moving to the country. Though he'd grown up in town, his grandparents, aunts, and uncles were farmers. One summer on vacation at Stockton Lake, Missouri, Steve met a fisherman from Douglas County who told him about the tranquility of the Ozarks.

The next summer Steve camped at Noblett Lake and became fascinated with Booger County. When his marriage ended, he moved to this farm with his children, Amy and Jim. He built a house and barn with sheds for pigs, rabbits, chickens, and goats. Steve worked part-time as a substitute teacher in Willow Springs.

Though he didn't have electricity or running water, Steve had a lot of free time. In the evenings he sat on the front porch and picked his banjo. He practiced with Charlie Hiler and other old-timers, most of them dead now, who helped him perfect his style and showmanship. Today, Steve plays with the Fantods, a quartet that presents an eclectic blend of folk tunes and bluegrass with the fun-loving, foot-stomping high energy of a traditional Ozarks hootenanny.

Steve found the word "fantods" in Mark Twain. Late at night, as the apprehensive Huck Finn cautiously slips through the snake-infested woods along the river, he finds a man lying on the ground. "It most gave me the fantods," Huck says. Like *booger* fantods is an obscure word that originated in dialects of the British Isles. It means the "willies," the "heebie-jeebies," scared witless, a state of extreme fear and nervousness. Fantods may be an American derivative of either "fantique" or "fanteeg," a blend of the words fatigue and phantasm, which originate in the Latin *fatigare*, to weary, and the Greek and Latin, *phantasma*, a specter or apparition.

The tasting room is that collection of log seats in the shade near the walk-in cooler. I'll have a Stout to remind me of the Emerald Isle. It's thick, dark, and pungent; though made with Arthur Guinness' eighteenth century recipe, American-grown ingredients and Ozark well water make it smoother and bitterer. Janet will have a Raspberry Cream Ale. Amber doesn't care for beer; she'll have a glass of water.

What will it be? How about an India Pale Ale? Early in the twentieth century English brewers discovered that by doubling the hops in pale ale they could ship beer to India without spoilage. Why not try a Porter? Porter comes from the Latin *porlare*, to carry; a porter is a workingman and porter the drink of nineteenth century workers. It's a heavy beer but sweeter and lighter than stout. In the spring Steve offers Czech Pilsner. Unlike ales that brew warm, pilsner, also known as lager, uses a different species of yeast that thrives in cool temperatures and takes twice as long to ferment. Brewers in Pilsner, Bohemia, discovered the process that for a long time was kept a secret. German immigrants brewed lager in St. Louis before the Civil War. Steve's pilsner has a sharp, crisp flavor. Perhaps Steve has some Irish Red, Vienna, or Cream Ale.

Is everyone's glass full? Let's raise our cups to honor Booger County's legends: fierce Osage, peace-loving Leni-lenápe, battle-weary Confederate Rangers, wrathful Baldknobbers, naive Henry Schoolcraft and Levi Pettibone. Here's to the grit of Walter and Ruby Braddock; Doc and Hester Osborn; Locke, Patsy, Shelt, and Nancy Alsup; Alabeth and Aaron Freeman. May they not be forgotten. We drink a tribute to Lee Cooley, Jack Vineyard, Doc Curry, Herb Sanders, and the Seven-Springers. Let's not forget the moonshiners. We'll clink our glasses to Booger County: clear streams, towering limestone bluffs, forested hills, pastures dotted with cattle and fine horses, amiable people waving from their porches.

I appreciate everyone who reads these chapters. For the past three years I've risen at 4:30 to write and rewrite. In my free time I've done research at libraries, read books, and interviewed dozens of people. On Saturday afternoons Janet and I have ridden our mountain bikes in search of Booger County's compelling stories. Thank you for joining us. May we meet someday!

References

Racetrack Hollow

Luckily, information about the early settlers of Booger County was collected during the 1930's in a WPA project called the "Missouri Historical Records Survey," which is now part of the "Western Historical Manuscripts Collection," University of Missouri, Columbia. The May 1987 issue of the Douglas County Historical Journal reprinted it. Other sources include:

"The Family of Simon Lakey," author unknown, Douglas County Historical Journal, May 1987.

"The History of Douglas County Missouri," Historical and Genealogical Society of Douglas County, December 1984.

"Hodge/Marler," submitted by Marion Conradi, Douglas County Missouri, History and Families 1857-1995, Turner Publishing Company, Paducah, KY, 1996.

"Omo," by Ethel Leach, Douglas County Historical Journal, December 1995.

Early Settlers in the East End of Douglas County, by Charles "Noel" Alsup.

In the autumn of 1999 I spent a Sunday afternoon with Cletis Upshaw, the Alsup/Upshaw family historian and longtime rural mail carrier in north-central Douglas County. We drove through the Denlow/Fox Creek/Coldspring area and stopped at Falling Spring, Racetrack Hollow, Denlow Cemetery, and the Shelt Alsup cabin site. The walls of Cletis' Norwood home are decorated with old photos of his colorful ancestors, including Locke, Patsy, Tom, and Shelt Alsup. Later, Cletis listened to my rough draft and made suggestions.

Many times as I wrote about the Alsups, I stopped after work at the Mtn. Grove home of Effa Giles, the oldest living Alsup (98). Effa clarified my information and provided Alsup family documents, including a short autobiography by Locke near the end of his life. Other information about the Alsups comes from:

"A Brief History of the Life of Jess Cox," Jess Cox, Douglas County Historical Journal, July 1975.

"The Fatal Horseride," Ernest Jenkins, Douglas County Historical Journal, December 1989.

"Fatal Affray in Douglas County," Missouri Patriot-Advertiser, 13 March 1879, reprinted in the Douglas County Historical Journal, May 1996.

"The Sheriff of Douglas County-1879," Gloria McKinley, Douglas County Historical Journal, May 1996.

Devil's Hill

During the winter of 2000 Ruby Braddock, in telephone interviews, told me the story of the Braddock Ranch. Ruby suggested that I call Gene and Shirley Mask for information about Siloam Springs. I visited with the Masks at their rural home near West Plains. They gave me photocopies of Jerry Dunn's "Pinebrook Inn" article and "Siloam Springs: Only Bubbling Waters Break the Stillness," by John Edwards, that appeared in the January 15, 1969, West Plains Quill. The series of articles on groundwater, written by Denise Vaughn for the West Plains Quill in the fall of 1998, were my source on Booger County geology. Denise used "Groundwater of Missouri," by Miller and Vandike (1998), as her source. W.D. Keller's Common Rocks of Missouri (University of Missouri Press, 1945) provided further information. Bill Plummer told the story of Peccary Cave to me.

Rippee

I spent an afternoon with Herb Sanders at his home in Ava in the spring of 2000. Further information about Booger County archaeology came from Herb's May 1986 article in the Douglas County Historical Society Journal, "Ten Thousand Years of Douglas County History," and from a transcript of a speech by Howard Curry about his excavations. "Assumption Abbey," by Tommy Roberts in the December 1991 issue of the Douglas County Historical Society Journal, was my only source concerning the Trappists. "Douglas County's Only Legal Hanging" and "The Execution of Ed Perry" originally appeared in the Ava Farm Record, February 4, 1897, and were reprinted in the December 1985 Douglas County Historical Journal. Nancy Weber's article about the Fleetwoods appeared in Douglas County Missouri, History and Families, 1857-1995, Turner Publishing Company, Paducah, KY, 1996. A special "Brown's Cave" issue of the Douglas County Historical Journal, May 1999, contained the following articles:
1. "Family Legends of Brown's Cave," by Herval Porter.
2. "The Wonderment of Brown's Cave," by Gladys Hutchinson.
3. "Brown's Cave—A Safe Haven For All," by Ken Brown.
4. "Brown's Cave," by Nancy Bolen.

El Dorado

Rude Pursuits and Rugged Peaks: Schoolcraft's Ozark Journal 1818-1819 was the principle source for this chapter. The edition I used had maps, introduction, and appendix by Milton Rafferty (University of Arkansas Press, 1996), biographical information about Schoolcraft, and details of his route. I used three sources for my material on the Osage: Kristie Wolferman's The

Osage in Missouri (University of Missouri Press, 1997); Terry P. Wilson's The Osage (Chelsea House Publishers, 1988); and John Joseph Matthews' Osages: Children of the Middle Waters (Norman: University of Oklahoma Press, 1961). Common Rocks and Minerals of Missouri, by W.D. Keller (University of Missouri Press, 1945), explained how lead and zinc ore are found and extracted.

Finding Vera Cruz

In October 1999 Janet and I cycled to Jack Vineyard's Bryant Creek home. For several pleasant hours we talked with him about Vera Cruz and the Civil War. Jack graciously allowed me to take home his manuscripts for the winter. Other sources for this chapter are:
"The Flood in Douglas County," Patriot Springfield, 7 June 1876, reprinted in the Douglas County Historical Journal, May 1999.
"Vera Cruz: Our First County Seat," by Barbara Devore, Douglas County Historical Journal, May 1985.

Uncivil War

Inside War: The Guerrilla Conflict During the American Civil War (Oxford University Press, 1989), by my former teacher, Michael Fellman, was the most important source for this chapter. An "intellectual historian," Professor Fellman focuses on the thoughts, feelings, and motivations of common people caught up in a relentless cycle of violence.
The 1838 Mormon War in Missouri, by Stephan Lesueur (University of Missouri Press, 1987), was my source for the Mormon odyssey across North America and their expulsion from Missouri.
Civil War on the Western Border 1854-1865, by Jay Monaghan (Bonanza Books, NY, MCMLV), provided most of my information about the Kansas/Missouri Border War and Price's raid across Missouri.
Nine Months in the Infantry Service: The Civil War Journal of R.P. Mathews, edited by Jeff Patrick (Greene County Historical Society, 1999), gave a first person account of life in Phelps Regiment during the Pea Ridge campaign. In 1861 Mathews was a student at the Christian College in Springfield, Missouri, who joined an ad hoc "Home Guard" Company.
Pea Ridge: Civil War Campaign in the West, by William L. Shea and Earl L. Hess (University of North Carolina Press, 1992), is a detailed, scholarly account of the decisive Federal offensive that "won" Missouri for the Union. Personal letters, memoirs, and official documents were used to tell how the Federal Army of the Southwest eventually defeated the Confederate Army of the West in a desperate, two-day battle.
Grey Ghosts of the Confederacy: Guerrilla Warfare in the West 1861-65, by Richard Brownlee (Louisiana State University Press, 1986), tells how the

Civil War in Missouri degenerated into insurrection, military tyranny, and ruthless guerrilla conflict that laid waste to much of the state.

Hardtack and Coffee or the Unwritten Story of Army Life, by John Billings (University of Nebraska Press, 1993, originally published in 1887), describes the everyday life of Federal soldiers in the Civil War. Billings tells how he and his fellow soldiers made camp, marched, kept warm in the winter, and dealt with lice, harsh military discipline, rain, and mud.

I am indebted to Jack Vineyard who graciously lent me the information he'd gathered about the Battle of Clark's Mill and life at Old Vera Cruz. Other sources include:

"The Battle of Pilot Knob," by Richard Brownlee in the April 1998 Missouri Historical Society Review.

"A Few Men But Many Widows: The Dan Fogel letters," edited by James Goodrich and Donald Oster for the April 1986 Missouri Historical Review.

"A Diminished Landscape: The Life and Death of Major Robert Henry Smith," by Kim Allen Scott in the July 1997 Missouri Historical Review.

Vanguard of Empire, by Lew Larkin, State Publishing, St. Louis, 1961.

Borderland Rebellion, by Elmo Ingenthron, School of the Ozarks Press.

"Refugees in Rolla, 1862-1863," by John Bradbury in the April 1993 Phelps County Genealogical Society Journal.

"The Civil War Letters of Colonel Bazel Lazear," in the July 1998 Missouri Historical Society Review.

"Battle of Hartville," Wright County Historical Society pamphlet.

From Douglas County Missouri, History and Families 1857-1995, edited by the Douglas County Historical Society and published by Turner Publishing, Paducah, KY, 1996, I took information about the following individuals and families:

The Collins family, especially Cornelius Collins, from John and Karen Trullinger and Zella Collins

William Thomas from Charles Thomas Stevens
James Robertson from Zada K. Purtle
Jesse B. James from Wayne J. Spence
Luke and Witt Marler from Zada K. Purtle
Newt Smallwood from Viola Dee Smallwood Cooper
Winfield White from Tom White
Joseph Lyons from Cheryl Hipp
The Todd family from Nancie Todd Anderson Weber
Jeremiah Heard from John M. Parker
James Wood from Ruth Coble Wintle
Elijah Sanders from Jerry R. Sanders
William Turner from Florence Silvey Garrison
Dan and Mary Hull from Kristie Lynn Towe
Lafe Gentry from James E. "Jay" Gentry, Jr.

Sylvester Freeman, Irvin King, Jessie Huffman, the Mankin family, Lewis Maxey, and Sterling Shipley: not attributed to any author.

Baldknobbers

Though I read numerous articles and accounts of the Baldknobbers, Baldknobbers: Vigilantes on the Ozark Frontier, by Mary Hartman and Elmo Ingenthron (Pelican Publishing, 1994), is far and away the best book on the subject and my principle source. I quote Judge Krekel from it.

"The Daniel Fogel Letters," edited by James Goodrich and Donald Oster, Missouri Historical Society Review, April 1986, provided the quotations I used to describe the post-Civil War Ozarks.

"The Infamous Elder S.G. Haws: Man of God or Criminal?" by Paul Bark and Ken Brown in the December 1998 Douglas County Historical Journal, furnished all of my information about Elder Haws.

Achilles Ellison's biography by Edwin Hailey in the Douglas County Missouri, History and Families 1857-1995, compiled by the Douglas County Historical and Genealogical Society, Turner Publishing Company, Paducah, KY, 1996, furnished data about the famous rescue.

Old Richville

My neighbor Eva Wood is the granddaughter of Myron Pease. She provided me with family documents and letters written by Myron that describe his childhood and early adult life. Eva sent me to see her kinsman, genealogist Herman Sneiderman, for more information about the Pease family. Herman's home is atop Bald Knob on the southeast edge of Mtn. Grove. Though it appears as a low hill from the square, Bald Knob is the third highest point in Missouri and has dramatic views to the south of the North Fork drainage. Jay Gentry's article in the December 1994 Douglas County Historical Journal, "The Old Steel Bridge," contributed the facts that I used about the picturesque bridge.

The Ruins of Omba

"In Spite of Hill and High Water," compiled and edited by Mabel Lovan, was my source for the story of the Osborns. Mabel was Bart's daughter. Marsha Tooley, her neighbor, kindly made a copy of Mabel's article for me. Faye Coble, whose husband, Buster, was the child of the tragic Cora Osborn, helped clarify details about the Osborns. In the spring of 1999 Faye went with me to Omba, where we discussed the life of Doc and Hester Osborn.

Champion

Over the years, as Janet and I have cycled past Champion, we have stopped to buy sodas and to chat with Duane. Though Duane related some of Champion's history, Virginia Andrews' "The Champion Store," in the May 1996 <u>Douglas County Historical Journal</u>, was my principle source of information about Champion. *Duane passed away in January 2002.

During the summer of 1999 I frequently visited with Effa Giles at her Mtn. Grove home to learn about the Giles family, especially Uncle Billy, Liz, Frank, Ralph, and Bill. That summer I was often a guest of Lee and Maggie Cooley. Lee and I spent a Sunday afternoon in the Tetrick area discussing old times as my truck bounced over the rough gravel roads. Lee loaned me a videotaped interview he'd made about his life and gave me a short autobiography.

In January 2001 I spent another Sunday afternoon driving through the Drury/Champion neighborhood with Lee's kinsman, Dain Lambert, whose farm is adjacent to New Hope. Dain and I looked at the Bob Day Spring, the Bakersfield School site, and Tetrick. We discussed the families in the area and the effects of the Dust Bowl and early 1950's droughts. Other sources include:

"The Weirdest Weather in the USA," Steve Koehler, <u>Springfield News Leader</u>, 6 January 2000.

"Charles Valentine Riley and the Roots of Modern Insect Control," Donna Brunette, <u>Missouri Historical Society Review</u>, April 1992.

<u>Insect Pests of Farm, Garden, and Orchard</u>, E. Dwight Sanderson, John Wiley and Sons, New York, 1915.

"Criminal Aspects of the Pendergast Machine," Lawrence Larsen and Nancy Hulston, <u>Missouri Historical Society Review</u>, January 1997.

"The Political Impact of the Depression on Missouri," J. Christopher Schnell, Richard Collins, and David Dillard, <u>Missouri Historical Society Review</u>, April 1996.

Topaz

During the winter of 1999/2000, whenever I stopped to buy gas, I took a few minutes to chat with Ray about his childhood, how he came to Douglas County, and his life as a storeowner. In November 2000, after Maria died, Ray and I talked in the back room of the store about Maria, her family, and her journey from Mexico to Missouri.

Pioneer Moses Johnson's reminiscences that were printed in the May 1989 <u>Douglas County Historical Journal</u> provided most of the early history of Topaz. Wayne Spence's short account of the Freeman family and Islet Dickman's article about Lawrence Smith in <u>Douglas County Missouri, History and Families, 1857-1995</u>, compiled by the Douglas County Historical Society and published by Turner Publishing Company of Paducah, KY, 1996, added to the story of Topaz. During the winter of 2000 I spent a Sunday afternoon with Joe O'Neal, the owner of Topaz, at his home beside the famous mill and spring. I also spoke with Eva Wood, ninety-five-years-old yet keen of mind, about the time she spent at Topaz working as a teenage clerk in the General Store.

In February 2000 I began to gather information about Seven Springs Farm. Back in the 1970's I was a neighbor and friend to "the farm" during its heyday. In person and by phone I talked to Paul Clark, Dave Ring, Patty Van Weelden, Jeff Dunshee, Jane Devries, Paul Goodwin, and Arrow Ross. Later, several of the Seven Springers read and amended my original manuscript.

Little Yeoman

Whenever I couldn't work during the cold, snowy January of 2001, I went to the Springfield Greene County Library and researched the Lenilenápe. Although I read many books, C.A. Weslager's The Delaware Indians (Rutgers University Press, 1909) was virtually my sole source. Elmo Ingenthron's Indians of the Ozark Plateau (School of the Ozarks Press, 1970) contributed some information.

Moonshine: It's History and Folklore, by Ester Keller (Bobbs and Merrill, 1971), provided data about the history of distillation and government efforts to control and tax liquor.

"Silent Teaching and Sat-Sanga," by Sri Ramana Maharsi, and "Truth Always Wins," by Baba Faqir Chand, helped me understand the meaning of Satsang.

Articles and photos in the August 9, 1979, West Plains Quill, by staff writers Jerry Womack and Frank Martin, told the story of the Satsang police raid in depth. Similar articles in the August 16, 1979, Cabool Enterprise and Douglas County Herald were helpful. Interviews with John Tickner and Marilyn Tickner helped me understand life at Satsang and the human side of the arrests.

Information about hemp came from Weeds of the North Central States, Bulletin 772, (University of Illinois, Urbana, April 1981), and "Incite," by Ted Williams, in the November/December 1999 Audubon magazine.

Index

Alsup, Locke 6-9, 11-12, 16, 20-21, 97, 114
Alsup, Shelt 2, 9, 13, 17, 19, 20
Alsup, Tom 12, 17, 97
Alsups 7-9, 11, 14, 18, 100, 104
Assumption Abbey 41-2
Bakersfield School 142, 146, 149
Baldknobbers 1, 107, 110, 112-119, 200
Barstow, Hiram 83-86
Benton, Maecenas 116, 117
Benton, Thomas Hart 76, 116-17
Berry, Jim 117, 118, 119
Blair, Frank 72-74, 77
Bob Day Spring 142
Boyd, Pony 116
Braddock, Ruby 24-28, 197
Braddock, Walter 24-28
Braddock Ranch 23
Brandt, Manny and Sandra 169-175
Brown, Tom 44
Brown's Cave 39, 42-3, 68
Burbridge, John 85-87
Burris, Johnson 98
Call, Bill and Ethel 148-9
Champion School 139
Cistercian Brotherhood 41-2
Clark, Paul 170, 172-5
Clinton, Bill 164-5
Coats, Bill 97
Coats, James 82
Coble, Buster 16, 163
Coble, Faye 16, 36, 163, 200
Coble, Henry 165
Coble, Nick 97
Coggburn, Robert and Andrew 115
Cooley, Lee 147-9, 151-4, 159
Cooley, Maggie 154, 157-8
Cox, Jess 19
Curry, Howard 39-41
Curtis, General Samuel 65-6, 79-81
Devil's Hill 23-4, 28
Devries, Jane 175
Doane, Herbert 147
Drury Store 147-8
Dunshee, Jeff 172-5
Ellison, Achilles "Kel" 113, 200
Ewing, Thomas 90, 95
Fleetwood, Billy 11
Fox Trotters 21
Freeman, Aaron and Alabeth 164
Fremont, John C. 76-77
Funk, Ed 118
Gentry, Lafe 98, 99
Giles, Frank 141-2, 149
Giles Family 140-2, 201
Glade Top Trail 107, 151
Goodwin, Paul 175
Hatfield, John and Liz 12, 13

Haws, Samson 114, 115, 200
Heard Family 100
Hemp 189-191, 202
Henson Family 139
Henson's Store 139
Hicks, Elmer 152
Hodge, Bud and Liz 14
Huffman, Jesse 102
Hull, Daniel and Mary 99
Hutchinson, Bart 163, 165
Jackson, Claib 72, 85, 95
James, Jesse B. 102, 164
Johnson, Winnie 126
King Family 102
Kinney, Nathaniel 110, 112-118
Krekel, Arnold 116
Lakey, Enos and Isabella 15
Lambert, Joe 149
Leni-lenápe 179-185
Little Yeoman Brewery 179, 192-194
Lyon, Nathaniel 73-76
Lyons, Joseph and Sarah 101
Mankin Family 100
Markley, Jane and Steve 192-194
Marler Family 102
Marmaduke, John 85-88
Martin, James 99
Mask, Gene and Shirley 31-32
Maxey, Lewis 101
McCall, Ray 161-2
McNeil, John 91
Middleton, George Washington 116, 119
Miles, Billy 118

Moonshine 116, 185-6, 202
Mt. Ararat Church 165-6, 189
New Hope Cemetery 142
New Madrid Fault 48
Old Steel Bridge 121
Osage 50-55, 185
Pease, Miles 121-6
Pease, Myron 121-5, 200
Pease Family 122-5
Pendergast, Jim 150-1
Pendergast, Tom 150-1
Perry, Edward 43
Pettibone, Levi 48, 49
Pike, Albert 81
Pinebrook Inn 30-31
Pope, John 91
Price, Sterling 73-76, 79, 80-82, 95-97
Quantrill, William 92-3, 103-4
Rafinesque, Constantin 184
Ramos, Maria 161, 177
Reynolds, Thomas 95
Richville 121, 124-5
Riley, Mary "Liz" 140
Ring, David and Valerie 170-75
Robertson, James 103
Ross, Arrow and Viki 173-5
Sanders, Elijah 100
Sanders, Herb 39-41, 60, 197
Sanders, Leonard 189-191
Satsang 187-192, 202
Schofield, John 89, 90
Schoolcraft, Henry 47-49, 56, 164, 197
Seven Springs 172-177, 202

Shelby, J.O. 82, 83, 88
Shipley, Sterling 100
Siloam Springs 29, 32
Skolnick, Robert 170-72
Smith, Bill 100
Smith, Joseph 68
Smith, Lawrence 165
Spaeder, Nick and Nancy 173, 176
Spangler, Beth 176
Spangler, Lizzie 99
Stillwell, Donald 166-8
Sweeton, Lydia Hicks 142
Taylor, George 117, 118
Tetrick 140-42
Thomas, William 101
Todd, Preston 16, 72, 75, 100, 101
Toothpick 162
Topaz 50, 161, 163-65
Upshaw Family 3, 196

Van Weelden, Leon and Patty 169-175
Vera Cruz 1, 2, 4, 12, 57-63, 65, 66, 83
Vera Cruz Road 8, 57, 61, 83
Vickery, Hardin 19
Vineyard, Jack 59-61, 198, 199
Walam Olum 184
Walker, Joe and Dave 113
White, Eva Lina 126
Wood, Eva 136. 200, 201
Wood, Henry and Sarah 164-5
Wood, James "Bushy" 100, 165
Wood, Russell and Joanne 165
Woodruff, John 29
Woods, James 102-3
Young, Peter and Frieda 187, 189, 191

To Order *Searching For Booger County*

Make your check or money order payable to:
Sandy Ray Chapin

and send to:
Boogeyman Books
PO Box 184
Mtn. Grove, Mo 65711 US

Include your name and mailing address.

Cost:
$15.00 per book
Add 0.78 sales tax if MO resident
For discounts on larger orders, contact us.

Shipping:
$4.00 for 1st book
$3.00 for each additional book

Also available:

Guided mountain bike tours
Guided birdwatching
Readings and talks by the author

About the Chapins

Amber   Sandy Ray   Janet

The Chapins have lived in Booger County for thirty years. Sandy Ray, author and map illustrator, is a carpenter and Marine Vietnam Veteran. Amber, chief editor and cover designer, studies architecture in NYC. As copy editor, Janet taught herself keyboarding on the new family computer and deciphered pages of Sandy's scrawl. During the week she drives the senior citizen's bus in Mountain Grove. Sandy and Janet's other daughter, Dana, is a 2001 U.S. Naval Academy graduate, currently in pilot training .

Avid mountain bikers, runners, and birdwatchers, Sandy and Janet also tend a large garden. In 1993 their vegetable plot won them a trip to Ireland in the PBS Victory Garden Contest. Viewers nationwide voted their garden into first place from a field of gardens from Alaska to Massachusetts. This is Sandy Ray's first book.